NATIONS OF THE MODERN WORLD

ALGERIA:
  Rebellion and
  Revolution

Joan Gillespie

CEYLON

S. A. Pakeman
Formerly Professor of Modern History, Ceylon University College. Appointed Member, House of Representatives, Ceylon, 1947-52

MODERN INDIA

Sir Percival Griffiths
Honorary adviser to India, Pakistan and Burma Association

IRAQ

Brig. S. Y. Longrigg
Formerly of the Government of Iraq and the Iraq Petroleum Company and one time Political Officer, Iraq
  and
Frank Stoakes
Director of Middle Eastern Studies, St. Antony's College, Oxford

JAPAN

Sir Esler Dening
H.M. *Ambassador to Japan, 1952-1957*

MALAYA

J. M. Gullick
Formerly of the Malayan Civil Service

PAKISTAN

Ian Stephens
Formerly Editor of The Statesman *Calcutta and Delhi, 1942-1951 Fellow King's College, Cambridge, 1952-1958*

TURKEY

Geoffrey Lewis
Senior lecturer in Islamic Studies, Oxford

YUGOSLAVIA

Muriel Heppel and F. B. Singleton

CEYLON

CEYLON

By

S. A. PAKEMAN

FREDERICK A. PRAEGER, *Publisher*

NEW YORK

Published in the United States of America in 1964
by
FREDERICK A. PRAEGER, *Publisher*
64 University Place, New York 3, N.Y., U.S.A.

© S. A. Pakeman 1964
Library of Congress Catalog Card Number : 64–16684

This Book is part of the NATIONS OF THE MODERN WORLD series

Printed in Great Britain

Preface

ANYONE writing a book in the series 'Modern Nations' is inevitably faced by the possibility that between the actual time of writing and of publication events may occur to make most unexpected changes in the situation as set down in the book – the political situation in particular.

Two Bandaranaikes, husband and wife, have been in power – almost *seriatim* – for seven years, at the time of writing. Though a general election is not due till 1965, an earlier one is always a possibility – unlike the U.S.A.: and this might conceivably radically alter the political situation – or equally, it might not. It is a big question mark, hanging at the end of the last chapter.

Designations are always a matter of difficulty when writing of people still living, many of whom I know personally. I have therefore deliberately cut out almost all designations and used plain surnames, or occasionally the equivalent where a knighthood is concerned.

The spelling of place names, and even of proper names, is another difficulty. No attempt has been made to use the correct Sinhalese spelling of these names, since some of the more well known might then be difficult for a non-Ceylonese reader to recognise. For instance, some of these might not even have heard of Lanka, or Sri Lanka, the Sinhalese name for Ceylon, so I have referred throughout to Ceylon as the island's name. I have used the letter 'w' rather than 'v'; these letters are interchangeable as far as Sinhalese is concerned. I have referred to the language as 'Sinhalese', when 'Sinhala' is more correct. In general, the spelling I have used is that which has normally appeared in the daily newspapers in the English language during the last ten or twenty years, and in such publications as motor maps.

I wish to express my thanks to Dr G. C. Mendis, my old student, colleague and friend, a pioneer in research, study and writing on the history of Ceylon, and the scholar and teacher who was responsible for getting the subject going in Ceylon University, for his kindness in going through the earlier historical chapters and setting me right on a number of points; also my indebtedness to his published works, especially *Ceylon under the British*, which has been a mine of information for me. I also thank Mr. Wykeham Dulling, Secretary of the Planters' Association of Ceylon, with whom in my last few years in Ceylon I had the most friendly relations, personal and official, not only for his helpful criticisms of the sixth chapter, which I much appreciated, but also for the useful information which he put together in the volume issued to commemorate the centenary of the Association for which he has done so much.

I further take the opportunity of acknowledging my debt to the work of Mr. W. Howard Wriggins, whose illuminating book, *Ceylon: Dilemmas of a New Nation*, gives a thorough and detailed account of the years immediately after I left Ceylon. His work has saved me a mass of research which would have been almost impossible for a busy person to undertake. I am grateful to him and his publishers, the Princeton University Press, U.S.A., for permission to use a most apt quotation, and to Dr. Mendis for forgiving me for stealing one without first asking him; it comes from his invaluable little book *Ceylon Today and Yesterday*, published in Ceylon. It is my regret that I could not have seen its forthcoming new edition before writing this book.

Last, but by no means least, I have made free and frequent use of the Ceylon Year Books, especially from 1952 onwards, and have dug in this rich mine of facts and figures for much useful material.

I have to thank the Ceylon High Commissioner and the Secretary of the Ceylon Association in London for so kindly and freely allowing me the use of their libraries and the borrowing of their books for protracted periods.

I also took the opportunity of consulting several Ceylonese friends on various points, and I thank them without naming them.

Finally I should like to say how much I appreciate the work of my typist, Mrs. J. de Lacy, who gave up so much of her scanty spare time to deciphering with remarkable success the manuscripts which I showered upon her – and my publishers for the exercise of great patience.

S. A. PAKEMAN

Contents

Map

Introduction

ALL COUNTRIES with long histories have always had at base a silent mass of peasantry, to whom no historians – other than economic historians – have ever paid attention, except on rare occasions such as the Jacquerie in France and the Peasants' Revolt in England, in medieval times, and the uprisings during the early years of the French Revolution: such occasions do not seem to have occurred in Asia. Countless generations of these peasants have left little trace of their lives, save when the spade of the archaeologist has turned up the remnants of pottery, of implements, and of ornaments made by the simple craftsmen who coexisted with them. Above them, emperors and kings, nobles and priests, fighting men and traders have acted and reacted, weaving the fabric of history as we know it. Even today, in most countries of the world, this substratum of workers, wringing a scanty living out of the land by constant, monotonous toil, are anything but vocal.

But, in contrast to all the centuries which have passed, in nearly all countries, there is one major change, one immense difference in their position. They have votes. This means that, being the mass majority in all countries except the highly industrialised, the ultimate political power lies in their hands. Very few of them have yet realised that the power is theirs, or understand that they can use it. But some are beginning to do so.

In the industrialised countries another element has entered – the urban worker. In those countries political power was wrung from or filtered down from the landholding aristocracies by or to the rising middle classes, and through them, almost by a process of evolution, to the workers in factories and mines, offices and shops, as well as to those working on the land. But in the non-industrialised countries political power has come straight down from kings, chiefs and nobles, the big landowners and the comparatively small middle classes, direct to the peasants, late indeed, but quickly. Moreover, to this last an outstandingly important qualification must be made: for in many of these countries the landholding and middle classes exercised but a modicum of political power, since it lay, for long or short periods of time, in the hands of foreigners, of European foreigners. And it has been the action of these foreign administrators that has, in the lands over which they have borne sway, by-passed these classes and, by the establishment of adult suffrage and the yielding of independence, planked the power fairly and squarely into the unconscious hands of the rural workers.

In none of these newly independent countries have those rural workers awakened – yet – to this fact; not in India or Pakistan, not in Malaysia or Indonesia, not in little Ceylon; nor have they in Africa, where many of the political leaders, if only a generation or two from their forbears who worked on the soil, are still the products of foreign education and foreign influences. Only in two countries have there appeared on the stage of history leaders straight from the peasantry – Stalin and (a much better example) Mao Tse-Tung; but in their two vast countries, being communist, where, anyhow for the present, there is the 'dictatorship of the proletariat', political power in the form of a free vote has not been put into the hands of the workers.

So, historically speaking, a vast question mark hangs over the near future. Will the rural workers, as and when they awaken, wish to place power, or allow it to slide, into the hands of leaders rising from among themselves in the communist way of Mao's China, or will leaders arise from out of them able and willing to work a system of free democracy? Or, again, will they be content to let the power rest where it is today, in the hands of professional men (especially lawyers), administrators, traders and technicians turned politician?

It is by no means impossible, or even unlikely, that the first signs of an answer to these questions may manifest themselves in the small island of Ceylon where, it would seem, the rural worker is beginning to awake, however slowly, to the facts of political life. It is perhaps permissible to regard Ceylon as a microcosm of Asian political and social development, even though every country has its own peculiar situation and problems arising from its history, its economic and social circumstances, and its environment. Hence a study of this small country may be worthy of a place in a series entitled 'Nations of the Modern World.' In this study no attempt will, or indeed can, be made to supply answers to these big questions. Nothing more can be done than to draw the picture, and try to trace whether, and why, these signs are there.

Chapter 1

The Place and the People

THE PLACE

GEOGRAPHY and climate lie at the root of a country's historical development. The first and basic factor is that Ceylon is an island in the tropics, a smallish island about 25,000 square miles in area, 270 miles from south to north at its longest, 140 at its widest, from east to west. It is usually described as pear shaped, not inaptly, with a peninsula at the top like a bent stalk of the fruit.

The next factor is that it lies immediately to the south of the great Indian sub-continent, to which in geological times it must have been joined, separated by a narrow strait, easily navigable by small boats for much of the year. To the south of the island the Indian Ocean stretches till it merges with the Antarctic. To the east and the west lie lands which, before the days of the steamship, lay distant several weeks' sail.

The island may be divided from the angle of relief into what is known in Ceylon as up-country and low-country, the former occupying about one-fifth of the country's area. The remainder, the low-country, is a large area consisting of the whole of the northern portion of the island, and a coastal belt of varying width. The up-country is a central mountain massif, mostly over 1,200 feet in height, rising in places to peaks and ridges of 6,000 to 8,000 feet. Around this is a belt which may be classified as uplands from about 300 to 1,200 feet. In the low country proper occur isolated rocks of heights from a few hundred to 2,500 feet in height, on one of which, on the very top, 800 feet high, a fifth-century king built a palace, and created, in the sheer rock of Sigiriya, the most fascinating of all the ancient monuments for which Ceylon is famed.[1]

The central massif has been likened to a natural fortress. It has two significances. The first is that it was used as such first by rebels and outlaws, but later by the Sinhalese kings themselves when driven from the lowlands by the European invader. There they maintained their independence for three centuries, with the result that there have

[1] See below, p. 38.

13

arisen certain differences as between the up-country, or Kandyan, and the low-country, Sinhalese, which, as we shall see later, had certain political and social effects. The second significance is that in the up-country grows tea, the export crop which is the foundation stone of Ceylon's economic wellbeing, the sheet anchor of her economy.

The next geographical consideration is rainfall. The south-west monsoon blows steadily from about May to August. Brought down by the central massif, the constant heavy rain has created what is known as the wet zone, which includes most of the up-country and the south-west coastal belt from about forty miles north of Colombo to a few miles east of Dondra Head, the southernmost point of the island. Throughout the wet zone the vegetation is rank and thick, except where it has been cleared for cultivation in the form of tea estates, rubber estates, coconut plantations and rice fields. This monsoon very rarely fails, though when it does the results are baneful. The other prevailing wind is the north-east monsoon, to which the rest of the island has to trust for its rain. It blows from about December to February. There is usually what is called inter-monsoon rain in October and November, from which all parts of the island benefit; September is as a rule a dry month, but sometimes heavy rain in that month has brought disastrous floods. This monsoon does not furnish the regular heavy rainfall which is expected, and usually obtained, from the south-west monsoon. The average rainfall is heavy, compared with that of countries in the temperate zones, but owing to the higher temperature of the atmosphere much of the rainfall is taken back by rapid evaporation. Hence the high humidity of the wet zone, and the fact that unless any part of the country receives an average of not less than seventy-five inches a year, cultivation cannot be carried on without artificial irrigation. Owing, also, to the heavy rainstorms which succeed a dry period, there is in some parts a recurrent danger of floods, whereby not only is damage done, but also many inches of rainfall are wasted.

The combined effects of relief and rainfall on the economy of the island are matters which will be considered later on in the book. But they have imposed conditions of basic importance on Ceylon's history from the angles of political as well as social development, the keynote to the understanding of which is 'artificial irrigation'.

RACE, RELIGION AND CASTE – THE COMMUNITIES

The outstanding fact about Ceylon as far as race is concerned is that for the last 1,000 years there has been a majority race, the Sinhalese, and a strong minority race, the Tamils. During this part of Ceylon history, before the coming of the Europeans, the two races were never united, often at war, and rarely prevailed the one against the other. Occasionally a single ruler was strong enough to have, at any rate, some control over the whole island, but such control never lasted long.

The two communities (this is a more apt word than race) have always been kept separate by language, religion and social customs. Though in some parts of the island, anyhow until recently, Sinhalese and Tamils lived peaceably side by side, they have never really mingled. Today there are no Sinhalese practising the Hindu religion, no Tamils who are Buddhists. Both Hinduism and Buddhism are highly tolerant religions, and co-exist comfortably, their supporters having a real respect for the other religion.

There is very little intermarriage today: there may have been some in the past, but the evidence for this is not at all clear. Social customs remain stubbornly different, except for those who have become 'Westernised', particularly the members of both races who are Christians, and those whose education has been through the medium of the English language.

It is probably true to say that it is only among these, the Westernised section of the population, that there has grown up, yet, any true sense of Ceylon as a nation. The term 'Ceylonese', used to describe an inhabitant of Ceylon, has comparatively little real meaning to the mass of the population. It is used in legislation and in law, and has particular significance in the Ceylon Nationality Act of 1948. But until the average Ceylonese regards himself as such firstly, and only secondly as a Sinhalese or a Tamil, there can be little prospect of a Ceylonese nation in the true sense of the word coming into being. As matters stand today, there may well be more likelihood of something like modern nations being formed in some of the tribally and linguistically divided countries of Africa, with their new independence, than in Ceylon.

The next chapter gives some account of the island's early history, going into a limited amount of detail on the origin and character of the Sinhalese. For the moment it is enough to say that they claim to be, and probably are in the main, of Aryan origin, that they came from Northern India, that they have their own language, manners and customs, and that the great majority are Buddhists.

The Tamils, in historical times, came from southern India. They are of the same race (Dravidian) speaking much the same language, (Tamil), having the same religion in much the same form, and having much the same customs, as some 50 million people in south India, most of whom are found in the State of Madras. However, they are in some ways distinct from the Tamils of India, and indeed call themselves 'Ceylon Tamils' – that is to say, except for 1 million workers, mainly on tea and rubber estates, whose forbears were brought over from the mainland by the British to provide a labour force for the plantations, for reasons which will be explained in detail in Chapter 6. These are generally known as 'Indian Tamils', and until recently few of them had permanent roots in the island. Most of them have always cherished the idea of returning some day to their native land and settling down there in their old age – though some of them were born in Ceylon and have never been to India; indeed, on some estates there are Indian labourers of the third and even fourth generations in Ceylon. They number about the same as the Ceylon Tamils, but they cannot be considered as really Ceylonese, even those families who have been for several generations in the island. A comparatively small number of them have been registered as citizens of Ceylon. The Sinhalese are very much against these Indian Tamils being considered as Ceylonese. Their attitude in this matter cannot, for a variety of reasons, be altogether surprising. The Indian Tamils have never mixed nor wished to mix, to any extent, with the Sinhalese of the Central and Uva provinces, where most of them are to be found working on tea and rubber estates. They have regular employment, and are reasonably well paid and housed in comparison with the Sinhalese villagers who are their neighbours.

There is, indeed, at the time of writing, an attempt on the part of the Government of Ceylon to get as many of them as possible sent out of Ceylon and back to India. It may be mentioned in passing that if this attempt were to meet with immediate success, it might well mean a temporary, and perhaps a permanent, collapse of the tea industry, and therefore of the economy of the island. Further reference will be made to these Indian Tamils when the plantation economy comes to be considered.

There were, till recently, many Indian Tamils in towns, particularly in Colombo, working as domestic servants (most European families had four or five), rickshaw pullers, dock workers and unskilled or semi-skilled labourers on the roads and railways and in other public services. These avenues of work are no longer, by legislation, open to them, and most of them have returned to India, except those in certain occupations like latrine workers, 'sweepers', which the Sinhalese mostly do not care to undertake.

There is one more large minority, over half a million, the members of which may generally be classed as Muslims; the name by which the Muslim community is known in Ceylon is 'Moors', an oddly anomalous term. It originated with the Portuguese, the first

European invaders, to whom Muslim and Moor were synonymous terms.

There is also a small section of the Muslim community who are Malays, mostly descended from soldiers who served in Ceylon in Dutch and early British times. Though they may have intermarried somewhat with other Muslims, they have on the whole maintained their solidarity as a community. One member of this community, the late T. B. Jayah, a prominent figure in the educational world, was a Minister under the pre-independence constitution, and later High Commissioner for Ceylon in Pakistan. The community numbers something over 30,000.

The Moors, like the Tamils, are divided into 'Ceylon Moors' and 'Indian Moors'. The former are of mixed origin; some of them may well descend from the Arab traders who frequented the coast of Ceylon in medieval or even earlier times: there are references in the old chronicles of Ceylon and of some Arab countries to support this – a most illuminating account of the island in the fourteenth century is to be found in the book of the famous Muslim traveller, Ibn Batuta. But most of them, commonly known as 'Coast Moors', are descended from Indian Muslims who settled in Ceylon. The Moors have always been and still are primarily traders, though among them are numbered many small shopkeepers and butchers. They are scattered throughout the length and breadth of Ceylon, but are most numerous in the Eastern Province, where they work on the land, and on the west coast, mostly around Puttalam, a coast town just in the dry zone about eighty miles north of Colombo: here too there are numbers of Moorish agriculturalists. There is another settlement, around a mosque of considerable antiquity, at a place on the south-west coast about forty miles south of Colombo named Beruwela. Though most of them speak the Tamil language, those dwelling in mainly Sinhalese areas use that language: with their customary adaptability they will probably use it much more now that it is the sole official language. In recent years the Moors have been inclined to support the Government of the day, of whatever party complexion, while standing up stoutly for their religious rights where need for such action might arise.

During the occupation of the Ceylon coasts by the Portuguese and Dutch, the Moors were regarded with disfavour by the invaders, by the former not only as being hereditary enemies on religious grounds, but also because the Muslims of south-west India had strenuously opposed the irruption of the Portuguese into Asian waters and Asian trade. By the Dutch they were regarded as trade rivals, particularly in the trade in cinnamon. But under the British

B

they received equitable treatment, and flourished considerably.

The Indian Moors are much more recent immigrants, who came from various parts of India in search of trade. Members of the wealthy 'Borah' community have exercised considerable influence in economic and even in political affairs. In recent years the Indian Moors have either shown a desire to become citizens of Ceylon or have returned to India.

Between them all the Muslims total about 5 per cent of the island's population of which they form a useful element, in particular from the economic angle. Unless their religious susceptibilities are at stake, they mix quite amicably with the members of the other communities in the island.

A small but highly important community is that known as the Burghers – again a somewhat generic term. The term Burgher, of course, comes from the Dutch, and is correctly used when it denotes the descendants of the Dutch who held the maritime provinces of Ceylon for a period of a century and a half before the advent of the British. When this took place many of those who had recently come from the Netherlands returned thither. But some remained, and practically all those of mixed blood stayed in the island which they had made their home. It had not, as in the case of their predecessors the Portuguese, been the policy of the Dutch to encourage intermarriage with the people of Ceylon, though this was done for a short period of time in the latter half of the eighteenth century. Those who remained in Ceylon after the British occupation, though Dutch speaking, soon began to adopt the English language, and the use of Dutch has gradually faded away; there are few, if any, alive today who can remember personally any of their forbears whose normal language in the home was Dutch. English became their language and, anyhow until recently, few of them had more than a working knowledge of colloquial Sinhalese or Tamil. They are, correctly, known as Dutch Burghers. They are proud of their community and very anxious to preserve it as such. Indeed, their club, the Dutch Burgher Union, has always been most exclusive, membership having been restricted to Dutch Burghers who could show several generations of forbears who had not married with Asians: the line was less strictly drawn in other Burgher clubs, particularly sporting clubs.

The term Burgher, however, has come to be applied indiscriminately to all people of mixed European and Asian blood. Until about a generation ago there were to be found some small communities of mixed Portuguese descent, known, quite irrationally, as 'Portuguese Burghers', some of whom still spoke in a patois based on Portuguese, their home language, and in living memory were able to attend, in certain Christian churches, services in that language. Most of them were low in the social scale, mostly living in towns, and included a number of craftsmen and mechanics. It was next to impossible for anyone from outside Ceylon to tell them apart from the average urban Sinhalese workers, especially as so many of the Sinhalese people during the period of Portuguese rule took Portuguese names – a glance at the Colombo telephone directory will show a great number of Pereras, de Silvas and Fernandos, of de Soyzas and Peiris's, just as a London telephone directory will disclose many pages of Smiths, Browns and Robinsons.

In addition to these 'Portuguese Burghers' there are, not un-expectedly, a certain number who descend from European fathers by unions sometimes regular, but more often than not irregular. There is a certain village up-country which used to be called 'Little England', no great distance from Diyatalawa, where was situated for some years of the latter part of the British occupation a naval and military rest camp.

The total number of Burghers in the widest sense in which the term is used – Eurasians might be more apt – amounts to roughly 50,000. The number may be diminishing, for some, particularly of the Dutch Burgher community, and of the first generation of mixed blood, have felt constrained, under the present régime, to quit Ceylon and migrate to the white countries of the Commonwealth, Australia and the United Kingdom in particular, where they have quickly settled down.

During the nineteenth century the Burghers occupied a highly important place in the social and economic life of the island. Owing to their education, which soon came to be conducted in the English language, and their Western ways of life, they were able to occupy many posts, mainly clerical, in the service of the Government and of mercantile firms. They also took up the legal, medical and teaching professions, often with outstanding success. And though, in the late nineteenth and during the first half of the twentieth century, more and more Sinhalese and Tamils entered these occupations and professions, the number of Burghers in them is still quite out of proportion to their percentage of the island's population. In the higher ranks of government service, since it has been opened more freely to the people of Ceylon, there were and still are members of the community who have risen to the top of what was till recently known as the Civil Service, and there are still first-rate Burgher lawyers, doctors, university and school teachers. Some of them have also taken to commerce, quite successfully.

The Ceylon Tamils have been in the island for a very long time. Indeed, some Tamil controversialists claim that they preceded the Sinhalese, and have even described themselves as the aborigines of Ceylon – probably a quite incorrect assumption. However, there is ample historical evidence that, well before the beginning of the Christian era, invasions from south India had begun, and that these continued sporadically all through the history of Ceylon up to the coming of the Portuguese early in the sixteenth century.

The Sinhalese epic chronicle the *Mahavamsa*, of which more later, tells the story of one of their great national hero-kings, Dutugemunu, in the second century B.C., driving back invaders from the Chola Kingdom in south India, and slaying their king. There were frequent invasions from the south Indian kingdoms of Pandya and Chola, especially after the ninth century of the Christian era. Not much is known of these kingdoms, but they were all Dravidians, that is to say, they spoke languages of which the modern derivatives are the Tamil, Telugu, Canarese and Malayali tongues, and their religion and social customs may be generally described as Hindu.

It is difficult to estimate the extent of south Indian influence on the history of Ceylon, particularly the extent to which there was any mixture of races. Some students of philology have laid great stress on the influence which the Tamil language has had on Sinhalese, others have strenuously controverted their claims. But it is clear that at the highest social levels there was considerable inter-action during the first millennium of Ceylon's known history. After the tenth century many Sinhalese kings took wives from the neighbouring royal families of south India, and the very last dynasty, extinguished by the British in the early part of the last century, was purely Indian, though bearing Sinhalese names and titles. It is more than possible that some tribes or groups who invaded Ceylon from south India and settled in the north and west of the island became 'Sinhalised': it has been stated that the for-bears of the Karawa (fisher) and Salagama (cinnamon peeler) castes, which are usually ranked next to the numerous Goigama, or cultivators, originally came from south India and became Sinhalese.

The Tamils, naturally, settled most in the north of the island, but also spread some way down the north-east and north-west coasts. Here, sometime during the ninth century, they founded an independent kingdom with its headquarters in the northern peninsula of Jaffna, until its independence was extinguished by the Portuguese in 1615. The Tamils remain the majority in the present Northern and Eastern Provinces, a fact which poses a political problem of first-rate importance.

The Jaffna peninsula is dry and – to the eye – looks barren. But the Jaffna Tamils, perhaps from the incentive provided by difficulty of cultivation, have for centuries worked very hard indeed to wring a living from its soil. They are industrious, thrifty, and calculating, which helps to account for their success in many walks of life, particularly during the period of British occupation, during which time they spread, though in some districts thinly, nearly all over the island, and were especially to be found in the service of the Government.

Up to the coming of the Portuguese, the Tamil Kingdom of Jaffna was often at war with the Sinhalese kings. It would seem that this has left a tradition of hostility between the two races. Throughout the British occupation it looked as if this might be dying down. The Tamils remained a distinct community, but they lived in peaceful co-existence with the Sinhalese, though there was little inter-marriage between members of the two communities, even when they were not sundered by differences of religion; as, for example, between the Christians of both races. But, sadly enough, the hostility revived in a marked form in the riots of May 1958. The causes of this will be examined further on in this book: but the immediate result was that many Tamil families living outside the Northern and Eastern Provinces lost their businesses, their homes, and sometimes their lives. There was a general movement back to the Tamil provinces, but they have now mostly returned to their former dwelling places.

It might be mentioned that a certain number of Ceylon Tamils emigrated to Malaya in British times, where they still form a most flourishing community.

RELIGION

The religious divisions of the people of Ceylon are easy to understand. The great majority of the Sinhalese are Buddhists, and of Tamils are Hindus. Moors and Malays practically all profess the faith of Islam. There are, however, about 700,000 of all communities who are Christians. All three of the European countries who between them occupied some or all of Ceylon for about four and a half centuries made efforts to propagate their faith. This was especially so in the case of the Portuguese, who gave strong encouragement to the missionary orders of their church, with the result that they left a considerable population of Roman Catholics: these survived a certain amount of persecution by the Dutch, and Roman Catholics are today the largest of the Christian denominations. The efforts of the Dutch to effect conversions to their brand of Christianity were less successful, and it is today only some, probably the majority, of the Dutch Burgher community who belong to the Dutch Reformed Church. The British in the early years of their occupation also sent missionaries to 'convert the heathen', and there are a few thousand Anglicans and other Protestant denominations such as Wesleyan Methodists and Baptists. No official statistics are available.

Throughout the occupation by Europeans there is little doubt that very many of the conversions were of a nominal character. If not impossible to enter the service of the governments, it was doubtless extremely difficult to do so during Portuguese and Dutch times for non-Christians. In early British times there was a strong bias in favour of Christians in this respect, though this died away, anyhow officially. It has frequently been stated, in controversy, that this bias continued to subsist, but this is not really a fair statement. Today it is sometimes urged that the reverse is the case.

The Christian churches are well organised, and in this sense they have an advantage over the Buddhists. The Roman Catholic Church in Ceylon is headed by an archbishop, who is a Sinhalese, and is closely knit. There are three principal missionary orders, dividing the island between them, the Benedictines, the Jesuits, and an educational order – the Order of Maria Immaculata. As far as this religion is concerned, there are certain political implications, to which later reference will be made. The Anglican Church is now part of the Church of India and Ceylon. There are two episcopal sees – Colombo and Kurunegala – under the general control of the Archbishop of Calcutta; in 1962 a Sinhalese bishop was appointed to this archiepiscopal see.

The importance of the way in which Christianity has influenced the course of development in Ceylon lies mainly in the field of education. In Portuguese and Dutch times this was entirely Christian, though the ancient Buddhist *pirivena* education struggled on bravely as best it could – and survived. During the early British times, especially at first, education was mostly carried on in schools run by Christian missionaries, among whom were certain American Congregationalists who worked in Jaffna: the latter's efforts were at first frowned upon by the British Government, but later encouraged: their influence on the educational development of the Jaffna Tamils has been very great. Of the leading boys' secondary schools at the end of the British occupation, only one was secular – the Royal College – about four were Buddhist, the remainder Christian, though in fact in many of the latter a large number of the pupils were not of that religion. The position in girls' schools was much the same. All these schools were run to a considerable extent on the British model. One of the best known, Trinity College, Kandy, was run very much on the lines of an English public school; most of the students were boarders, organised in houses, and considerable importance was placed on team games, such as cricket and rugby football. Much of this was due to a famous headmaster ('Principal' is, however, the term used in Ceylon), Rev. A. G. Fraser – a successor of his, Robert Stopford, is now the Bishop of London. Fraser succeeded in imbuing many of his pupils with what may be called 'the public school spirit', and his example was followed in other of the boys' secondary schools. These schools for a number of years had the passing of either the Cambridge Senior or the London Matriculation examinations as the goal of their senior pupils; and neither examination was in any way tailored to suit local conditions.

The significance of the two main religions of Ceylon, Buddhism and Hinduism, in particular the former, will emerge as the book goes on.

CASTE

To the outside observer caste in Ceylon is an unobtrusive, even hidden, subject, so much so that the following paragraphs are written with some reluctance. The caste system of the Sinhalese differs, and has always differed markedly, from that of India, so greatly that there has been no necessity to lay legislative stress on caste, as has been the case on the mainland, where the practice of untouchability is not only illegal but unconstitutional. When the constituencies for parliamentary elections were delimited, some trouble was taken in certain areas to arrange that some of the lower castes or sub-castes would not be without a good chance of representation in Parliament. It would appear that there is often a tendency for a voter to vote for a candidate of the same caste as himself. Beyond this, caste would seem to have comparatively little influence on politics.

In general the Sinhalese do not care to discuss the question of caste with any non-Sinhalese, unless they happen to know him very well. The average Western-educated Ceylonese will say that caste is a rapidly decaying influence in the social system. This is doubtless true, but it exercises, perhaps occasionally only, subtle influences that rarely appear on the surface, except in the matter of marriage. Marriages in Ceylon are generally arranged, and those between members of different castes, or even of sub-castes, are uncommon, though not unknown. Even in comparatively Westernised Colombo, so states the only authority who has in recent times made any study of the subject, '95 per cent of the marriages are endogamous'.[1]

The principal peculiarity of caste among the Sinhalese is that more than half of them belong to the highest caste, the Goigamas, or cultivators. There is little or no trace of Brahmins (priests) or Kshatriyas (warriors), though the caste usually held to be next in order to the Goigamas, the Karawas (fishers), claim to Kshatriya origin. However this may be, it seems likely that members of this caste are of Indian origin, though now completely 'Sinhalised'. The same may well be true of the Salagama caste (cinnamon peelers). These two, and the Durawa caste, are considered the three superior castes below the Goigamas. There are a number of castes inferior in status to these in the caste hierarchy, such as that known as the Dhobi caste (washers), though a number of this caste have risen to high positions in the Government and in other spheres such as the professions. There are also many sub-divisions among castes, the Goigamas in particular. Strictly speaking there are no untouchables, as in India, though for many centuries an inferior caste known as Rodiyas, and one or two others, suffered social disabilities in such matters as the use of wells. Even this is tending to disappear, though the Rodiyas continue to exist under the stigma of being very low caste.

Among the Tamils caste divisions are more live. Here, too, the highest caste is that of the cultivators (Vellalas). Some years ago the Principal – a European – of a certain Christian school in Jaffna, which had hitherto been attended only by boys of this caste, held a meeting with the parents of boys at the school and told them that he proposed to admit a boy of lower caste. Both parents and pupils agreed to this proposal, but when the boy arrived the school servants refused to serve him with food at mealtimes. This the Principal countered by arranging that his own personal servants should serve the boy. But the boy refused to be served by them, because, according to him, these servants were of too low a caste to serve him with food!

The real solvent of the caste system has been economic. The Karawas in particular, during the nineteenth and twentieth centuries, took up profitable lines of occupation and some of them prospered exceedingly. The influence of government by the British has been another solvent, for during almost the whole of their occupation of Ceylon they refused to make any caste distinctions, particularly in the matter of admission to the service of the Government.

[1] Bryce Ryan *Caste in Ceylon* (Rutgers University Press), 1953. Some of his conclusions have been heavily criticised in Ceylon.

So that, as the upper ranks of the administration became more open to Ceylonese, some members of castes comparatively low in the hierarchy rose to high positions in government service. Thus caste distinctions have tended to become more and more penetrated, or even superseded, by class distinctions. Wealth and high position in the government service or in the professions has created these class divisions which, anyhow till quite recently, have been very marked. The real gulf has come to be between the Western-educated, i.e. those whose education has been almost entirely through the English language, and those whose education has been in Sinhalese or Tamil – as well as those who have received no education at all.

In a sense, too, European residents could be considered as something in the nature of a caste – a point which will be considered at a later stage of this book.

By and large, caste today, though still very much in existence, plays little part in the political and a decreasing part in the social life of Ceylon. The occupational character of caste, which was not improbably its origin, or certainly the origin of many castes and sub-castes, hardly counts for anything today; it may be put this way, that while most if not all the fishermen are Karawas, most Karawas are not fishermen. There are still certain acts that people of higher caste will not perform, certain occupations that nothing would persuade them to enter. Inter-caste marriages are rare, and take place only among either the well-educated and Westernised, or among the urban poor – though in the latter case the word 'marriage' is often not the correct description of the marital condition.

However, caste is still there, pervasive beneath the surface, and has influences which are not at all apparent to a foreign observer. In the words of the above-quoted writer 'as long as family units persevere, caste will survive'.

Chapter 2

Ancient and Medieval Ceylon

T HE MIGRATION of races and tribes is a fascinating subject which has led to much historical speculation, owing to the lack of records for the most part. Ethnological and other scientific studies are doing something to throw light on these, but as yet they have not gone very far in Ceylon. Every such migration has to end somewhere, and this usually happened when the migrants reached some impassable natural obstacle, such as an impenetrable forest or mountain range – or the ocean.

Ceylon being an island just off the apex of the great inverted triangle which is the southern part of the Indian sub-continent, and easily accessible from it, it might be expected that the island would have received waves of migrants in prehistoric days, before the advent of the Sinhalese from India, which may with some likelihood be assigned to the sixth century B.C. There are traces of prehistoric man – palaeolithic and neolithic – in Ceylon, and there has survived, even to this day, the remnants of a primitive tribe known as Veddas, who were till recently in the hunting stage of human existence.[1] There are only a few families left in the jungles of the Eastern Province, but without doubt a great number of the Veddas have been Sinhalised, and in early times – perhaps later on, too – there was probably some intermixing of blood between the Veddas and the Sinhalese. Legend speaks of tribes called Yakkhas and Nagas (demons and snakes). There is a section of opinion among some Tamil controversialists that these early tribes were of Dravidian race, but there is no real evidence to prove this contention. More probably they were stone age peoples, rather like some of the forest tribes of south India, the Bhils and the Gonds, to whom it would appear that the Veddas are akin.

These primitive peoples undoubtedly practised some form of animistic religion, and some of its cults may survive, underlying the forms of Hinduism which the Sinhalese brought with them, and the Buddhism which they later adopted. Buddhism was, and is, a most

[1] Seligman's *The Veddas* is still the authoritative work on the ethnology of these people.

tolerant religion and, like several of the other great world religions, made comparatively little attempt to upset or do away with many of the superstitious practices which are found among the peoples whose leaders adopted one or other of these religions. Research is needed to go into the question of which such non-Buddhist practices among the Sinhalese village folk descend from those that they brought with them, and which they absorbed from the peoples who inhabited Ceylon before they arrived.[1]

The Sinhalese were a race from north-western India, though some authorities favour a north-eastern origin. Possibly both are right, and there may have been more than one stream of immigration. Their descendants claim to be of 'Aryan' stock, which may well be the case. Certainly the Sinhalese language is in origin an Aryan dialect, though it would appear to have been greatly influenced and modified by other languages, of Dravidian origin, particularly Tamil.

According to legend, the Sinhalese came in one wave, led by a mythical hero named Vijaya. This is the legend as given in the *Mahavamsa*, the ancient chronicle of Ceylon,[2] which includes Sinhalese with other names of a totemistic character, so that it is possible that these tribes may have come to the island at various times between the fifth and the third centuries B.C. Little is known of their social customs beyond what can be sifted from the chaff of myth and legend, which does not amount to much. The Sinhalese invaders practised agriculture and were acquainted with the use of iron, which would account for their speedy success over the indigenous tribes, who may not have progressed further than the hunting stage, using stone weapons and implements. The degree of their civilisation can only be surmised, but from the geographical factors enumerated earlier, the fact that they settled in the northern part of the island, and hardly penetrated for a long time to the wet zone, would imply some knowledge of artificial irrigation.

The immigration of the Sinhalese is the first major event in the history of Ceylon. The second was the introduction of the Buddhist religion during the second half of the third century B.C.: the date usually assigned is B.C. 247. At that time the great emperor Asoka

---

[1] N. D. Wijeyesekera, *The People of Ceylon*, (*passim*) (Gunasena & Co., Colombo).
[2] The *Mahavamsa*, written in Pali, the sacred language of Buddhism, was probably compiled during the sixth century A.C., and was based on an earlier chronicle, and a long tradition of history handed down orally by Buddhist *bhikkhus*. (monks is the closest English translation of this term). It is a remarkable document, being a continuous history, unique in Asia, up to the middle of the fourth century It was afterwards continued, in what is known as the *Culavamsa*, by various hands up to the middle of the eighteenth century.

bore rule over most of India, and was acknowledged as supreme ruler by the kings and rulers of the whole sub-continent. The king of the Sinhalese was Tissa, who was sufficiently in touch with the state of India to send the Mauryan emperor an embassy. In return, Asoka recognised Tissa's kingship and sent him a message recommending him to adopt the teachings of the Buddha – the Dhamma. According to the *Mahavamsa*, Asoka sent his son Mahinda, who had taken the vows of a bhikkhu, to preach the religion. The Sinhalese king gladly accepted it, and became known as Devanampiya Tissa, the first word signifying 'beloved of the gods'.

By this time the Sinhalese kings had established their head-quarters at Anuradhapura, which was to remain their capital city for nearly a thousand years. Here was founded a *vihara* (which may be translated as monastery) and here, brought by Mahinda's sister, a Buddhist *bhikkuni* (nun), was planted a branch of the sacred bo-tree (*ficus religiosa*) under which the Buddha was sitting when en-lightenment came to him. The tree is still there, just alive, and the oldest historic tree in the world.

This, briefly, is the story of the coming of Buddhism as told in the *Mahavamsa*. The force of historical criticism is being brought to bear on it, to the effect that the introduction and spread of Buddhism were probably of much slower growth: but however modified or even discredited, the essential fact is that the story is implicitly believed by the people of Ceylon. Buddhism became the sole religion, and spread over the country and above the mass of local cults – the worship of Hindu gods and minor local deities, the propi-tiation of demons and spirits, and so forth, which remained, and still remain, a substratum beneath it.

BUDDHIST RELIGION AND PRACTICE

Since Buddhism is a living force, possibly the strongest in present day Ceylon, some consideration of its nature as a religion is necessary before touching further on the ancient and medieval history of the island.

Gautama Buddha, an Indian prince who lived in the sixth century B.C., was appalled when he found out for himself the extent and depth of human suffering. It seemed to him that it was caused by desire, by the ceaseless struggle of human beings to get something. He therefore determined to find a way of freeing himself from human desires and passion. Accepting, as he did, the basic Hindu concep-tion of the rebirth of the individual as some body, human or animal,

depending on his actions in his previous life – his *Karma*[1] – only by
limiting desires could the individual be born into a higher state of
life, and the Buddha described how this could be done, by following
the noble eightfold path – right understanding, right thoughts, right
speech, right action, right means of livelihood, right effort, right
mindfulness and right concentration. By practising this kind of self-
control through successive lives the individual would ultimately
arrive at a condition called *nibbana* (often written *nirvana*) and find
himself free from desire, free from the cycle of rebirths: he would
become what is known as an *arahant*. In order to do this, it would be
necessary first of all to free himself from the ordinary cares of life by
taking vows and becoming a bhikkhu, who lives a life not unlike that
of one of the more severe orders of Christian monks.[2] The bhikkhu
must live a life of poverty and celibacy, depending for the neces-
saries of life on the alms of the charitable and pious. The teaching of
the Buddha is collectively known as the *Sasana*, the order of bhikkhus
as the *Sangha*.

Buddhism is, then, not an organised religion in the ordinary
sense of the word. The individual who wishes to attain *nibbana* must
cut himself off from ordinary life. But there is another ideal, which
developed somewhat later: it can perhaps be best summed up as
'service'. The individual should perform meritorious acts with the
purpose of serving, and saving, others, after the example of the
Buddha himself; by so doing throughout a series of lives he would
become known as *Boddhisattva* – one destined in the end to be a
Buddha. The importance of this is that the bhikkhu with this ideal
does not withdraw within himself, but deliberately tries to serve
others, to do which he must necessarily be more in touch with the
outside world. Hence it is that bhikkhus have taken at various times,
and perhaps today more than ever, some part in public affairs.

It must not be thought that the Buddhist religion applies only to
bhikkhus. For the ordinary person who has not taken the vows there
is a moral code laid down, included in which is the prohibition of
taking life and the encouragement of purity, by following which he
(or she) may hope to acquire such merit that the next rebirth will be
into a higher sphere of life. There is nothing in this code to prevent
the ordinary layman from continuing to follow the religious practices

---

[1] Karma is defined by Buddhists as 'the law of moral causation'. This constant
succession of birth and rebirth is not what is sometimes called the transmigration
of souls, of which the basic idea is of an undying spark of God – the soul inhabiting
a succession of bodies. Buddhism acknowledges neither a supreme deity nor the
soul.
[2] A bhikkhu, however, is at liberty at any time to renounce his vows, and this is
by no means unusual.

of his forbears, provided they do not include the sacrifice of living creatures or impure ceremonial practices.

Certain ceremonies have grown up under the mantle of Buddhism which have a strong appeal to the laity, and to the ordinary Sinhalese person they mean a great deal. Every full moon night (*poya*) sees in the Sinhalese towns and villages processions, in many of which women clad in white predominate: they walk along, chanting *sadhu, sadhu* (good, or holy), to the Buddhist temples, where they offer flowers and listen to sermons by bhikkhus. Flowers are also placed at the foot of the sacred bo-trees and shrines, incense is burned, and those visiting the temples repeat the five precepts of the moral code. The greatest of these full moon days is *Wesak*, in May, when the Buddha's day of birth and of enlightenment is celebrated – a day once described to the writer by a Sinhalese as 'the Buddhist Christmas day'. Paper lanterns, many of them elaborate and some quite beautiful, are lit and hung outside houses and shops: and some quite large panoramas, often representing scenes from the Buddha's life, are displayed. In towns today much is done with coloured electric lights – efficient but much less attractive. The Sinhalese have a considerable talent for decoration, and any Sinhalese town or village on Wesak night is a thing of beauty. Another great festival is *Poson*, full moon day in June. Still another great occasion is the famous *Perahera* at Kandy, which is a series of nightly torchlight processions of relics borne on the backs of gaily decorated elephants (over 80 of them on the final night) accompanied by Kandyan chieftains, in their picturesque, if somewhat feminine-looking, traditional attire, and by male dancers in their striking costumes. The Kandy Perahera is more than a religious procession. It is witnessed by thousands of villagers, the bright saris of the women making the crowds an attractive spectacle in themselves, as well as by visitors from all over the world – and it is well worth seeing.

Many villagers also have their own processions on full moon nights. Buddhists in general, especially the villagers, have a fondness for going on pilgrimages. These are usually nowadays to the ancient sites and shrines, such as Anuradhapura and Polonnaruwa, the ancient and medieval capitals of the Sinhalese kings, Mihintale, where Mahinda is reputed to have first preached the Buddhist way of life, and Tissamaharama, away down in the south-west of the island. Another great place of pilgrimage is Kataragama, tucked away in the southeastern jungle, and difficult to access – this place is, in fact, a famous Hindu shrine of remote antiquity. They go to Kandy, to the *Maligawa* (Temple of the Tooth), whenever there is an opportunity to view the tooth relic of the Buddha, and above all to Sri Pada, better known to the world as Adam's Peak, a sugar-loaf mountain 7,000 feet high in the southern part of the central mountain massif, on top of which is a depression reputed to be the footprint of the Buddha – or of Adam, if the pilgrim happens to be Muslim or Christian. The climb up the steep path is no easy matter even for the young and vigorous, though many older people take it, using to help them in their ascent iron chains placed there by a pious Sinhalese king in medieval times.

All these pilgrimages, though there is much of the holiday spirit about them, have a strong religious significance. (It is worth noticing that the addiction to pilgrimages among the people of Ceylon has not been disregarded by the Roman Catholic Church, whose devotees visit their own jungle shrine, known as St. Anne's, at Madhu.) At all of them Buddhist bhikkhus are likely to be involved, carrying out certain religious or ceremonial duties, and thus coming into contact with the laity.

There are other occasions, too, which draw them together – marriages, funerals, sickness, and the chanting of *pirit*, which is chanting by a number of bhikkhus to avert misfortune. In times past the bhikkhus seem to have played a very large part in village life: this is still to some extent the case to this day.

The average Sinhalese, man or woman, especially in the villages, has a strong belief in magic and in astrology. Many ceremonies are regarded as bringing good fortune and averting the influence of evil spirits and demons. Most Sinhalese would never dream of starting on a journey unless under auspicious circumstances, usually determined by an astrologer – and this applies to many highly educated people.

Ancient cults and beliefs may well lie deep rooted in Sinhalese practice and behaviour; but, however this may be, the vast majority of the Sinhalese are, at least outwardly, fervent Buddhists. The preceding paragraphs have tried to indicate how closely mixed up Buddhism is with the life of the people – the Sinhalese people. They have remained faithful to the Buddhist religion and way of life throughout centuries of Hindu influence and, at times, domination, albeit mild and tolerant, and persecution or neglect by European rulers for four and a half centuries – one and a half in the case of the Kandyan people. And now that these rulers have gone, it looks as if Buddhism has come into its own again. An outward and visible sign of this is what is known as 'The Buddhist Committee of Enquiry', set up not by government action, as is usually the case with such committees at the present day, but by certain leading Buddhist laymen. The publication of the Committee's findings – a naturally biased document – had a strong impact on public opinion in the island, and a quite remarkable influence on recent political developments.[1]

THE SINHALESE KINGDOMS

Though the rulers of Ceylon appear to have had some contact with the kingdoms of the Indian mainland before the advent of Buddhism, there is no doubt that the abundant contacts with them, and to a lesser degree with Burma and Siam, were due to this event. The close touch with India became political after a time, but whether in its political, religious or cultural aspect it was the most important external influence in Ceylon for the next 1,800 years. The Buddhist connexion brought to Ceylon the art of writing, a tradition of learning, and through these were developed the arts of architecture, sculpture and painting. The Sinhalese soon became a civilised people; they attained a high degree of civilisation, the centre of which was the capital city of Anuradhapura, the ruins of which still attest what must have been considerable magnificence.

There was one other area of Sinhalese settlement, away down in the dry south-east of the island, known as Ruhuna. But there is very little knowledge of this: it seems to have centred around Tissamaharama, of which not very much more than traces exist. Right up through the centuries Ruhuna was a semi-independent or occasionally a totally independent principality.

Not only was Anuradhapura the city of the Sinhalese kings, it was also from the outset the headquarters of the *Sangha* – the order of bhikkhus – and here was sited the *Maha Vihara* (great monastery). Their *dagobas* – vast domes of brick – are there to this day, in ruins or, sometimes, rather unfortunately restored by pious Buddhists. When they were first built, as huge relic chambers, they were topped by erections resembling gilded spires: one of them was described by the famous Chinese traveller, Fa Hien, as four hundred feet in height, and adorned with gold, silver and gems. The first of them to be built, according to the *Mahavamsa*, was erected by the first Buddhist king, Devanampiya Tissa – the Thuparama dagoba. They are not unlike the Indian relic mounds (*stupas*), but those in Ceylon have their own characteristics.

For many centuries the Maha Vihara remained the centre of the simplest and purest form of Buddhism – the *Theravada*. Later on variants of the religion appeared, but the Mahayanist form, which spread over northern India (for a time), China, Tibet and Japan, though it appeared in Ceylon, never made much headway, and

[1] See below, pp. 180–1.

Ceylon today, like Burma and Thailand, the two other main Buddhist countries of Asia, kept the older form, usually called the *Hinayana*. Buddhism spread – how quickly is not known – surely all over the country, and to this day the sites of ancient vihares are still coming to light in what is now dense jungle country. Before the bhikkhus had *vihares* built for them, they dwelt in caves, and the oldest inscriptions extant in Ceylon are to be found under the drip ledges of some of these caves.

It is a remarkable fact of Ceylon's history that it was in the flat northern part of the island, the dry zone, that this early civilisation flourished. This part came to be known as the *Rajarata* – king's country. Then, as now, the staple food of the people was rice. The growing of rice requires water, and in the dry zone water is far from plentiful. Hence, for the successful cultivation of rice there, artificial irrigation was necessary in order to feed a population of any size. There is evidence from foreign travellers that Anuradhapura was a fairly large city, though the numbers of its population have been grossly exaggerated by some writers. Without doubt, however, it must have been quite a fine city, and probably quite beautifully laid out. There is little that remains of its civil architecture, though the remains of the royal baths, if the ruins are correctly identified as such, are very striking. In any case, it is clear that the people had to be fed, and a remarkable system of irrigation was developed by the Sinhalese over many generations – a very astounding and admirable achievement in early civil engineering.

The irrigation system in a flat country must, of course, be based on the conservation of water in reservoirs and the construction of channels to supply water to the maximum possible acreage around them. The ancient Sinhalese constructed reservoirs with remarkable skill. Some of them were of considerable size, great artificial lakes, and many of these 'tanks', which is the English word by which they came to be known in Ceylon, were skilfully connected with each other to form a vast irrigation system. Modern irrigation engineers have evinced much admiration for the way in which the ancient Sinhalese succeeded in their irrigation schemes, which are far from easy, even to their modern counterparts. There are a few rivers which, rising in the central mountain mass, run in a northerly or north-westerly direction. Whenever there is a shortage of rain they are apt to run dry, and in any case evaporation is rapid. In the flat country the rivers are shallow and sluggish, owing to the very small drop in levels and the nature of the soil, so that the construction of these early irrigation systems was a remarkable practical feat. They required constant attention, and their construction and maintenance

C

must be regarded as the leading feature of early Sinhalese economic history – little as is known of it.

These tanks, large and small, were to be found in hundreds all over the Rajarata. Many villages constructed their own, whenever these happened to be adjacent to a stream which could be dammed: but the average village tanks depended on the annual rainfall, and could not, like the big ones, be regarded as storage tanks.

The history of the wet zone in the early days is obscure. Most of it was dense jungle, possibly inhabited by scattered tribes of Veddas, but also by Sinhalese who, from political or other reasons, had felt compelled to quit their homes in the dry zone. As a Ceylon historian puts it, the wet zone was 'the home of rebels and defeated causes'.[1]

The coast regions must have been of some importance, but they attracted very little attention from the writers of the *Mahavamsa* and its successors. It is only every now and then that any mention is made of such secular matters as trade, in elephants, in spices and in gems. Most of such evidence derives from foreign travellers, and from coins found in Ceylon. There is evidence that before the Christian era Arabs and Greeks were trading in those commodities, and later on Persians and Chinese. The Sinhalese themselves, however, do not seem to have been to any extent travellers or traders.

The kings, or maybe often just the local rulers, presumably levied some sort of duties or licences to trade on the foreign importers. Their main revenue, however, was the grain tax; and all the king's subjects had to render him some kind of service, which varied considerably according to the status of the person concerned. With a crop like rice, growing as it does in water, the agricultural population can never have been fully employed. Then, as now, prepared rice, the staple article of their diet, must have been supplemented by the edible products of the coconut palm, and by vegetables; but the growing and preparation of these is not to any extent time-consuming. It was during the intervals of cultivation that the people were able to carry out the work which they owed to the king, known as *rajakariya*. It was by means of this kind of labour – forced labour often enough, perhaps – that the great dagobas were piled up, and the bunds (embankments) built across the rivers for the construction of the tanks. When it is remembered that, for example, the tank known as Minneriya had (and has) a bund several miles long and about 50 feet high, it becomes clear that a very large labour force must have been employed, and very carefully organised. This particular tank is 4,560 acres in extent when full of water – and, incidentally, is then a very beautiful sight. It was fed by a canal 25

[1] G. C. Mendis, *The Early History of Ceylon*, (Colombo Apothecaries Coy.).

miles in length, dug in the fourth century A.C. Another canal, which brought water to Anuradhapura, was 54 miles long, and irrigated 180 square miles; for the first 17 miles of this canal the gradient is only 6 inches to the mile, which aptly illustrates the ability of the irrigation engineers of those times.

The people of Ceylon in those early days seem to have been homogenous in race (except in so far as they interbred to a greater or lesser extent with the Veddas or other aboriginal tribes); in language, for the Sinhalese tongue spread all over the inhabited parts of the island – today the few remaining Veddas speak a dialect of Sinhalese; above all, in religion, and without doubt it was the Buddhist religion which was the most binding force. During the early centuries the king at Anuradhapura seems to have been the reasonably undisputed ruler of the Sinhalese, though in the more remote principalities, like Ruhuna, those who ruled there often bore little more than a nominal allegiance to him.

But there soon came to be another set of invaders, for from the second century B.C. onwards there were sporadic irruptions by various adventurers from southern India. Till about the ninth century A.C. the Anuradhapura kings managed either to hold them off or to drive them out before they could establish a permanent foothold in the island, but by the fourteenth century they had been able to accomplish this. In the intervening centuries, one or other of the south Indian kings on a number of occasions partially conquered the *Rajarata*, though their success was never either complete or lasting. It must be remembered that these invaders were of Dravidian race, speaking Dravidian languages, and professing the Hindu religion – Dravidian is not perhaps quite a scientific term from the ethnological angle, but it is the most useful general term for the peoples of southern India.

There are three Sinhalese kings whose memories are specially honoured among the Sinhalese. The first of these was Devanampi-yatissa, already mentioned, in whose reign and with whose hearty encouragement the religion of the Buddha was introduced. The next, perhaps the most cherished by the Sinhalese, was Dutugemunu, who reigned in the second century B.C. Not long before he came to the throne two sets of adventurers from India had invaded the island – the Mahavamsa describes them as 'Damilas', i.e. Tamils: the second, a Tamil warrior named Elara, took Anuradhapura and reigned there for forty years. The chronicle gives him the character of a just and good ruler. Dutugemunu was descended from the rulers of Ruhuna, members of the royal clan. He wrested Ruhuna from his father and brothers who ruled there, then brought an army north and defeated Elara in battle – according to the almost epic story, slew Elara in single combat, both kings mounted on elephants. This victory enabled him to set up his throne at Anuradhapura, where he redeemed his somewhat dubious earlier career by restoring the city, building the great Ruwanwelisiya dagoba and the 'brazen palace' – probably a wooden building, with a metal-covered roof resting on a veritable forest of pillars and with some religious significance. The facts to be specially noted are that he freed his country from the Tamils and encouraged the Buddhist religion.

The third hero-king, Parakramabahu I, came a thousand years later, in the twelfth century A.C. He gained fame in much the same way as Dutugemunu – fighting successfully against the south Indians, and restoring and cherishing Buddhism. During the tenth and eleventh centuries Ceylon had fallen into the hands of the powerful rulers of the Chola kingdom. Anuradhapura was deserted, and many of the buildings were destroyed by Rajaraja, a great king of that realm, who made Ceylon a province of his kingdom, with its capital at Polonnaruwa. But after his time the Chola kingdom started to break up, and the Sinhalese king Vijayabahu I succeeded in temporarily expelling the invaders; he did not re-occupy Anuradhapura, possibly because the invaders may have done too much damage to the complicated irrigation system, but also because the more central position of Polonnaruwa enabled the king to exercise more control over the other districts of the island. Vijayabahu was the ruler of the *Malayarata*, which comprised the central hill-country: much of this was thick jungle, except for rice fields, mostly in terraces on the hill-sides. But it had the advantage of being highly defensible – as was proved time and time again during the next 800 years. He established his rule over Ruhuna with considerable difficulty, and when the Chola kingdom in India became weakened by internal troubles, regained the Rajarata, taking over Polonnaruwa as his capital. His descendants for the next hundred years fought among themselves, till the advent of Parakramabahu, known as 'the Great', who by a mixture of force and cunning brought the whole island under his rule. His claims to greatness rest largely on the fact that he was able, with at any rate initial success, to carry the war into south Indian territory, reversing what had been the usual course of events. He also restored and beautified the capital city, undertaking a big building programme. The ruins of Polonnaruwa, in their decoration particularly, show strong south Indian influence. He also carried out big irrigation works, including a vast tank known as the *Parakrama Samudra* (Sea of Parakrama). It would seem, however, that all this was very costly, and the Sinhalese monarchy never appears to have recovered from the severe economic burdens caused by the activities of Parakramabahu. None the less, in popular legend Parakramabahu is one of the great names living in Sinhalese memories, both as a defender of Ceylon against the Dravidians and a strong supporter of the Buddhist religion and of the Sangha.

During nearly the whole history of Ceylon, up to the beginning of the sixteenth century, the danger from south India was intermittent. From the ninth century onwards it was pretty constant. After the time of Parakramabahu I the south Indians managed to get a firm foothold in the north of the island, and the Tamil kingdom of Jaffna-patam had become well established by the fourteenth century: it kept its independence, except for a short period in the reign of Parakramabahu VI and his two successors in the fifteenth century, till the early seventeenth, when it was extinguished by the Portu-guese. For several reasons, possibly of security from the strategic angle, the Sinhalese kings moved their capitals further south and south-west, and by the time the Portuguese reached Ceylon, early in the sixteenth century, the capital was situated at Kotte, a few miles from Colombo.

Thus, during these centuries following the quitting of Anurad-hapura, the dry zone became less and less populous – maybe due to the onslaughts from India, the destruction of the irrigation system, or the increase of malaria – and the Sinhalese began to penetrate into the centre and, particularly, the south-west of the island, where most of them are to be found today. As they cleared the thick jungle they found good soil, and no lack of water for the growing of rice.

During all this period the Sinhalese remained staunchly Buddhist. The Buddhist religion went through some vicissitudes. The Indian invaders do not seem to have indulged in persecution – Hinduism is a thoroughly tolerant religion. But they did pillage, and even destroyed vihares, and built some Hindu temples, at which the Sinhalese people, or some of them, did not hesitate to worship. It is an interesting fact that one of the most famous Hindu temples was sited at Devendra (now known as Dondra), the southernmost point of the island.

But Buddhism itself does not seem to have been greatly influenced by its constant contact with Hinduism during these centuries. At various times sects deemed to be heretical found their way into Ceylon, including the Mahayanist form of Buddhism. But these did not last, and the simpler form, the Hinayana, maintained itself in Ceylon.

The kings kept in close touch with the Sangha, and acquired

merit by the gift of lands to vihares, together with the services owed
by the people on those lands; also by building new vihares or
restoring old ones.

The history of the Sinhalese monarchy is on the whole not very
remarkable. Some kings were noted for saintliness or scholarship –
or both. Many of them, for instance Mahasen and Dhatusena,
made notable contributions to the great irrigation systems, constructing new bunds or enlarging old ones; Parakramabahu I was
particularly famed for this. A few of them were notoriously wicked;
a reigning queen (there were few of them) poisoned several successive husbands. One fifth century king, Kassappa I, came to the
throne after putting the king, his father, to death, as well as all the
other members of his family on whom he could lay hands. The story
is that one brother escaped – and that it was foretold to Kassappa
that this brother would ultimately bring about his death. Be that as
it may – and it worked out that way in the end – Kassappa quitted
Anuradhapura and had built for him a new capital, which is one of
the wonders of Ceylon. He had a palace constructed on top of a
great rock 800 feet in height called Sigiriya, the lion rock, accessible
only by a narrow gallery and a perilous climb up a sheer rock face.
Below the rock he laid out what must have been a series of beautiful
water gardens. The remains of the palace still lie on top of the rock,
the gallery is still there, and skilful archaeological work has discovered and restored the water gardens. The rock itself resembles
a crouching lion, and Kassappa had it carved that way. It is held
that one rock face was covered with paintings. This may be so, but
anyhow, half-way up it is a tiny cave, inaccessible but for a modern
iron spiral staircase, and on its wall still survive mural paintings of
high artistic merit. The rock is one of the most fascinating sights in
Asia, and conveys to the visitor a vivid impression of the high level
of architectural planning and artistic skill which the Sinhalese kings
had at their disposal a millenium and a half ago.

With the coming of independence, then, the Sinhalese people not
unnaturally cast their minds back to this long pre-European era.
The romantic tradition of a glorious past somehow survived, despite
the fact that it was a comparatively short time before independence
that the history of Ceylon came to be to any extent taught in the
schools; long enough, however, for the younger adult generation to
have some knowledge of it. Politically this is of importance, for the
two main characteristics of this history are the close interdependence
of the Government and the Buddhist Sangha, and the feeling that
the Tamil is the hereditary enemy who destroyed the ancient cities
and made a permanent settlement in the land of the Sinhalese.

To the historian, the history of Ceylon before the coming of the European invader shows an island whose people had a certain sense of racial unity, maintained largely through the Buddhist religion, but, after the tenth century, rarely united effectively under a single ruler: a kingdom rather weaker than the neighbouring kingdoms of southern India, and therefore coming every now and again completely under the control of one or other of them, yet maintaining its identity by trying, and often succeeding, in playing off one of them against the other; but ultimately having to retreat to that part of the island which was more defensible than the ancient northern part – and of the latter, some given up to Tamil settlers, the rest deserted and reverting to jungle. Economically, a peasant economy, with the people living largely on rice as their staple food, the products of the coconut palm and some vegetables, and a rather thin, if profitable, trade on the west coast, carried on almost entirely by foreigners, some of whom – the Muslims (later called Moors)[1] – settled in the island for trading purposes. Culturally, a tradition of learning derived from India, based on a classical language, Pali, and maintained largely by the order of bhikkhus, the Sangha; a tradition of craftsmanship, in relation to sculpture, decorative carving, painting and architecture, some of much merit, and greatly influenced through the centuries by the culture of the mainland, yet keeping its native characteristics. Socially, a condition perhaps most easily described as feudal, the relations between rulers and ruled, and between the various grades of society, being based on services in return for the holding of land, interlocked with a pervasive but not too rigid caste system.

[1] See above, p. 17.

Chapter 3

The First Two European Invaders

O N this static society, in nearly all respects very much inward-looking – for the age-long menace from south India tended to die away after the collapse, in the sixteenth century, of the great kingdom, sometimes termed 'empire' of Vijayanagar – descended an entirely new menace. This came from a far distant continent, from a race of white people professing a different, and a militant religion, with a lust for conquest and a complete lack of understanding of, combined with some contempt for, the people of Ceylon, their religion and their culture. It was, of course, a part, an early part of that amazing world movement which goes by the name of 'the expansion of Europe', and which lasted for well over four centuries. It is only today, as it were, that it has come to an end, after covering the whole world. This may perhaps be best illustrated in two not unconnected ways; the first, that the Afro-Asian countries command a majority in the General Assembly of the United Nations, the second, that 'colonialism' has been coined as a 'dirty word' to define the movement.

The impact on Ceylon of these successive waves of European conquest did not have a really vital effect in changing the island people till well after the advent of the third, the British, for neither the Portuguese nor the Dutch, nor indeed the British at first, seriously tampered with the social system and the institutions of government based upon it: what they did was to adapt it for their purposes. Nevertheless, their coming had one major effect. From the earliest times influences from the mainland of India had been very strong. It is only one of the accidents of history that the island was never absorbed into one or other of the Indian kingdoms – it nearly happened more than once. But once the Europeans had come, with that new phenomenon to Asia, sea power, the old contacts were cut off, or at least greatly diminished, and it is only in comparatively recent times that they have been renewed.

Pioneers in this world movement, as it affected Asia, were that remarkable nation, the Portuguese. Historians often ascribe their voyages and discoveries to the quest after the trade in spices, under-taken in order to bypass the big block of Muslim countries of western Asia; and, indeed, in this there is much truth. But there was also the lure of the fabulous wealth of Asia, of which the few medieval travellers had told the story, the tradition of the splendour of the Asian kingdoms, with which a profitable trade, or perhaps from which an even more profitable plunder, might be secured.

The Portuguese first came to Ceylon early in the sixteenth century, arriving to begin with by the accident of weather. They were made quite welcome at Colombo, off which their ships had anchored, and expressed their wish to trade with the subjects of the Sinhalese king, then at Kotte. The Sinhalese were not unused to voyagers arriving for that purpose. Greeks and Romans, Persians, Arabs and Chinese had at one time and another come in much the same way, though only the Arabs had settled. So much was this the case that the *Culavamsa* (successor of the *Mahavamsa*) did not even bother to mention their arrival. Another chronicle, the *Rajavaliya*, however, refers to them as a race of great beauty, who ate stones and drank blood (i.e. bread and red wine) and who were willing to give two or three pieces of gold for one fish or one lime.

The newcomers had to face the hostility of the Muslim traders and of the Malabars of south-western India. The latter had some ships of war, but it was not long before the superior sea power of the Portuguese mastered them; and it was sea power that enabled them to hold their conquests. This achieved, they soon saw the weakness of the Sinhalese kingdom at Kotte, so near to Colombo, where they decided to establish their trading headquarters. By 1519, only 19 years after Vasco da Gama had turned the Cape of Good Hope, they had built a fortress there.

The headquarters of the Portuguese in Asia was at Goa (where they remained till almost yesterday), but whereas expansion was not possible from that base into the interior of India, this was not so in Ceylon. By taking advantage of the divisions between the rulers of the Sinhalese kingdoms, who were various members of the royal family, they finally succeeded in extinguishing all of them except the *Udarata*,[1] the kingdom of Kandy, which remained impregnable in the mountains. They also brought under their suzerainty the Tamil kingdom of Jaffna, soon after the middle of the sixteenth century, and early in the next century extinguished it. The Portuguese made several expeditions into the *Udarata*, as did their successors, the Dutch. But although they usually managed to reach Kandy, all the expeditions proved failures, partly owing to the nature of the country, the guerilla tactics of the Sinhalese, and that insidious enemy the malarial mosquito. The Kandyan kingdom survived into the time of the British occupation.

[1] Formerly called *Malayarata* (see p. 36.)

The Portuguese therefore held little more than the west coast, and some way into the interior of the island. But it was a remarkable exploit, taking into consideration the distance from their home country, the comparative scantiness of their population, and the heavy equipment they wore in a tropical climate; not only these, but also the political troubles at home, for from 1583 onwards Portugal itself had come under the rule of Philip II of Spain. But the story of the Portuguese in Ceylon is on the whole an unsavoury one. The captains-general often used most underhand methods in their dealings with the Sinhalese rulers; a few of them were men of quite atrocious character. One of them used to toss his prisoners into a river to waiting crocodiles. Those Portuguese who settled in the island, however, got on quite well with the Sinhalese, and inter-married with them freely. But the soldiers who came had only the intention of getting their hands on what wealth they could gather, by any means, and getting back as quickly as possible to their native land.

Yet there was another group of Portuguese who differed widely from these – the missionary priests and friars. It was a professed object of the Portuguese to 'convert the heathen', and in this they had a remarkable degree of success. Some of the people of Ceylon undoubtedly adopted Christianity for the loaves and fishes; but many were genuine converts, and to this day there are many thousands of Roman Catholics in Ceylon, especially on the west coast. They built churches and schools, not hesitating to destroy Buddhist and Hindu temples, such as the famous shrine at Dondra, and to take over the temple lands for their maintenance.

On the whole the Portuguese interfered but little with local laws, customs, and methods of administration. What they did was to put their own people, or Christian converts on whom they felt they could depend, into the higher posts. A certain number of the Sinhalese adopted Portuguese ways of living and, conversely, some of the Portuguese settlers adopted many Sinhalese or Tamil customs, according to the race of the women they married.

For most of the sixteenth century the Portuguese were content to trade, using the Sinhalese kings as puppets, particularly one un-fortunate monarch who was a convert to Christianity. More than once they were in serious danger of being driven out, in particular by the ruler of one of the adjacent kingdoms, Sitawaka, by name Rajasinha I, who was unusually warlike and showed definite military skill. Their situation, indeed, sometimes seemed desperate, the Portuguese being penned in their fortress of Colombo, and only saved by the arrival of reinforcements by sea from Goa or Cochin.

Towards the end of the century they embarked on more ambitious schemes of expansion, suppressing the kingdoms of Kotte and, later, of Jaffna, hoping to get as complete a control of the whole island as they had of its western coastal strip. But they were never able to conquer the kingdom of Kandy, despite several attempts. It was as a reaction against these attempts, in the thirties of the seventeenth century, that the king of Kandy called in a new power – the Dutch.

The Dutch had turned their eyes Asiawards during their life and death struggle with Philip II of Spain and Portugal. They realised that to destroy the Portuguese monopoly of trade with Asia would be damaging to their enemy and profitable to themselves. Their main interest came to be farther east than Ceylon: Batavia (now Djakarta), in the great island of Java, was to be their headquarters. Early in the seventeenth century their ships appeared off Ceylon's east coast, and they opened relations with the kings of Kandy.

The Portuguese realised that the east coast was open to the Dutch, and one of their more capable captains-general, Constantine de Saa, sent an expedition thither, which took Trincomalee, incidentally destroying there a famous Hindu temple and building a fort on its site. He also seized the other east coast port, Batticaloa. However, not long after this, the Portuguese suffered a major defeat in one of their fruitless raids against the Kandyan kingdom, in which de Saa was killed. The Portuguese power was in serious danger from the Sinhalese but, as before, Colombo held out and was relieved by sea.

It was in 1636 that the Kandyan king, another Rajasinha (the Second), a man of odd character but considerable ability, realised that it was not in his power to drive out the Portuguese. He therefore entered into renewed negotiations with the Dutch – the earlier negotiations had come to an abrupt end when a Dutch vice-admiral who went to Kandy offended the king and was murdered. Rajasinha hoped with the aid of the Dutch to drive out the Portuguese and reclaim all the land they had held, in return for extensive trading privileges.

Sea power in the Indian Ocean was already passing into the hands of the Dutch, and in the fourth decade of the seventeenth century first some ports on the west coast of Ceylon and then the important harbour of Galle, in the south-west, fell into their hands. After a temporary respite, due to the fact that the Portuguese in Europe had thrown off the yoke of Spain, the Dutch completed their task of driving out the Portuguese, in 1656, by the capture of Colombo, after a desperately brave resistance by the weak Portuguese garrison, and finally, two years later, by taking the last Portuguese strongholds in the north, Mannar and Jaffna, again after a determined resistance.

Rajasinha demanded that the territories taken from the Portuguese should be handed over to him. But the newcomers managed to avoid this, saying that the king had not paid them certain sums promised by him for their assistance. The Dutch saw themselves as the successors of the Portuguese, and above all were determined to take and keep in their hands the profitable cinnamon trade. Moreover, Colombo was a useful staging post on their way by sea to Batavia. They held on to the east coast ports of Trincomalee and Batticaloa and, on the west coast, especially the important harbours of Colombo and Galle. In these places they built strong forts – all of which still stand, except that of Colombo, where only the name remains. Rajasinha was furious, but could do little.

It may be mentioned here that more is known about this monarch than any other of the Sinhalese kings, for in 1660 an English merchant sailor was captured on the east coast, and spent nineteen years in the kingdom of Kandy as a prisoner. His name was Robert Knox: in the end he escaped and wrote a fascinating book on his experiences,[1] from which has been derived much information about the kingdom of Kandy at this time, and the life of its people.

The curious relation between the Dutch and the Kandyan kings differed markedly from the arrogant attitude of their predecessors. The Portuguese had insisted that the Sinhalese rulers were the vassals of the king, and should pay tribute on that account; they had even induced one of the Sinhalese kings to make over his kingdom to the king of Portugal. The position of the Dutch was, in theory, that they were the king's allies, and – he always insisted – subjects. They were in fact the servants of the *Vereenigde Oost-Indische Compagnie* (United East India Company) whose main purpose was trade[2]. The Dutch Governor-General at Batavia was quite specific in his instructions to the Dutch Governors in Ceylon that the kings of Kandy must as far as possible be placated and 'kept sweet' by suitable presents made at intervals. They often had to put up with insulting treatment in their efforts to obey these instructions.

In practice the difference between the rule of the Portuguese and that of the Dutch was not so great. They were in Ceylon. Ceylon was, or could be, both useful and profitable. Therefore they were determined to stay there, as the Portuguese had done. For about the first hundred years of their stay in the island, the extent

---

[1] Robert Knox, *An Historical Relation of Ceylon*.
[2] Copper coins are often come across in Ceylon with V.O.C. on them.

of territory in their possession was rather less than the Portuguese had half-possessed. But the Dutch held on to all the ports that were of any strategic importance, and this for a long time prevented a Kandyan king from having relations with any foreign countries, unless it were on some religious affairs; they could also interfere with his supply of salt.

Like their predecessors, the Dutch were in many matters content to take on the administrative system they found in Ceylon, and this, as mentioned earlier, was based on that which the Sinhalese rulers had used for centuries. In the later years the Portuguese administration had markedly deteriorated; the officials were in many cases both corrupt and incompetent. They had made considerable use of native officials, many of whom had turned Christian for gain, and who, to varying degrees, had adopted Portuguese manners and customs, and that language. It was not surprising, then, that on various occasions, when it looked as if the Portuguese might be driven out, these officials intrigued or openly sided with the Kandyans. The same is true of the armed levies, which they raised in some numbers and which were quite liable to desert to the Sinhalese kings if it seemed to their advantage, and if a war, or even a battle, seemed to be going against their masters.

There are very few records remaining of the Portuguese administration of Ceylon, though there may be some in Portugal which await the research student. They seem to have been destroyed by the Portuguese before they surrendered to the Dutch. There are, however, some contemporary histories, particularly 'The Temporal and Spiritual Conquest of Ceylon' by a Jesuit, Father Queyroz, which is a quite remarkable work. The author set out to show that the loss of Ceylon was due to the failure of his countrymen to observe the laws of God and the precepts of morality. The Dutch, however, kept more careful records, nearly all of which are, fortunately, extant in the Ceylon Government archives; they have been put into good order and are a mine for historical research into the period. This has already been started in the Ceylon University.

The Dutch found the administration in a state of chaos, but they set to work and constructed a reasonably orderly machine of government, much on the former basis. They did their best to encourage agriculture and develop some crafts; but above all, they paid very special attention to the cinnamon trade. For most of their occupation they were dependent on the wild cinnamon, much of which grew in the Kandyan king's domains; there was even a special caste of cinnamon peelers (chalyas), whose duty it was to bring the cinnamon to the king, or direct to the Dutch. These wily traders got the spice at very little cost, as the cinnamon peelers did their work on a service tenure basis, and the Company were thus able to make large profits.

The Dutch Governors were, on the whole, able and just men, as their memoranda to their successors (many of which are in the Ceylon archives) go to show. There was one notable exception, but he did not last long, and was severely punished for his cruelty and misdeeds. They reorganised the administration, much on the same lines as before, as far as the collectors of taxes and dues, and the rendering of services on the basis of land tenure, were concerned. They set up a system of schools, primarily for the training of minor members of the administration, locally recruited, but also for proselytising purposes. The main posts were held by Dutchmen, but some of the lesser ones by the offspring of those who settled in Ceylon and intermarried with the people – though generally, un-like with the Portuguese, intermarriage was not favoured by the authorities. Sinhalese and Tamils who espoused the religion of the Dutch Reformed Church were often given government posts. The Roman Catholic religion was unpopular with the authorities, and at times was actively persecuted. But it had taken deep root, and survived, though with difficulty, throughout the century and a half of Dutch rule – it is, incidentally, an odd historical coincidence that all three of the European countries who bore rule in Ceylon were each there for about this same period.

The Dutch also improved communications, by making a few roads and constructing a system of canals in a section of the coastal belt, particularly around Colombo. Some of them are there still. They were partly as outlets for flood water, as well as means of communication.

But the most important feature of their occupation concerned the law. Nothing much is known of how the Portuguese ran their legal affairs – it seems to have been a mixture of the customary laws of the people and rough justice – or injustice – of an arbitrary or military type. This did not appeal to the orderly minds of their successors, under whose rule a legal system was established, based on the Roman-Dutch law, with a high court of justice, from which there was an appeal to the court at Batavia, civil courts, and a *land-raad*, for cases about land in districts outside the three 'com-manderies' centred at Colombo, Galle and Jaffna.

In addition to this, one legally minded Governor had the cus-tomary laws of the Tamils codified; the code was known as the *Thesawalamai*, and is still the basis of one of the systems of law which run concurrently in Ceylon.

The Roman-Dutch law remains the basis of the law of Ceylon to this day, though considerably modified by the impact of British law in certain respects – company law, for instance. It is the main legacy of the Dutch occupation to Ceylon; the other, as explained in the first chapter[1], is the Dutch Burgher community.

During the years of the Dutch occupation of the maritime provinces, the Government had constant trouble with their own people, due to the fact that they were always illicitly engaging in private trade, which was very hard to put down. As the eighteenth century went on, their international position grew weaker, owing to the exhaustion which was a consequence of their final struggle with Louis XIV of France. They emerged successful from the War of Spanish Succession, but it was Britain which really reaped the fruits of victory. In Ceylon the administration tended to deteriorate in quality, despite the efforts of several able Governors.

Towards the middle of the eighteenth century an important change took place in the Kandyan kingdom. It had become the practice of its kings to seek for brides from the royal houses of the south Indian kingdoms, instead of, as formerly, from noble families among the Sinhalese. So that when, in 1739, the line of Rajasinha II died out, in the person of his grandson, the kingdom passed to the deceased king's brother-in-law, who was by race south Indian. Under Rajasinha the Buddhist religion had declined – he was no great patron. His son tried unsuccessfully to get bhikkhus from Siam in order to revive it. But when the Indian came to the throne, he took the Sinhalese name of Sri Vijaya Rajasinha and became a Buddhist, taking up his adopted religion with great enthusiasm. He was successful in getting some bhikkhus from Siam, the Dutch Government helping in the matter by providing the necessary shipping, and the result of this was a remarkable religious and cultural revival.

In mid-century the Dutch Government tried to tighten up the revenue collecting system. It also introduced the plantation system into the growing of cinnamon, which meant that the Kandyan kings would not so easily be able to upset the trade by interfering with the collection of the cinnamon in its wild state. The Dutch had always been most particular to keep their tight monopoly of the trade, which involved very strict control of the ports to prevent illegal export.

The new revenue measures provoked discontent which in 1760 culminated in open rebellion. This was fostered by the king of Kandy. But worse still, from the Dutch point of view, was his

[1] See Chapter 1, p. 18.

attempt to establish relations with the British, now the coming power in India. The Dutch, therefore, though unwillingly, decided they had to take strong measures against him. They invaded and captured Kandy though, like their predecessors, they were unable to hold it with a garrison. However, the king had suffered much by the war and in 1766 accepted peace terms which put the Dutch in a very strong position: they got full control of all the ports of Ceylon, a complete monopoly of trade, and the king undertook not to make any attempt to establish relations with other European powers.

But the tide of world affairs was turning against the Dutch. During the wars consequent on the War of American Independence, in the seventies and eighties, when the Dutch were involved in war with their former allies, the British, the Madras Government sent a fleet which captured Trincomalee. The British had for some years cast eyes of envy on this magnificent natural harbour, since in the naval actions against the French fleets in eastern waters its possession would have been invaluable to them. However, in this particular series of naval engagements the French had, quite unusually, something like naval parity, and benefited by the genius of Admiral Suffren. They recovered Trincomalee, which at the end of the war in 1783 they handed back to the Dutch. But the Dutch were to hold Ceylon only for another 13 years.

At this point the effects of nearly three centuries of European impact on Ceylon may be considered. The first consequence was the breaking of political contact with the mainland of India. The sixteenth century was the heyday of Muslim rule in the sub-continent – the time of the great Akbar and the Mogul emperors who succeeded him. Though these monarchs were immensely rich and powerful, they made no serious attempt to extend their direct rule over southern India; but the kingdoms there had all they could do to keep their ends up, and had no time for aggression against Ceylon.

Another consequence was the separation between what was at first the Tamil kingdom of Jaffna, and later a district or, in Dutch times a *commanderie*, and the Sinhalese parts of the island: that part of the country remained a separate unit. The north central part of the island, the old *Rajarata*, was almost entirely given over to jungle: there was a sparse and scattered population south of the Jaffna peninsula in the district known as the Wanni. But probably most of the communication, which was largely that of civil and military personnel, was by sea between Colombo and Jaffna or Mannar.

The continuing existence of the independent kingdom of Kandy was a constant feature of these centuries. The Sinhalese people there, not being exposed to European influences as were those in the low country, tended to grow somewhat apart from them, though the latter would gladly have come in with them had it ever been possible to get rid of the invaders.

These two points, the separation of the Tamil-inhabited areas from the Sinhalese and, to a lesser degree, of the Kandyan from the low-country Sinhalese, have had and still have direct bearing on subsequent history and on the present political situation; though during the period of the British occupation these separations ceased to be so marked, they were always there, and cropped up every now and again.

When the confused state of the country under the petty Sinhalese kingdoms of the fifteenth and sixteenth centuries is considered, and the fact that both the Portuguese and the Dutch interfered comparatively little with the old administration and social mode of existence, it is probable that the average villager in the occupied areas was not unduly worried by the change of masters. It was only at or near the top of the social scale that this could have been keenly felt, and even here the landholding classes were largely used by both sets of foreigners for local administration of the age-long semi-feudal type, particularly by the Portuguese. Only a comparatively small area of the island was under foreign rule, though this was the most thickly populated and prosperous. The number of Europeans in Ceylon at any time, apart from the military forces, cannot have been very large, and it is easy to overestimate their influence, and the changes which their presence brought about. Except for those who adopted the Christian faith, or were employed in the administration, the impact of these Europeans on the society of Ceylon in general may not have been so very great; the same is true of the first thirty or so years of the British occupation.

D

Chapter 4

The Coming of the British

T HE legacies of the Portuguese and Dutch occupations have already been indicated. That of the British is infinitely greater, though it has so recently become entitled to the term 'legacy' that it is by no means an easy task to estimate or even to define it. One of the main purposes of this book is to make some kind of estimate, not of the extent but of the nature of British influence in Ceylon. Whether the legacy is to be a lasting one, or comparatively evanescent, is on the knees of the gods.

There is no need to dwell at any length on the take-over by the British. It was basically due to the circumstances of the wars against revolutionary France. Even though by the last decade of the eighteenth century it had become fairly clear that the British and not the French were in the way of becoming the paramount power in India, there was always the possibility that French success in Europe might revive the still by no means negligible French influence in Asia. The British East India Company had been approached by Kandyan kings for an alliance against the Dutch, and there is no doubt that the valuable cinnamon trade was something of a bait; but more so the harbour of Trincomalee, as was clear during the wars which developed following the revolt of the American colonies. After the outbreak of the French Revolutionary wars, the exiled Stadtholder of Holland, who was a refugee in England, sent instructions in 1795 to the Dutch Governor in Ceylon to admit the British to Ceylon as a security measure. From the British point of view this had strategic importance.

The Governor and his Council were very undecided about this, but when they heard that, as a result of the French invasion, a Batavian Republic had been instituted, replacing the former United Provinces, albeit under French control, the Governor refused to obey these instructions. Consequently the Madras Government fitted out a sufficiently numerous and well-equipped expedition, and without much difficulty had by 1796 taken over the territory in Ceylon held by the Dutch. The take-over was materially aided by an extremely odd transaction. Hugh Cleghorn, a professor at St.

Andrew's University, was a personal friend of Count de Meuron, the proprietor of a Swiss mercenary regiment which the Dutch had hired to swell their military establishment in Ceylon; it was under the command of his brother. Cleghorn suggested to Henry Dundas, Secretary of State, that the de Meuron Regiment might be bought over by the British. Dundas welcomed the suggestion, and sent him out to clinch the transaction. This was brought off, and the Colombo garrison robbed of about half its strength, so that little more than a token resistance was put up by the Dutch forces.

It was not at first certain whether the British occupation would be permanent, or only a wartime necessity. But both the Government in Britain and the East India Company were anxious to keep Trincomalee and the coastal strip which the Dutch had held and, at the break in the French wars occasioned by the Treaty of Amiens, it was settled in that treaty that the occupation would be permanent: the Dutch possessions further east, however, were to be returned.

For the first few years of occupation the administration was of a mixed civil and military character, under the East India Company: it soon came to be almost completely civilian.[1] The territory was administered by a Revenue Department, which made a sad mess of it. Instead of carrying on the Dutch system of administration through local officials, a number of East India Company men were brought over from Madras – which must have been a strain on the establishment there. Those who came were not of high calibre. A few were British, the rest Madrassis, whose main idea seems to have been to use the revenue system to which they were accustomed in Madras to enrich themselves as rapidly as possible. Two unpopular measures, a tax on coconut palms and the abolition of service tenures, made matters much worse, and open revolts broke out.

The Governor of Madras, Lord Hobart, heard of this trouble and appointed a commission to investigate the causes. It was fortunate that the military Governor at the time happened to be Colonel de Meuron, former commander of the Swiss mercenary regiment which the British had bought over. He knew local conditions, and strongly advised a reversion to the Dutch administrative system. His advice was taken. Reports of the unsatisfactory state of affairs reached London and the British Government formed the idea of removing the control of Ceylon from the East India Company and making it a Crown Colony. The influential Company raised strong objections and an unsatisfactory compromise was reached, by which the Com-

[1] See C. R. de Silva, *Ceylon under the British Occupation 1795–1833* (Colombo Apothecaries Co.)

pany kept control of the collection of revenue, and of trade. In
1798 the Government sent out the Hon. Frederick North to be
Governor. He was to take control of the civil and judicial administration and to have some military powers (this was soon a source of
trouble); the Company kept its trading privileges. Hugh Cleghorn
was sent to be Principal Secretary. North sent back the Madras
officials, and carried out the recommendations of the Commission
by restoring the Dutch system of making use of indigenous officials.
A few civil servants, some of remarkable youthfulness, came out
from Britain. This system lasted on, with a certain number of
modifications, for well over thirty years. The evils of the 'Madras
system' are still a byword in Ceylon.

The dual control with the Company was not a success, and in
1801 the British Government decided to revert to its original plan
and make Ceylon a Crown Colony, though leaving to the Company
the monopoly of the dwindling cinnamon trade.

There is no need to go into details of the first three decades of
government by British Governors directly under the Crown.[1] There
were during the period four of them: North, Maitland, Brownrigg
and Barnes; the three last were all high ranking soldiers. They were
all quite able men, North perhaps the least able, and they set up a
tradition of incorruptibility. The main interest of the earlier years
lies in the relations with the king of Kandy.

It seemed to North that an independent state in the interior was
something of an anomaly. So when he was approached by some
Kandyan chiefs, who resented having as their sovereigns members
of the South Indian Nayakkar family, he turned a favourable ear to
their suggestions. The whole proceedings were far from creditable,
and the expedition which he sent to Kandy was a bad failure, for
much the same reasons as all those which preceded it in Portuguese
and Dutch times. Kandy was easily enough captured, but the
garrison became stricken with fever, and its commander was
eventually induced to surrender weakly to the Sinhalese; after
which practically all that was left of it was massacred. At this time
(1803–4) the British Government had plenty on its hands with the
renewal of the European war. North's successor, Sir Thomas
Maitland, made no attempt to wipe out the stigma on British arms,
but wisely concentrated on improving the civil and judicial administration of the territory under his control. His measures included the
introduction of trial by jury, really the work of a very able legal
official who became Chief Justice, Alexander Johnstone.

[1] See H. A. J. Hulugalle, *British Governors of Ceylon*. Associated Newspapers of
Ceylon, 1963, and C. R. de Silva, *op. cit.*

Sir Robert Brownrigg, who succeeded Maitland in 1812, however, made up his mind that the problem of the Kandyan kingdom
must be finally and firmly dealt with as soon as opportunity arose.
The Kandyan king, who took the name of Sri Wickrema Rajasinha,
was growing more and more unpopular with the chiefs, with whom
intrigues were reopened. In 1815 the king committed an act of
barbarous cruelty on some Sinhalese traders who were British
subjects, and this gave Brownrigg the opportunity for which he had
been looking. The French wars were as good as over (except for
the Hundred Days and Waterloo) so there was no particular
difficulty from the military angle. There was hardly any resistance to
the expedition. The king fled, but was captured, and sent to confinement in India.

The events consequent upon this need some careful consideration,
for they were to have many repercussions in the future. The fact that
the British took and kept the Kandyan kingdom marks a big change
from the circumstances of the two previous occupying powers, in
that Ceylon for the first time in many centuries came under, and
was to remain under, a unified rule.

The circumstances of the invasion of Kandy by the British forces
were, nominally at least, that they had come in on the invitation of
the Kandyan chiefs to rescue an oppressed people from a tyrannical
ruler. The Governor, therefore, on behalf of the British Crown,
entered into an agreement, styled a Convention, with the chiefs and
headmen acting on behalf of the Kandyan people. This declared the
king and his line deposed, and vested the sovereignty in the
Sovereign of the British Empire, to be exercised through the Governor
of Ceylon. 'The rights, privileges and powers' of the chiefs and headmen 'lawfully approved by the British Government, and to all
classes of people the safety of their persons and property, with their
civil rights and immunities according to the laws, institutions and
customs established and in force among them' were to be maintained. It goes on: 'The religion of Boodhoo (Buddha) is declared
inviolable, and its rites, ministers and places of worship are to be
maintained and protected.' Torture and mutilation were prohibited.
'Subject to these conditions, the administration of civil and criminal
justice and police over the Kandyan inhabitants of the said province
is to be exercised according to established forms and by the ordinary
authorities, saving always the inherent rights of Government to
redress grievances and reform abuses.'

The original idea of the British seems to have been to treat the
Kandyan kingdom in much the same way as a protected 'Native
State' in India: but the way in which events fell out seemed to

Brownrigg to justify his course of action, taken on his own initiative. Possibly, as has been suggested, the fact that the taking of the Kandyan kingdom coincided in time with the victory of Waterloo prevented any public or parliamentary interest being taken in it. But certainly it was a great disappointment to Ehelapola, the chief who had been most prominent in the intrigues with Brownrigg – and whose family had suffered brutal treatment in consequence from the Kandyan king – that he was not made king, nor any attempt made to set up a Sinhalese as king. The chiefs soon found themselves far less powerful, and the bhikkhus were not at all satisfied with the loss of influence which British rule entailed: they were also, in all probability, nervous of Christian proselytism. The people, though in general they had been somewhat oppressed by their former rulers, particularly the headmen, but bound to them by the ties of caste and custom, had no wish to be ruled by foreigners – possibly the memory of Portuguese raids into the kingdom in the time of their forbears was still in their minds.

Anyhow, as a result, there was a very serious uprising in 1817, to which all the prominent chiefs save one were parties, open or secret. The British were in real danger. But with dissension among the chiefs, a lack of any concerted effort, and with reinforcements sent from India, the danger lessened. It was, however, sufficiently acute the next year to convince the authorities that really severe measures were necessary, and some villages were burned, crops destroyed and livestock seized. The rebels threatened, but were never able, to cut the British line of communications – a stratagem on which in the past the Kandyans had always relied. Eventually the rebellion collapsed.

At the end of 1818 the Government issued a proclamation which threw all the blame for the rebellion on the chiefs, and took away many of their powers. Although they kept some of their former administrative functions, they were in future to be strictly controlled by the British authorities. They lost the power of charging fees, and of making minor appointments, and were to be paid salaries instead of collecting the revenue themselves and recouping themselves from it. A new system of taxation, based on taking a proportion of produce, and certain judicial reforms, lost them both power and influence. The view taken by the British Government, then and since, was that the Kandyan Convention of 1815 was abrogated by the rebellion, and that the 1818 proclamation took its place. This has, however, never been accepted by leading Kandyans. In particular the Buddhists, both bhikkhus and laymen, have always felt that the religious clauses of the Convention have been studiously ignored or, at the least, neglected. Their feeling has had important repercussions in very recent times, as will be shown later.[1]

During the governorship of Brownrigg's successor, Sir Edward Barnes, two developments of great significance to the future of Ceylon began to shape themselves and towards the end of his tour of duty there came an even more important development. The two first owed much to him personally.

After the 1818 rebellion, the Government's scheme for preventing a fresh outbreak, or nipping in the bud any attempts at revolt, was to construct a number of small forts dotted about the island, and garrisoned by a small number of regular troops, British, or Malayan mercenaries, the latter either taken over from the Dutch or attracted from Malaya. The traditional Kandyan method of defence, by restricting entry to the kingdom to narrow jungle paths, was got over by widening them: but even then communications remained difficult. Barnes decided to withdraw most of these garrisons and to concentrate on the improvement of communications by the construction of roads, particularly a road from Colombo to Kandy. Previously to this most of the roads in Ceylon, in the low country, were not much better than dirt tracks, almost unusable in the heavy monsoon rain time; but the work of roadmakers in Britain like Telford and Macadam had introduced metalled roads, and their example was followed in Ceylon. A fascinating account of the building of these roads is to be found in the autobiography of Major Skinner, a military officer who came out to take a commission in the Ceylon Regiment at the age of 14, and who spent 'Fifty Years in Ceylon' (the title of his book), during most of which he was employed by the Government in the construction of roads and bridges, for which he had shown a special aptitude. Barnes' policy was most effective, and the work of improving communications, carried on by his successor, was effective in giving Ceylon one of the best road systems in Asia. The labour employed to build these roads in the time of Barnes was under the old *rajakariya* obligation – labour service in return for the holding of land. The construction of the Colombo-Kandy road, completed in 1821, was a fine piece of civil engineering, and a high pillar at the top of the Kadugannawa pass, erected to commemorate this, still stands. At a sharp turn in the pass the road was tunnelled through a large rock. A legend grew up that as long as the road ran under the rock, Ceylon would continue to be ruled by foreigners. Ceylon is now free, but the road still runs under the rock!

The Colombo-Kandy road, and certain feeder roads, very soon

[1] See below. Chapter 13 p. 181.

came to have a significance other than military. With the end of the war, there was, and continued to be, little danger of wars in Europe, or of any war in Europe spreading to Asia, so that the harbour of Trincomalee, the possession of which had been one of the major reasons for the taking of the Kandyan kingdom, was less important. But the new significance was owing to another factor for which Governor Barnes was to some extent responsible. This was the clearing of up-country jungle for the planting of coffee. Neither the growing of coffee nor the idea of plantations was new. The Dutch had introduced the plantation scheme for the cultivation of cinnamon, and had experimented, with little success, with the growing of coffee. For the latter a certain elevation was necessary. In 1823 an Englishman named Bird opened up land for coffee in the neighbourhood of Kandy. His success, and that of other pioneers, impressed Barnes, who encouraged the project and soon had a coffee plantation opened up for himself. The difficulty was transport. But with the construction of the Colombo-Kandy road, and feeder roads, the difficulty could be met. The means were admittedly slow – a maximum of two miles an hour by bullock cart – but it was economically possible, and the growing of coffee went on apace. The plantation industry, first of coffee and then of tea and rubber, became the main prop of Ceylon's economy.

During these first thirty years the Governor ruled autocratically, with the aid of a civil service. North had some difficulties with the military authorities, but the other three were all high ranking soldiers, so that they had in their hands the executive and legislative powers as well as the command of the forces, and a considerable amount of judicial power too. They were undoubtedly well intentioned, within their limits, and able – the three last particularly – and did their best to govern with benevolent efficiency, according to the instructions originally given to North by Dundas, the Secretary of State, in 1801. Briefly, these put all power except the judicial into the hands of the Governor, but the stipulation was that this power must be exercised for the benefit of the people of Ceylon. The country was to be made as far as possible self-supporting by developing its economy, and the Treasury in London was to have direct – if distant – control of revenue and expenditure. This was in case public opinion at home should come to consider Ceylon a burden on Britain's resources at a time when they were being heavily strained by war expenditure. The Governor was to practise 'a humane, enlightened, liberal and steady policy' which, Dundas hoped, would secure the loyalty of the people to the British Government. It is to these Governors' credit that they did their best to follow their instructions, especially when it is remembered that several months, or even as much as a year, might elapse between the sending of a dispatch to London and the receipt of the answer – two long and fairly risky sea voyages.

The Governors were aided by a Council, but this was entirely advisory, as it consisted of officials, of whom the Chief Secretary and the Chief Justice must always be members, and two or three of the other principal officers, such as the Commissioner of Revenue, when such a post was in being. In Kandy, to begin with, was stationed a Resident. This post was held by Sir John D'Oyley, a most able man, to whose diary most of the knowledge of the Kandyan territory is due. Later on the territory was administered by a Board of Commissioners.

The more important of the ranks of the administration were filled by civil servants sent out from Britain.[1] They were first brought out under North's governorship, having been selected personally by the Secretary of State. Some of them came out very young, in their 'teens, yet were pensionable after only twelve years' service. They were strictly forbidden to engage in private trading, and were strongly encouraged to make themselves familiar with the Sinhalese language. Their pay seems to have been adequate.

As well as the civil servants and the military, there were some technical officers. As early as 1803 a Medical Establishment was started, and a little later we find a Civil Engineer and a Surveyor-General – later combined into one post. These were the embryos of what became the Medical, Public Works, and Survey Departments, which have had a continuous history up to the present day. Their work has been, with rare exceptions, unspectacular, and their personnel has often been rather looked down upon by members of the civil service. But their contribution, with that of other technical and professional departments created later, to the social welfare and progress of the people of Ceylon has been very great, if comparatively unnoticed.

On the judicial side there were developments of an important character. In 1801, by royal charter, a Supreme Court of Judicature was set up, presided over by a Chief Justice; also a High Court of Appeal, which included the Governor. From both of these there were appeals to the Privy Council. The process of change-over from the Dutch legal system was fraught with many difficulties, and there were the further complications of several different kinds of law applicable to different communities. Furthermore, with an auto-

---

[1] Collins, *Public Administration in Ceylon*, Chaps. IV and VI (Oxford University Press).

cratic executive in the hands of one person, the Governor, there was always the possibility of a clash with the judicial authorities; and this happened on several occasions.[1] One Chief Justice, Sir Alexander Johnstone, was sent back to Britain by Maitland to get instructions. But the results of his representations to the Secretary of State had political and constitutional implications to which Maitland took strong objection, as limiting his powers as Governor. The Charter which Johnstone had brought back was amended – largely because of a change of Secretary of State in Britain – and the net result, but a very important one, was the introduction of trial by jury, the first introduction of this procedure into Asia. There were several high judicial officers appointed from London, but many of the others came from the Dutch Burgher community.

Another set of British to come to Ceylon were the missionaries. These were of various denominations, but the Church of England occupied an official position. Early arrivals were the American missionaries at Jaffna, referred to in a previous chapter:[2] a certain number of the people came over to various forms of Protestant Christianity, though they were never as numerous as the Roman Catholics, whose religion had taken deep root in the island, and who were now at liberty to practise it without governmental hindrance. In the development of Ceylon the important part played by the missionaries was in the educational field, of which more later.

Finally there were a certain number of Europeans who came to Ceylon for business, mostly connected with the export and shipment of cinnamon. To begin with they were not at all favoured by the Governors, who were afraid of harm being done by unscrupulous European adventurers. Europeans were prohibited from acquiring land, though this prohibition was fairly soon reversed. Many of them were agents for British trading firms. During this period, however, they were mostly of no particular account.

[1] C. R. de Silva, *op. cit.*, Chapter X.
[2] See Chapter 1, p. 22.

Chapter 5

The Colebrooke-Cameron Reports

THE early thirties of last century were a turning point in Ceylon's history, for they mark the beginning of two essential, though often conflicting, features of colonial rule. The first of these is that, for the nationals of the colonising power, economic advantage is to be gained by investing capital in a colonial territory and thereby developing it. This goes nowadays by the name of 'economic exploitation'. To the 'exploited' colonies it has brought both good and ill effects. It differs from the earlier type, that practised by the Portuguese and the Dutch in Ceylon, for instance, who derived their economic advantage from a monopoly of trading, particularly in cinnamon, and invested no capital, except in so far as the latter started some cinnamon plantations, late in their occupation. The newer exploitation, involving the investment of capital, carried with it the seeds of development, and it was as a rule more or less held in check by the colonial governments. The absence of such checks in undeveloped territories could and did lead to great evils, of which an outstanding example is the collection by forced labour of wild rubber in the Congo, by which what was really a concession to an individual caused great suffering to the inhabitants of the country. This evil was remedied by the concession being handed over to the Belgian Government – which, strangely enough, had no experience of governing colonial territories, and became a colonial power by accident. The newer exploitation was not based on forced labour. It gave employment to some of the nationals of the country, by which they acquired certain skills – though owing to certain conditions which will be explained later, the number of these was far less than it might have been. It involved the opening up of waste or uncultivated areas, and the improvement of communications. It was revenue producing, developing the natural resources of the country and making its economy viable. But such profits as accrued, and they were often considerable, were, except in so far as they were ploughed back into the enterprises, likely to be sent out of the country as the rewards for the risks taken by the investors of the original capital and their successors. In Ceylon, of course, these enterprises took the form of the plantation industries, and gave a direction to the economy of the island which its critics have attacked for leading to a lack of balance in the economy.

The second feature of colonial rule is that the political and cultural ideas of the colonial powers are bound to filter through to the people of the colonies, in some cases being deliberately encouraged, in others discouraged, even actively. As far as Britain is concerned it was impossible for that country to develop parliamentary democracy, on the basis of an extending and finally a universal franchise in the homeland, without that political idea filtering through to her colonial peoples. The medium of filtration was the 'western-educated' young men who received part or all of their education in Britain, and those of both sexes who were educated in the schools and colleges of the colonial country on British lines, by British or other European teachers – such as the Roman Catholic teaching orders – and through the medium of the English language; and this applies not only to the political but also to the cultural ideas of the colonial countries. Where there is foreign rule, the ways of living of the foreigners are always likely to be the envy, and sometimes the admiration, of those sections of the ruled who come into direct contact with them, and often attempt to adopt or at least to imitate them.

In the case of the African colonies, where there was little or no previous culture, Western political and cultural ideas had a free run. But in the case of India and Ceylon, the tradition and continuity of an ancient and high culture, very different from that of the West, with religion as its basis, managed to survive and, as time went on, to revive.

In Ceylon, the first feature, economic development or exploitation, came in through the introduction and growth of coffee planting, with its ancillaries of import and export and of banking firms. These developments will be traced in a later chapter. On the political side, the second feature came initially as a result of the Colebrooke-Cameron Report of 1833.

Taking this feature first, it is desirable to cast a backward look at the thirty odd years which preceded the Report, and to review the attitude of the British Government to the acquisition and subsequent administration of Ceylon during these years. Once it had been finally determined that the acquisition of Ceylon should be permanent, the important thing is that its government was taken out of the hands of the East India Company, and that it became a Crown Colony, the first of its particular type. The alternative would have been to have left it to the Company to form part of its curiously ramshackle collection of territories, in which case Ceylon would presumably have become one of the provinces of British India. This might well have been the case had it not been for the failure of the 'Madras system' in 1797,[1] with its novel and objectionable methods of revenue raising, and the greed and corruption of the officials who ran it – all the more objectionable to the Sinhalese, possibly, as these officials were Tamils, their traditional enemies: hence the action of the Secretary of State, Henry Dundas, in taking the step of bringing Ceylon directly under the Crown.

This action raised a new kind of problem in British colonial history. The former colonies of the 'First British Empire' had been left, to a considerable degree, to manage their own affairs. Even when the American colonies, except Canada, broke away, the old plantation economy of the British possessions in and near the Caribbean, with their accompanying political institutions of partial self-government run by a planter aristocracy, offered no real precedent for Ceylon. Dundas was conscious of this, and to his mind the best precedent was to be found in the administration of the Company's possessions in India. He wrote in 1802, 'It was far from being proposed to assimilate that Island or its Government to our Colonies in the West Indies. But, on the contrary, whatever experience has shown to be politically wise in the Government of the British territory on the Continent of India and appears as the case in this instance applicable to Ceylon, it is the inclination of His Majesty's Government to preserve or to adopt.' Hence, rule by autocratic Governors was the characteristic of the governing of Ceylon up to 1833, as indicated in the previous chapter.

At this time there was no specific Secretary of State for the Colonies, nor Colonial Office, which developed about the middle of the century. Nevertheless interest was shown, every now and then, by the British Government and by Parliament in what was going on in the new possessions which had come under British rule as the result of the wars with France. As early as 1822 it was decided to set up a Commission of Inquiry to look into the affairs of some of these colonies. In that year Robert Wilmot, an Under-Secretary of State, moved the appointment of the Commission. Its primary objectives were Mauritius and the Cape of Good Hope; but it was decided to extend its scope to Ceylon also, though this was not regarded as being so pressing as the other two. The same Robert Wilmot, who since 1822 had changed his name to Wilmot-Horton, and been knighted, came out to Ceylon nine years later as a civilian Governor following three

[1] See above, Chapter 4, pp. 51–2.

military ones, and was to put the recommendations of this Commission into practice.

Eventually, in 1829, a Commissioner came out to Ceylon. He was Major William Colebrooke, a regular soldier, of a somewhat unusual type. He had in fact served on two occasions with the forces in Ceylon, which was helpful. He was joined by a legal colleague, Charles Cameron, whose assignment was to look into the administration of justice in the island. Colebrooke spent two years in Ceylon, and Cameron a year. They presented their reports in 1832, four by Colebrooke, on the Administration of the Government, on Revenue, on Compulsory Services, and on Establishments, and one by Cameron, on the Judicial Establishment.[1]

Cameron was strongly influenced by the politcial and social ideas current in Britain at the time, and in particular those stemming from the political philosopher Jeremy Bentham, with his doctrine of 'the greatest good of the greatest number'. Colebrooke had served for a time under the celebrated Stamford Raffles. B. H. Farmer in his recent book 'Ceylon, a Divided Nation', doubts if he was also a Benthamite, but his Reports show that he was influenced by similar ideas, and by the growing humanitarianism of the time, of which the most striking example was the successful movement for the abolition of the slave trade and slavery – an institution which had subsisted almost unquestioned all over the world from the earliest times. Anti-slavery came to be one of the outstanding features of British colonial policy. The twenties, too, were a period in which the agitation for political reform was growing in strength, and which succeeded with the passing of the Reform Act of 1832.

As Dr. Mendis points out, the recommendations made in these Reports are worthy of careful study, for their implementation laid the foundations of developments which were to lead ulñimately to the independence of the premier Crown Colony, as Ceylon came to be known. And it was the example of Ceylon which was to be that followed by the British Government in giving independence to other Crown Colonies, and thus transmuting the old British Empire into the Commonwealth of Nations. This example was, of course, contemporary with the giving of independence to India, and there is no doubt that the process of constitutional change on the sub-continent had considerable effect on the parallel developments in Ceylon, and on the minds of those working and agitating there for political advance.

[1] G. C. Mendis '*The Colebrooke-Cameron Papers*' (Oxford University Press), 1956, which gives an excellent and detailed survey, with documents, of these Reports.

Constitutionally, the important recommendation was the limitation of the autocratic powers of the Governor, thus departing from the policy of Dundas as set out in 1802, in his instructions to Governor North. This was to be done by the institution of Executive and Legislative Councils, and by removing the Governor's powers of imprisoning and banishing without trial. His judicial powers were also to be removed.

In these respects the first set of instructions sent out by the Secretary of State, Lord Goderich, followed the recommendations pretty closely, though they were somewhat modified after criticisms by Governors Barnes and Wilmot-Horton. The final decision which set the constitutional pattern throughout the nineteenth century, and later, was that the Governor should not be excluded from proceedings of the Legislative Council, as Colebrooke had recommended; and he continued to preside over the deliberations of that body until 1924, in practice, and 1931, in theory. The same was the case with all the other colonies, and one of the first signs of approaching independence has, more often than not, been the appointment of someone else, such as a Speaker, to preside over their legislatures.

The Executive Council was to have brought before it all matters of importance, save under circumstances of extreme urgency. The Governor could act against the opinion of the majority, but in this eventuality he had to report his reasons to the Secretary of State. The composition of the Council was as follows: The Commander of the Land Forces, the Colonial Secretary, the Colonial Treasurer, the King's Advocate (predecessor of the Attorney-General) and the Government Agent for the Central Province (i.e. part of the land covered by the former Kingdom of Kandy). The Governor was instructed to have copies of the Minutes sent to the Secretary of State.

The Legislative Council was to consist of 15 members, of whom 9 were to be officials – the Chief Justice,[1] the Commander of the Land Forces, the Colonial Secretary, the Auditor-General, the Colonial Treasurer, the Government Agent for the Western Province, the Surveyor-General and the Collector of Customs at Colombo. The other 6 were to be selected from the chief landed proprietors and the principal merchants of the island. Colebrooke had recommended 'provision being at once made for the appointment of any respectable inhabitants, European or native', and Goderich's first instructions laid down 'equal proportions from the respectable European Merchants or Inhabitants and the higher classes of Natives': this would 'secure at once the advantage of the

[1] In later years the Chief Justice was replaced by the Attorney General.

most exact local information, and the still greater benefit of convincing the population that laws made for their government proceed from persons participating in their own interests and general opinion, who will divide with the higher officers of the Government at once the credit and responsibility of legislative measures'. The Legislative Council was to have the power of lawmaking, subject to a somewhat limited veto by the Governor. Minutes were to be kept and sent to the Secretary of State halfyearly. All laws and business, however, could only be introduced on the initiative of the Government. The first 6 unofficial members were 3 Europeans, 1 Burgher, 1 Sinhalese and 1 Tamil.

Another most important recommendation of Colebrooke's was to do away with the separation of the Kandyan territories from the rest of the island, and similarly with the Tamil north. Thus Ceylon was unified under one administration – the first time for many centuries. The island was divided into five provinces – the number was subsequently increased to nine – with a Government Agent in charge of each.

Rajakariya, the centuries-old feudal concept of labour in return for the holding of land, he recommended for abolition, and this was done. This meant that the villager was no longer tied to the land, and that the possibility of his becoming mobile now existed: though in point of fact it was to be a long time before villagers came to move about the country much – except on pilgrimage to holy places, as many of them had done for centuries, as a rule once in a lifetime. As we shall see, *rajakariya* had been very useful just previously in the making of roads into the up-country. But its abolition was very desirable as a step in the emergence of Ceylon from medievalism.

Colebrook, as – presumably – a follower of Adam Smith's ideas, came out strongly against monopolies; as a consequence, the old monopoly of the cinnamon trade, which was all that remained of the East India Company's privileges and connexion with Ceylon, disappeared. It had actually become of very little value, owing to competition from other countries. Other monopolies, such as fish and salt, and all forms of government trading, were brought to an end.

Cameron's Report also made for unification. His aim was to make the administration of justice more efficient and free from any kind of discrimination between Europeans and the people of Ceylon, and between rich and poor. As the result of his recommendations, all courts were brought directly under the Supreme Court by allowing appeals to that court. A uniform system was set up covering the whole island, which was divided for judicial purposes into three circuits: these again were divided into districts, and a District Court set up in each, with full civil and limited criminal jurisdiction. The jury system was retained, and the right of *habeas corpus* introduced by writ from the Supreme Court. The Roman-Dutch law remained the principal law of the island, but those who wished to keep their customary laws, like the Kandyan and Tamil customary law, could be judged by them. A Charter was issued in 1833 giving effect to the legal changes. The result of this was to bring about a stable judicial system in Ceylon, which has earned for itself general and profound respect. It did perhaps have the result of encouraging the strongly litigious tendencies of the people, to some of whom going to law is almost a hobby. But taking the system by and large, the rule of law is one of the legacies of British rule which has come in for very little criticism, and to which a great compliment – that of being taken for granted – is paid. To this day any encroachment on the freedom of the judiciary by the executive power is watched with the gravest suspicion, and angrily opposed. As a very recent instance may be quoted the action taken by the courts in the trial of those accused of attempting a *coup d'état* against the present Government,[1] at the time of writing these words *sub judice*.

There is a further feature in the reports of both Commissioners worthy of note, the recommendations that the higher posts should be open to the natives of the country. Colebrooke wrote in his Report on the Administration:—'The prospect of future advancement to situations now exclusively held by Europeans will constitute a most powerful inducement with the natives of high caste to relinquish many absurd prejudices and to qualify themselves for the general employment. With this view, it would be highly expedient that the intention to open the civil service to His Majesty's native subjects should be publicly declared.' Cameron, too, in a letter to the Secretary of State in 1832 wrote:—'A Native who has for some years been subjected to this discipline (i.e. as a paid court assessor) . . . may, I think, be very safely placed in the more arduous and responsible office of a Judge of original jurisdiction' (at a salary, incidentally, of one-fifth of that paid to a European Judge) 'and by such an appointment the honourable ambition of the upper class of Natives will be safely gratified, and the great mass of the people will be bound by ties of affection to a Government which ceases to withhold offices of power and emolument from its Native subjects.' If these recommendations had been carried out in the spirit in which they were made, it is not improbable that the path of Ceylon to independence,

[1] See below, Chapter 15, p. 199.

E

comparatively smooth as it was, might have been easier and quicker. If, for instance, a local man had been appointed to an official position which would have given him a seat on the Executive Council, a considerable amount of bitter feeling among the Western-educated might have been avoided. However, throughout the nineteenth century no such appointments were made, and the Executive Council remained exclusively European in composition.

One further recommendation made by Colebrooke had to do with education. Partly in pursuance of his suggestions for bringing 'natives' into official positions, up to and including the civil service, he came out strongly in favour of the use of the English language as the medium of instruction. He wrote – wrongly as it ultimately turned out – that 'it would be impracticable for individuals, even of the most respectable classes, to support the expenses attending the acquirement of a liberal education in Europe', and that the measure formerly adopted of 'sending young Cingalese to Europe, and maintaining them at English universities' was too expensive. Education should therefore be conducted locally by religious societies, as far as possible, and the existing government schools should be reformed by being placed under a commission, with a strong clerical bias; the teachers appointed by the commissioners should be competent to give instruction in the English language. This idea of a Schools Commission bore fruit. The final words of his recommendations on education may be quoted:—'The education afforded by the native priesthood in their temples scarcely merits any notice. In the interior the Bhooddist priests have evinced some jealousy of the Christian missionaries, but the people in general are desirous of instruction, in whatever way offered to them, and are especially anxious to acquire the English language.' For a very long time this was the general attitude of the Government to the ancient *pirivena* education. It is not surprising that a committee of inquiry set up by some Buddhist laymen a few years ago,[1] in the chapter on education in its report, was white hot with indignation.

The instructions given to the Commission at the outset laid particular stress on the duty of the Commissioners to make a report on the revenues, 'their present extent and possible augmentation', and on the expenditure, 'the possibility of reducing it within the ordinary resources of the Colony', and other financial matters. It was for the recommendations made on this score that Colebrooke's report deservedly came in for heavy criticism at a later date. They had the effect of seriously weakening the civil service by too drastic

[1] *The Betrayal of Buddhism* (abridged report of the Buddhist Committee of Inquiry) Colombo, 1956.

a cutting down of salaries, and doing away with their pensions. The establishment was perhaps somewhat swollen, but the remedies were too severe. The service in consequence suffered a marked deterioration, from which it did not recover till the forties, when the efforts of two successive Governors were successful in improving the terms of service and arresting the deterioration in its personnel. In the days of nineteenth century *laissez faire* in ideas, and a strict respect for the taxpayer in practice, it was a feature of British colonial policy to make colonies, as far as it could be done, pay their own way. At the time this seemed to be the right and proper policy and one which was followed in Britain itself, though under very different circumstances. It is due to this that the detractors of 'colonialism' make the case that the British Government made no real attempt to raise the standard of living of colonial peoples, but were content to sit by and let their nationals exploit the economy of the colonial territories for their own profit.

Considerable attention has in this chapter been devoted to the recommendations of this Commission, the greater part of which were adopted by the Government. The reason for this comparatively detailed treatment is that they laid down the pattern of political and constitutional practice in Ceylon until the early part of the present century. The movement towards political advance in some sense developed from this pattern, in another sense was a reaction against it. But the general results of the Commission were more significant, as has been well pointed out by Dr. G. C. Mendis in his little book 'Ceylon Today and Yesterday',[1] where he calls the Colebrooke reforms 'a dividing line in Ceylon history', marking, as they do, the 'transition in Ceylon from the medieval to the modern' and 'the most definite turning point in the whole course of Ceylon history'. Such a pronouncement from the first Ceylonese to undertake a scientifically-minded study of his country's history is worthy of respect. To sum them up, what the reforms brought about were: the beginnings, however faint, of constitutional government, ultimately to develop into parliamentary democracy on 'the Westminster model' in the first British colony of non-white people to become an independent member of the Commonwealth of Nations; the break-up of a semi-feudal organisation of society on a largely caste basis – however hard this basis died or, more correctly, is dying – making possible the substitution for it of a society based on individual relationships on an economic basis, with a background of commercial capitalism; equality before the law based on a unified

[1] G. C. Mendis, *Ceylon Today and Yesterday*, Associated Newspapers of Ceylon, 1957.

system of justice (though not of laws), with the two pillars of *habeas corpus* and trial by jury (the latter had, in fact, been brought in earlier); the freeing of trade by the abolition of government and Company monopoly; and, above all, the complete unification of the whole island under a single uniform administration.

These reports were the work of two men, to whom much credit must go, although their names are only faintly known to history. The results of their recommendations, as taken up by the British Government in London, represent something new in colonial policy, the deliberate grafting of British ideas of constitutional government, the rule of law, and efficient and incorrupt administration for the good of the governed on an ancient civilisation based on ideas and practices which can best be described as feudal. A similar line of policy was pursued in India: but the circumstances of a vast subcontinent differ widely from those of a small island colony.

Nevertheless these ideas need to be looked at in the light of the times in which they began, and, indeed, of most of the remainder of the nineteenth century: and here we cannot but note the calm assumption that what was good for Britain must needs be good for everyone else: the lofty disregard of and disrespect for any religion but Christianity, so that the world was divided into Christians and 'heathens'; the ignoring of any but Western culture (with the very notable exceptions of a few 'orientalists'); the suspicious attitude towards any governmental activity other than defence, the maintenance of law and order, and the raising of revenue; the shadier side of the midde class virtues; and the unspoken, complacent, unshakeable conviction of British – one may almost say English – superiority which has always had such a maddening effect on 'foreigners and colonials'. But as the nineteenth century drew to its close, and the twentieth wended its stormy and dangerous way, these attitudes of mind invisibly died away, till today no one boasts of being an imperialist, and even in Britain itself 'colonialism' is becoming a word which makes the average Briton feel embarrassed and uncomfortable, faintly ashamed of the old Empire and – perhaps – faintly doubtful about the new Commonwealth.

Chapter 6

The Economy Under the British

THE carrying out of the British colonial policy referred to earlier – colonies to be self-supporting as far as possible – was by no means easily attained during the first thirty-odd years of the British occupation. Ceylon had few economic assets. The economy was mainly a peasant economy, which meant that the Sinhalese villagers were – except in times of calamity such as floods and droughts – self-supporting, but on a low standard of life – they lived under a natural rather than a money economy. They grew enough rice for themselves in good seasons, though under the existing tenures they often had to part with a fixed share of their produce to their landlord or feudal superior – a landowner or a Buddhist vihare, usually. Where coconut palms grew, they yielded something extra in the way of food: oil from the nuts had various uses; shelter was obtained from weaving the big leaves into *cadjan* with which they could roof their huts; the husks were used to make charcoal for cooking; toddy, an alcoholic drink, could be made from the unopened flowers tapped before the nuts mature, (though this meant the loss of a crop of coconuts) and from this could be distilled arrack, a highly potent spirit. These are only some of the uses of this palm tree.

For the villagers in the dry zone, life was even harder.[1] Most of them, until the old irrigation system began to be restored, eked out a pitiful existence, having to rely usually on a small village tank for the supply of water for which they depended on one season's rain. If the rain failed, their plight was woeful. They were, more often than not, too, stricken by malaria, or diseases arising from malnutrition.

The chiefs and the larger landowners, including the vihares, drew revenues from the customary services owed by the tenants and, as

---

[1] For a fascinating study of this life, see Leonard Woolf, *The Village in the Jungle*; cast in the form of a story, it draws a remarkably accurate picture of the decay of a remote dry-zone jungle village. For a more cheerful picture, this time of village life in the more prosperous wet zone of the south-west, see J. Vijayatunga, *Grass for my Feet* (Edwin Arnold).

above, from a fixed share of the produce. There was hardly any middle class among the Sinhalese and Tamils in rural districts: the small traders were usually Moormen, and of course there were a certain number of craftsmen.

There was a long established export trade, in precious and semi-precious stones, pearls – when there was a successful fishing of the pearl banks every so many years, areca nuts, which had a market in India, elephants (the Ceylon elephant is very trainable), again to India; some coconut products; above all, spices, and in particular cinnamon.

In Chapter 4 reference was made to the starting of coffee growing in plantations, and to the encouragement given to it by the Governor, Sir Edward Barnes. It was shown to be potentially profitable, and when the problems of transport were solved by the building of roads, coffee planting went ahead fast. World markets were there, ready to be entered. What was required was land on which to grow it, enterprise, 'know-how', the investment of capital, and the labour to work the plantations.

The land was there, in the Central Province, the old Kingdom of Kandy. Much of it was dense hilly jungle, but it could be, and was, cleared. It was mostly uninhabited, for the Kandyan villagers lived in the valleys, on the slopes of which they grew their rice, hill paddy, in narrow terraces, as they do to this day. Most of the land was held to be Crown land, and it was sold to prospective coffee planters at a very low price indeed. But the Kandyan villagers, once the land for plantations was cleared, lost some of their customary rights. They could no longer use the jungle for fuel, for pasture, for hunting, or for the occasional, if wasteful, 'chena' cultivation.[1]

When the work of clearing was in process, the villagers were ready and willing to undertake it. But once it was done, they would not work on the plantations – carry out the steady, regular work which was essential. They held it to be beneath their dignity to work for wages, and preferred to continue cultivating their own lands, or those of which they were tenants. The work of carting the coffee, and the various crafts which were necessary on the estates, were mainly carried on by the low-country Sinhalese, who were accustomed to work for Europeans, and to live under a money economy. The planters' difficulties in finding labour for their estates were overcome,

[1] 'Chena' cultivation is of the same type as that practised by primitive agricultural communities, as in early Anglo-Saxon England. It is done by clearing an area of jungle or burning off grass on open downs, and raising one or two crops there: then moving on to another patch: the 'chena' lands are usually uncultivable for several years after the crops have been taken from them.

from about 1837 onwards, by importing labour from southern India. The story of Indian Tamil labour on the plantations will be told later on in the chapter. It was, ultimately, to have momentous consequences.

Enterprise, as conditions were, and capital could only be got in any quantity from abroad. The Governor, Sir Edward Barnes, set an example of enterprise by himself opening up a coffee plantation, and he was followed by some members of the civil service. Up to 1810 Europeans had been prohibited from buying land, but this ban was lifted by Governor Maitland. Civil servants were not allowed to engage in private trade, but there was no prohibition against going in for agriculture. Though without doubt those who acquired land and went in for planting coffee must have seriously neglected their administrative duties, this did help to bridge something of a gap in their fortunes, for during the thirties the economies resulting from the recommendations of Colebrooke's report hit civil servants very hard.

It was after the middle thirties that coffee planting became financially attractive. The representations of Sir Edward Barnes to the home Government that the import duty on Ceylon coffee should be brought down to the same level as that on coffee from the West Indies – the famous Blue Mountains Jamaica coffee – were successful. There was at this juncture a drop in the export of West Indian coffee, and Ceylon coffee managed to infiltrate into the world market. The possibilities became known in Britain, and enterprising individuals with capital, say two or three thousand pounds, came out to Ceylon. The sales of Crown land went up enormously; in nine years 294,526 acres were bought. The price was absurdly low to begin with, and the story of these sales is not always very edifying. Some coffee estates were quickly re-sold at fancy prices.

To begin with, the Sinhalese took no part in this cultivation. The landowners had little or no capital, nor did they show any enthusiasm for large-scale agriculture: there was no mercantile class with liquid assets to invest, though later on some Sinhalese people, as will be shown, accumulated some capital and went in for coffee planting. So it was left mainly to immigrant Britons to show their enterprise, to come out to Ceylon, take up land and try their hand at clearing the jungle and planting coffee. Some of them lost their money through ignorance or incompetence; not all of them were very desirable types. But many made good; they acquired the minimum of 'know-how' about soil conditions and the best methods of cultivating the coffee tree, and those who did so found it was possible to grow the trees, do the necessary processing, and show a profit after the lapse of as short a time as three years. And by the forties Ceylon coffee really began to boom.

The life of a planter in these early days was by no means an easy one. He usually had to put up with the most makeshift quarters. It was next to impossible to get the kind of food to which he had been used, or to get the food cooked in a palatable way. He had to look after his own health, and that of his labour force, as best he could.

The boom time which ensued after Ceylon coffee became able to enter the British market on the same terms as coffee from the West Indies did not last very long. In 1847 a severe financial crisis which hit Britain brought about disaster; the bottom dropped out of the market and a number of planters were ruined. Estates bought for several thousand pounds were sold for a few hundreds. However, the corner was turned and in the fifties and sixties coffee estates increased and prospered rapidly. The sale of Crown lands for the planting of coffee, which had dropped markedly, was resumed: in 1857, for example, no less than 19,795 acres were alienated. The year before that there existed 404 plantations with 80,950 acres under coffee.[1] In the early seventies the annual export amounted to between 800,000 and 900,000 cwt. It is hardly an axaggeration to say that Ceylon was ruled by 'King Coffee'.

During this period the lives of the planters became much more comfortable. They were able to get bungalows built, to bring out their wives, and to get away, albeit infrequently, from their estates and travel down to Colombo by train, for the Colombo-Kandy railway was completed by 1867, which also, of course, made a big difference to the transport of coffee. It is interesting to note that private enterprise for one reason or another failed with the contract for the construction of this railroad, so that it had to be undertaken by the Government. Hence from the outset it has been a state enterprise, the Ceylon Government Railway. During the next eighteen years it was extended still further into the mountains so as to tap various planting districts: it also ran along the south-west coastline. But its main object was to serve the interests of the planting industry; which, of course, entailed the bringing of revenue to the Government.

With the development of the coffee industry came that of ancillary occupations, banking and agency houses, and shipping. Some of the older firms in Colombo, such as George Stuart and Co., date back to the early coffee days. The Ceylon Chamber of Commerce was established as early as 1839. In 1854 was founded the Ceylon

[1] For these figures and other information the author is indebted to the centenary volume of the Planters' Association of Ceylon, issued in 1954.

Planters' Association, and the two of them came to exert considerable influence on the political as well as on the economic affairs of
the island. Both these bodies have performed very useful services to
business and planting. The work of the Planters' Association in
improving the lot of the estate labourer, in initiating the agricultural research institutes, and in other directions must be com-
mended.

The coffee industry was never organised on a large scale. Those
who came out from Britain to embark upon it were mostly individuals with a limited amount of capital, who bought a few hundred
acres of land, and had it cleared and planted. Their agricultural
knowledge was all too frequently minimal: but it could be acquired
and, as mentioned above, an estate could be made to pay in a
minimum of three years' time from its opening. Coffee soon became
the major export industry of Ceylon, suffering only the one setback
in the late forties. It was not long before some of the low-country
Sinhalese took to coffee planting, and many of them did quite well
out of it. Most of the Ceylonese planters came from castes other than
the Goigama. Some of these began by entering into contracts with
planters for transport by bullock carts, or for building. Yet others
came up to practise their craft of carpentry – the Dutch had
established a flourishing carpentry industry at Moratuwa, fifteen miles
south of Colombo (it still flourishes there), and it was members of the
Karawa caste who practised it. Some of these men made enough
money to be able to take up land and start coffee plantations,
usually though not invariably of comparatively small acreage. An
appreciable quantity of coffee, too, was grown by the more enterprising villagers on small holdings. It has been estimated that, when
coffee production was at its zenith, from one fifth to one quarter of
the crop exported was produced by Sinhalese planters and small
holders. The export figures for 1870 were, plantation crops, 885,728
cwt., others, 168,300 cwt., totalling just over a million cwt.

But the reign of King Coffee was drawing to a close. It was in
1869 that a leaf disease was first observed – orange-coloured spots
on the leaves of the coffee tree. This was a fungus known as *Hemileia
vastatrix*. The Royal Botanic Gardens at Peradeniya, near Kandy,
were notified, and the Director issued a strongly worded warning of
the danger to the industry. But planters were optimistic, owing to
the sporadic nature of the disease; they hoped, and led themselves to
believe, that it was only temporary. By the end of the seventies,
however, the disease had taken firm hold, and in the eighties the
industry gradually collapsed. The export of coffee had by 1889
dropped to under 100,000 cwt. The ravages of the disease, too,

coincided with keener competition from other coffee-producing countries.

Many planters were ruined: their estates seemed worthless, and they sold them at fantastically low prices. The situation seemed desperate. But it was saved, first by the planting of cinchona, from the bark of which tree quinine is derived; and then of tea. The original impetus for the cultivation of tea came, like the warning on coffee, from the Royal Botanic Gardens. Attempts had been made in the forties and fifties to introduce the growing of tea, and had proved practicable; but coffee then seemed to be too profitable to bother with other crops. Planters who had hung on to their estates, and others who bought up derelict plantations, hastened to replant them with tea – after some had temporarily carried over with cinchona – and by 1881 13,500 acres were under tea. By 1889 the acreage had increased to over 200,000. In 1888 23 million lbs. were exported – it may be noted that 74 years later (1962) the total export had grown to 447.9 million.

Thus the new crop prospered exceedingly. It had to be worked on a more or less scientific basis from the outset, for the processing of tea was much more difficult and complicated than the drying of the coffee berry. The process requires shelter, in a sizeable building known as a factory, wherein is housed a mass of expensive machinery. Some of this machinery was invented, and even manufactured, locally, but much of it, including the power engines, had to be imported from Britain. This meant that capital was required to buy and install this machinery. The Sinhalese who had managed to acquire coffee estates, sometimes on borrowed capital, had nearly all been ruined by the coffee crash, and were unable to raise the capital necessary to run a tea estate. The consequence was that nearly all the owners of tea plantations were Europeans, the vast majority from Britain. For some time the tea industry continued, like coffee, to be run by individual private enterprise. Men with capital came out from Britain, bought estates – at first at very low prices – or managed to acquire Crown land and open up tea estates in the high jungle, some even up to 6,000 feet, which had been too high for coffee. The extent of this sale, however, had to be limited by the Government, as too much clearing would have had adverse effects on the forests and on the water supply. In point of fact the way in which much of the jungle was cleared, and the crops planted, led to an alarming amount of soil erosion; only in recent years is this being checked by better methods of planting the tea bushes, known as contour planting. Though tea can be grown at almost any elevation, the high grade tea for which Ceylon became famous is produced at elevations over 3,000 feet – the greater the elevation, the better the quality is likely to be, though this is not always the case; some of the very best tea grows at 4,200 feet.

In the late nineties there was something of a slump in tea. This had the effect of hastening a process already started in the organisation of the industry. Recovery from the slump was effected by better methods of cultivation and more mechanisation in the factory. This meant larger injections of capital, which came to involve estates passing out of the hands of individual owners into the control of companies, and often the joining together of several small estates into a big one, which could be more economically worked. Some individual estate owners formed companies from their own estates, keeping the bulk of the shares in their own hands or in those of their families, but with deaths and the need for raising more capital, and other causes, the shares often came on to the market. The owners sometimes worked the estates themselves, but often put in managers, and lived at home on the proceeds. Some of the tea companies (and other plantation companies) had their head offices in Britain, and became known as sterling companies, as their shares are quoted in sterling. There are others whose head offices are in Ceylon, with their shares quoted in rupees, and hence known as rupee companies. There has long been quite a lively share market in Colombo, and several prosperous firms of brokers. More and more the process of estates passing out of individual proprietorship went on, so that by, say, the end of the first world war the number of European estate proprietors had become comparatively small. Hence the majority of planters were coming to be the employees of companies, and known as estate superintendents, over whom the agency houses in Colombo exercise control, not always appreciated.

But a more important effect of the tea slump of the nineties was the stimulus given to a new cash crop – rubber: the introduction of rubber growing into Ceylon by the bringing of *hevea* rubber seeds out of Brazil in the seventies is an interesting story.[1] Rubber grows best at elevations lower than tea, and is mostly found in the foothills of the central massif. In the development of rubber plantations Ceylonese[2] planters have played a quite prominent part. Rubber was

---

[1] See E. F. C. Ludowyk, *The Story of Ceylon*, (Faber) pp. 203–4. The story told there is not completely accurate; the correct story may be found in Rutherford, *Planter's Notebook*, 1931.

[2] For the remainder of this book the word 'Ceylonese' will be used to designate the permanent inhabitants of the island – the word used by Europeans, governments included, was for a long time 'natives'; but this has rightly passed out of currency. Where it is necessary to distinguish the various communities (a term preferable to 'races'), the necessary designations – Sinhalese, Tamils, etc. will be used.

never planted on a scale so extensive as in Malaya or Java, but it became Ceylon's second most important export crop. The rubber estates in European ownership (mostly by companies) were about half the total acreage under rubber. In the opening years of the present century, some large fortunes were made in rubber planting in Ceylon. But rubber has always been a highly speculative world market, and when tea recovered, as it soon did after the slump, it was the most stable element, and the largest, in the island's export economy. The uses of rubber, of course, increased immensely with the development of the automobile industry all over the world, which was well on its way by the beginning of the First World War, at which time the acreage under rubber in Ceylon amounted to about a quarter of a million.

The third export crop was that of coconut products. Whereas tea and rubber were new crops, the coconut palm had been growing in Ceylon from time immemorial. Some of the old landowning class, and other Ceylonese who had in one way or another made money – as by the practice of law – used their ancestral or their purchased lands to plant coconuts on a large scale. Coconuts are a comparatively easy crop to cultivate and to work, and it was not necessary to have a large labour force on a coconut as it was on a tea plantation; the temporary work of neighbouring villagers at the appropriate seasons, in addition to a small nucleus of permanent employees, was usually adequate. The majority of coconut products went for domestic use, but when coconut plantations were formed an export crop was possible. Copra (the dried white meat of the coconut) was the usual form of export; but there was a certain amount of coconut oil extracted from that commodity and exported. Copra and coconut oil are the basic elements for making margarine. There are other products, such as desiccated coconut, also exported. The material left after the oil is extracted, locally known as *poonac*, makes a good cattle food, and some of this is exported to India. Fresh coconuts, too, are exported in considerable quantities, as also is coir, for rope, yarn, mats, and the stuffing of mattresses; coir is made from the coconut husks – a village industry. There is some sale, not only from the larger plantations but also from those of under 50 acres and from villagers' gardens; the marketing of the last of these has usually been a matter for middlemen, as it still is in part, though the development of the co-operative movement and of agricultural marketing boards between the two world wars and subsequently have been helpful to the small producer.

Ceylon is deficient in minerals, on the whole. The only important mineral that has been mined on a large scale is the lead ore, graphite, commonly known as plumbago, found mostly in the south-west of the island. In the early years of the present century a considerable demand for this product arose from the steel industry, and this was greatly stimulated by the need for munitions in the first world war. The mining of graphite became a very profitable occupation. It was almost entirely undertaken by Sinhalese on whose lands it was found, or who acquired such lands. Some of them became wealthy from the proceeds of the plumbago industry. It was from this source that the first three Prime Ministers of independent Ceylon (all related) obtained their not inconsiderable fortunes. Other minerals on a small scale are found in Ceylon, to which later reference will be made; but these were not exploited before the first world war, and some of them still await any noticeable development. There is, however, a possibility of iron mining on a big scale, as large deposits of iron ore have recently been found which may prove to be commercially workable.

The marketing and shipping of the export crops and commodities was at that time, and indeed till quite recent years, almost entirely in the hands of European firms. Among these were few of any size, though two or three were branches of firms with connexions spread widely over southern Asia. On the whole, though, they were small but prosperous, confining their activities to Ceylon. They undertook agency duties, export and import, broking, shipping, insurance, and lighterage. There were two or three engineering firms who undertook repairs to shipping and estate machinery, and imported and sometimes manufactured the latter. Motor garages, in the earlier days of the automobile industry anyhow, were started before the First World War, almost entirely by European firms.

Retail trade on any large scale was carried on mainly by Europeans and Indians. In the towns of Colombo and Kandy and in the hill station of Nuwara Eliya were several large European-owned and managed stores, selling a variety of articles. Smaller retail concerns were to a considerable extent owned and managed by Indians, mainly from north and central India. This was particularly the case with the import and sale of textiles. Another activity of the Indians was the lending of money. Some of them, known as 'chetties', sometimes operated on quite a large scale. On a smaller scale Colombo and other places were perambulated by Pathans, commonly called 'Afghans' big, picturesque and rather terrifying men carrying stout sticks, who lent small sums at exorbitant rates of interest, and made their debtors scared and miserable when they failed to pay up in time.

By the beginning of the First World War, banking, which had had a somewhat variegated history in Ceylon, had come very largely into the hands of the big commercial banks operating throughout Asia, such as the Imperial Bank of India, the Chartered Bank of India, Australia and China, the National Bank of India, the Mercantile Bank of India and the Hong Kong and Shanghai Bank. There were also a couple of local banks up-country. Insurance, too, was almost exclusively in European hands. Some of the small firms conducted insurance business as the agents of big companies; one or two of these companies later opened offices of their own in Colombo.

On all three of the main cash crops was imposed a small export duty, and on their prosperity depended to a great extent the revenues of the island. Other revenue came from customs duties on a wide range of imports, excise duties, and miscellaneous items such as salt, a Government monopoly, pearl fisheries (occasionally), licences, stamp duties, and a poll tax, later abolished.

Another important source of revenue was shipping and harbour dues. In the old days the port of Galle, in the south-west, was the principal harbour from the commercial angle. The magnificent harbour of Trincomalee was too far away to be of any commercial use, valuable, or potentially valuable, as it was from the angle of naval strategy. Galle harbour was not safe during the south-west monsoon, owing to a submerged rock near the entrance. Colombo was an open roadstead, though much used when the weather permitted. But Colombo was the obvious terminus for the products of most estates, being the commercial as well as the administrative capital of the island. It had been a trading centre and a port of call, on a small scale, for centuries. But in the seventies two matters for consideration arose, the need for the export of coffee throughout the year, and the increase of shipping to and from Australia and southern and eastern Asia, which was bound to ensue after the opening of the Suez Canal in 1869. After some hesitation it was decided in 1873 to build a breakwater, and this was completed by 1882. Further breakwaters were built, and by 1906 Colombo harbour was completed – the largest artificial harbour in Asia – and a graving dock constructed. By 1911 the tonnage of shipping calling at Colombo had risen to over 7 million, giving employment to dock workers and furnishing revenue to the Government, as well as profits made by firms such as marine engineering, lighterage, and coal importers. Colombo had become one of the busiest and most important ports in the world – it was coming to be called 'the Clapham Junction of the East'.

It was explained earlier in this chapter that the Kandyan

villagers did not, for various reasons, wish to do regular work on the newly opened coffee estates, and that once the jungle was cleared they went back to their normal village life. They were not attracted to these, even though the work was seasonal – unlike tea, for which there is work all the year round. But near at hand there was a vast reservoir of unskilled labour. In the barren and overpopulated districts of southern India life was very hard, and the level of subsistence low. It is not clear to whom the idea of drawing on this labour first occurred, but they seem to have come seasonally soon after the start of the coffee plantations. In the forties a system of regular recruitment was begun.

In those early days the conditions of the Tamil 'coolies', as they were then called (the use of this word in Ceylon to describe estate labourers was ultimately forbidden by legislation) was highly unsatisfactory. The worst feature was the journey from India to the up-country. The labourers were brought down in gangs by a leader known as a *kangany*. After crossing the narrow Palk strait, they had to make their way on foot through the waste lands of the North-Central Province (as it is now); and on that long trek many of them died. Later on they were brought to the port of Mannar on the west coast by sea: but this constituted a serious danger to the health of the colony, as cholera and smallpox were endemic in the parts from which they came, and even bubonic plague was a fell disease they might bring with them. After some time, largely on the initiative of the Planters' Association, quarantine camps were established, with medical facilities. Eventually a well organized centre, known as the Coast Agency of the Ceylon Labour Commission, was established at Mandapam in south India, through which all immigrant labourers and their families had to pass. This was paid for by contributions from the estates, and was under the supervision of the Planters' Association, with the co-operation of the Governments both of Ceylon and of Madras.

The labourers lived in 'coolie lines' on the estates, which consisted of long, low, one storey buildings, with a number of small rooms, usually ten, and usually one family to a room. Some of these lines were unhealthy and insanitary, though probably an improvement on the conditions under which the labourers lived in their home-lands. They were paid regular wages and were issued with a free weekly supply of rice. On the whole, planters did their best to look after their labour force, and in one way and another their welfare was improved – medical facilities were made available, better lines, built, and eventually estate schools set up for the children. These improvements were due partly to the growth of interest and the taking of action by the Governments of India and of Ceylon, and partly to the efforts of the Planters' Association.[1]

It is, of course, not at all surprising that the conditions of Tamil coolie labour in the last century stirred up no particular feelings of indignation; free enterprise and *laissez faire* were the economic shibboleths of the period and applied just as much to the factory worker in Britain or India as they did to the estate worker in Ceylon, or elsewhere.

There was one feature of these labourers' conditions of life which had a most restrictive and unjust operation. The journey from India to Ceylon plantations could not be undertaken without cost, and the immigrant labourers rarely had any funds to meet such cost. The usual method was for the cost to be met by the recruiter, the *kangany*, usually from a fund furnished by his employer: a little cash might be advanced to the immigrant, and, according to the immemorial custom of the East, the *kangany* got his rake-off, probably from the immigrant as well as from the planter. The cost was debited to the immigrant and had to be paid off gradually from his wages. He was given a *chit* (piece of paper) known as a *tundu*, stating his indebtedness, and was not allowed to leave the estate until the debt stated on the *tundu* was discharged. Debts would often be increased by advances of pay made for marriages and other festive occasions, so that the unfortunate labourer whose *tundu* showed a large load of debt was virtually tied to the estate. This practice was abolished in 1921 on the initiative of the Planters' Association. It cost the industry about £4 million sterling; but there is no doubt but that this greatly improved the relations between the employers and their labourers.

Indian Tamil labourers took other kinds of work, too,[2] but whatever their occupation, nearly all of them could only be described as temporary immigrants. The object with which members of this poverty-stricken, thrifty, hard-working race came to Ceylon was to make and save enough money to return in their old age to their native land (it was called 'going back to their coast'), buy a plot of land, and spend there what was left of their lives. Those employed on estates lived their own lives, mixing little with the Sinhalese villagers, and having very little contact with anyone outside the estate, even the Tamil labourers on neighbouring estates, except on occasions such as marriages. When reasonably well treated, as they

---

[1] See E. F. C. Ludowyk, *op. cit.*, pp. 195–9 for a severe criticism of the system of Indian estate labour, and Harry Williams *Ceylon, Pearl of the East*, (Robert Hale) pp. 222–55 for an account, sympathetic, if perhaps highly coloured, of the lives and work of estate labourers, though by a man with full personal experience of running an estate and looking after his labour force.

[2] See above, Chapter 1, p. 16.

usually were, they were quite content to stay on the same estate all their working lives. Some of them, however, occasionally paid visits to their 'coast', but usually returned; many of the later generations have never been to India and do not particularly wish to go there. The presence of these, today about a million alien folk, has raised major political as well as economic problems for the Governments of independent Ceylon.

The aim of this chapter has been to sketch the economy of Ceylon as it was when the people of the country began, slowly, to run their own affairs. The process was begun, as it was throughout the British colonial Empire, in the political field, and political preceded economic independence – which has not even yet been achieved. Economic independence is really rather a foolish term, as the only possible way to attaining a full economic life, for an individual or for a country, is by economic interdependence. But many among the Ceylonese feel that their independence must needs be incomplete till all their trade and industry has come into the hands of their nationals. Considering what had gone before, this is a not altogether unnatural feeling, though of doubtful economic wisdom.

To sum up the economic situation, then, as it was when their country was on the verge of being handed over to the native-born Ceylonese, when the process of securing control of their own affairs, say 1913, was starting. It is clear from the foregoing that economic power was to a major extent in the hands of non-nationals. The tea industry, on which the economy of the island principally relied, was almost entirely under European management and control; the rubber industry was about half under Ceylonese ownership, but the agency side to a great extent European-controlled; though coconuts were mainly Ceylon-owned and managed. Export and import, shipping, banking, insurance, and much of the retail trade, except quite small shops, were run by non-nationals. The upper classes of the Ceylonese still held their often extensive lands, after the old semi-feudal pattern. The rising middle classes consisted of the small landed proprietors; members of the professions – lawyers, doctors and teachers; holders of, with a few exceptions, subordinate posts in the government services or, with hardly any exceptions, in European mercantile firms and stores (the Indian firms employed almost exclusively their own nationals); and those who pursued miscellaneous occupations, like contractors and small shopkeepers. The mass of the people, about 3 million in number, save for a growing urban proletariat of unskilled labour, dock workers, etc. (not very large) subsisted under a peasant economy – small owners, tenants and unskilled labourers, living near, on, but too often below the margin of

F

subsistence. They produced rice and other foods mainly for their own consumption, and were able to supply their meagre clothing and easily constructed shelter; there was little animal husbandry, and what there was, of an inferior quality. They were always very hard hit by climatic disasters such as drought and floods.

Except for a politically minded section of the new middle class, the people of Ceylon seemed reasonably contented with their lot. As Asian countries went at the time, Ceylon was comparatively prosperous, with enough revenue to run the government services with fair efficiency, maintain public utilities like roads, railways, bridges and postal and telegraph services at a quite high level, and, in the larger towns, water, gas and electricity services; provide an island-wide medical service; primary education for a proportion of the children of Ceylon; with the help of the assisted schools, some secondary education, for the most part in the English language; and there was the beginning of a very limited amount of welfare, though most of this was carried on through voluntary agencies, often run by Europeans. Also, in rural districts, irrigational facilities were steadily enhanced and improved and some effort was made to improve methods of cultivation through the Department of Agriculture and its officers.

For the Europeans, the period between the opening of the twentieth century and the outbreak of the first world war was their heyday. Tea and rubber prices were good, though that of rubber was subject to variation, often upsetting; so that, on the whole, trade was booming. Medical facilities were plentiful, and tropical medicine had made strides enough to ensure a reasonable standard of health, despite the climate. Estate labour was quiet and well behaved. Salaries were in general adequate. Planters had free accommodation, often in pleasantly situated and commodious bungalows. Social life was pleasant and plentiful, assisted by good communications by road and by telephone. Urban employees were not yet disturbed by political agitators. The business and planting communities, especially through the Chamber of Commerce and the Planters' Association, carried great weight with the Government. Living was not unduly expensive, and imported luxuries came in at low tariffs. The social life of the European community and some of its implications will be considered in a later chapter.

The people of Ceylon, as a whole, were not politically conscious. They accepted the existing order of things, and had real respect for their European masters. Only – there was a section, mostly of the rising middle class, especially its upper ranks, who were not content and who did not accept the existing order, and it was this section which was the mainspring of the movement in the direction of political independence. It was in the decade which included the First World War that the movement really got under weigh.

Chapter 7

The Constitutional and Administrative Position Under British Rule

T HE CONSTITUTIONAL régime which was established after the Colebrooke recommendations lasted, with a few modifications, till the early years of the present century. It was a marked step forward in colonial constitutional development, a step for which most of the other colonies of the British Empire in Asia and Africa had to wait until this century, after one or the other world wars: even in India the parallel development came later.

But the essential feature of European colonial rule, the British included, was efficient and reasonably impartial administration. Constitutional progress up to a point was well developed in the British colonies before it had made even a beginning in the possessions of other colonial powers. This may well be due to the fact that Britain was the only one of those powers which had colonies of settlement, where the population was largely white and of the home stock, and where constitutional development was in consequence only to be expected. How far this influenced British thinking on colonial policy concerning non-white colonial peoples would make an interesting historical study, though not one to be pursued here.

In this chapter will be outlined the constitutional set-up from which Ceylonese self government developed, and the administrative structure which was gradually made over to the leaders of the country in the period of increasing self government which preceded full independence.

The history of constitutional affairs in the seventy-seven years from the constitution of 1833 to that of 1910 was mainly concerned with the relations between the Government and the business and planting interests as represented in the Legislative Council where, despite the official majority, they exerted great influence. Though constitutional development was meagre, it had its importance in the limitations placed on the executive power, and exercised by the unofficial minority which, be it remembered, included a few representatives of the permanent population.

The composition of the Executive and Legislative Councils is given in Chapter 5 (p. 63). That of the Executive Council remained strictly official and British all through the nineteenth century: it might have been better if a few unofficials had been added. In the Legislative Council the representation of the three most important communities, the Sinhalese, the Tamils and the Burghers – the last of them the most politically active – was maintained, and after about fifty years a Kandyan Sinhalese and a Moor were added.

In the fifties and sixties demands were made by the Europeans, supported by the Burghers, for an unofficial majority. In 1864 they formed an association, the Ceylon League, with this end in view. But this was steadily opposed by the Government in Ceylon, supported by the home Government, the argument being used, perhaps justifiably, that an unofficial majority would serve only the interests of European planters and merchants and of the small community of Burghers, but not of the mass of the people. Sir Henry Ward, an able mid-century Governor, in a dispatch wrote as follows:

'In a Colony, the population of which consists of seven or eight thousand Europeans, a small though intelligent class of Burghers, and two millions of Cingalese, Tamils and Moormen . . . you cannot introduce the principle of Representative or Responsible Government. . . . The Government must for many years hold the balance between European and native interests.'

The members of the Legislative Council were always nominated, though in the fifties Sir Henry Ward allowed the Chamber of Commerce and the Planters' Association to recommend one member each for appointment; and this concession continued. It is worthy of note that some of the European unofficial Councillors on occasion put forward the opinion that there should be more Ceylonese on the Council. But though the Council was a body in which bills could be introduced, under certain conditions, by any of its members – a concession which had been obtained – and though it could, and did, deal freely and frankly with the financial estimates, the Governor and the Executive Council always had the last word, and in cases of dispute the official view had to prevail. Nevertheless the Executive did feel an obligation to give the views of the unofficial members really serious consideration. This was quite naturally the case, seeing that the European unofficials, always the most vocal, represented the views of those upon whom the economy of the country, and hence its revenue, had to depend. Similar considerations carried on till well after the date of full independence. The Governors of Ceylon during this period were on the whole men of ability,[1] except perhaps Lord Torrington, who may not unfairly be described as a placeman. It was during his tenure of office that the only really serious trouble during this period occurred. In 1848 – a notable year for rebellions – a revolt broke out. It was not, perhaps, altogether Torrington's fault; there is no doubt that the deterioration of the civil service was a contributory factor. But with proper handling the trouble need not have issued in open revolt;[2] and the measures he took after the revolt had been quelled partook of the nature of panic. It was for his mishandling of the situation that he was attacked in the Parliament of Westminster – the only occasion during this period that the affairs of Ceylon attracted the keen attention of that body. Mr. Gladstone took a prominent part in the attack on the Government. The result was Torrington's recall, as well as that of the Colonial Secretary and a senior civil servant.

After the above-mentioned agitation for Council reform in the sixties, the Legislative Council went on quietly with its normal functions. The agitation for reform now came from outside it, from that section of the Ceylonese middle class which was, at last, becoming politically minded.

The main burden of the administration was on the shoulders of the civil service. The efforts of the two Governors preceding Torrington, and of his successor, were successful in rehabilitating the service from the deterioration consequent upon the mistaken economies of the thirties. The rates of pay were made adequate and pension rights restored. Thereafter it can fairly be said that the civil servants carried out their duties on the whole with zeal and efficiency.[3] After 1856, entry to the civil service had to be gained through open competitive examination. The rewards and opportunities were not as great as those for the Indian Civil Service, or for the top grades of the civil service at home; but though, with notable exceptions, the Ceylon civil servants as a body cannot be described as of outstanding ability, they carried out their duties conscientiously and well. For many years they were mostly drawn from the honours schools of the English universities, after a public school education, and they had the defects as well as the virtues of their type; for

[1] See the recent book by H. A. J. Hulugalle, *op. cit.*
[2] For an account of these events, see G. C. Mendis's *Ceylon under the British.*
[3] For the history of the civil service and other government services see *Public Administration in Ceylon*, by Sir Charles Collins, (Oxford University Press).

instance, they did not mix readily with the Colombo businessmen or the planters, they were inclined to look down socially on the personnel of the technical and other government departments, and they were suspicious of the rising Ceylonese middle class, especially in the towns. Many of them always preferred to be stationed in rural areas, anyway out of Colombo, partly for financial reasons, partly to be more 'on their own' than was possible under the direct eye of the heads of the administration. They got on reasonably well with the rural population, both the larger landowners and the villagers. If, as many of them did, they took the trouble to make themselves really well acquainted with the Sinhalese or Tamil languages, or both, and constantly toured their districts, on horseback or on foot (one very celebrated Government Agent used to go all round his province on a bicycle), they earned the deep respect of the local people, who admired, if they did not imitate, their rectitude and incorruptibility. Few of them, however, can be said to have really endeared themselves to the people of Ceylon – a notable exception being the Government Agent just mentioned.

During the nineteenth century the civil service was drawn almost exclusively from people coming from the British Isles – the term 'European' is that generally used in Ceylon, and indeed in India and Africa, too, to denote anyone of the white races, even, to their manifest annoyance, Australians and Americans. This term is accordingly used in this sense throughout this book. In 1875 a Tamil, Mr. (later Sir) Ponnambalam Arunachalam, went to an English university and was successful in the competitive civil service examination. Though he was a man of ability, he never got further in the civil service than Registrar-General, which was something of a side-track, though he made a remarkable success of organising his department and was rewarded with a knighthood. Subsequently he became a prominent political leader. A few other Ceylonese emulated his example, perhaps the best known of whom was Sir Paul Pieris, who did much for the study of Ceylon's history and antiquities. But it was not until a date between the two world wars that a Ceylonese was appointed to a post as Government Agent, in charge of one of the nine provinces, and the top post of the service, except of course for the Colonial Secretary and his Deputy. There were a few Indians and two West Indians recruited to the Ceylon Civil Service. The service was divided into grades, and a special Grade V was instituted for those Ceylonese promoted for merit from the ranks of the clerical service: but they never got very far. As time went on, and especially in the present century, the British element in the service tended to change somewhat, ceasing to consist almost entirely of ex-public schoolboys, and reflecting in this way the type of graduates from the two older English universities.

The leading official was the Colonial Secretary, and the next senior was the Colonial Treasurer. The Colonial Secretary in particular, and his immediate subordinate staff, were likely to be considered for promotion to high positions in other colonies. The most important officials after these two were the Government Agents of the nine provinces; their functions were similar to those of District Commissioners in the Indian Civil Service; each had one or two Assistant Government Agents. Technically they were revenue officers. In the nineteenth century they also exercised judicial functions, and the post of District Judge was held by a civil servant, who in all probability had no legal training at all. In addition, there were several posts such as the heads of the Customs, Excise and Postal departments which were normally filled by civil servants.

With the improvement of communications, particularly the introduction of the telegraph and the telephone, and the closer touch thus made possible with headquarters in Colombo, the average civil servant was less able to act on his own, and inevitably more immersed in office routine – paper work – than formerly. The advent of the motor car in one way made it easier for the civil servants to get around their areas; but on the other hand they seem to have penetrated rather less than their predecessors into the more remote parts. One Assistant Government Agent had the bright idea of a motor caravan; by some odd quirk he was posted to a rather wild district with only one single road! The later civil servants, though they all had to pass examinations in Sinhalese and Tamil, became, with brilliant exceptions, rather less acquainted with these languages, partly owing to the fact that they got about their areas rather less, and partly because, with the spread of English education, all the members of the clerical service and many other Ceylonese with whom they came into official contact spoke English fluently.

There were a few, rather too few, civil servants who took a genuine interest in the languages, customs, history and antiquities of the people of Ceylon. But most of them, anyhow in the latter years, were too occupied with their purely administrative duties, or the social life among the government servants in their headquarters, or, in the towns, Colombo particularly, in that of the European community, to pursue such interests – which was perhaps inevitable, but unfortunate.

It was not until constitutional change got really under way after the first world war that Ceylonese in any numbers entered the civil service. Though various attempts were made to bring them in during the nineteenth century, the fact that the civil service examinations were held only in London was a big obstacle to this. The opening of the Ceylon University College in 1921, at which the students sat for the external degree examinations of the University of London, greatly widened the field of prospective Ceylonese candidates for the civil service, and this was accelerated three years later when the civil service entrance examination took place simultaneously in London and Colombo. There was, quite naturally, a constant drive from the politicians to increase the Ceylonisation of the service, and indeed of the other government services too. Regulations were introduced to this end as early as 1920,[1] and by degrees the proportion of Ceylonese civil servants was increased; the last Europeans to be recruited came out in 1937. The figures read as follows:

1920	79 Europeans,	11 Ceylonese
1930	83 ,,	55 ,,
1940	49 ,,	81 ,,
1950	11 ,,	124 ,,

During these thirty years to enter the civil service became the aim of nearly all the academically able young men in the island. To these, the winning of a high honours degree (external) of London University, or, if their parents could afford to send them, or if they could borrow the necessary money to go to one of the British universities, Oxford or Cambridge preferably, was coveted and striven for not so much because of the academic attainment but as the best way to get into the civil service. The position of a civil servant was very highly regarded. This was reflected in the fact that young civil servants were able to command high dowries in the marriage market. But it is fair to state that, by and large, the Ceylonese who entered the service absorbed the high traditions which they found there, of hard and intelligent work, and incorruptibility. They formed a 'steel frame' which kept the government of the country going in the often difficult circumstances of increasing self-government and then independence. But they were also inclined to pick up the somewhat exclusive attitude of superiority of which civil servants are apt to be accused. It has been, rather disappointingly, alleged that too many of them made little effort to get to know

[1] Collins, *op. cit.*, pp. 101–2.

the people of their areas in the way in which their predecessors, the nineteenth century Europeans, had done. To begin with, they rightly continued the tradition of holding themselves aloof from politics. This may or may not have been maintained in recent years; but in Parliament and in the press of recent years, they have been accused of meddling. What truth there is in such allegations is difficult to judge. The politicians on their part have been apt to dislike the civil service and its mentality, the final result of which dislike has been the abolition of the service as such, as a relic of 'colonialism', and the substitution of a single graded administrative service. This is so recent that no estimate of its success is possible. But certainly, for the period of transition from a colonial to an independent status, both the Ceylonese and European members of the civil service did a really good job. It is, perhaps, a pity that a civil service entirely manned by Ceylonese did not have a rather longer tenure of administrative power, for they did not have, as the Europeans had, the prospect of being transferred to high administrative posts in other British colonies, as Chief (or Colonial) Secretaries and Governors, a process which had taken from Ceylon some of the most able and promising administrators: so that their hopes of promotion were necessarily confined to Ceylon. When the European civil servants departed, a number of them on proportionate pension before the normal age of retirement (55), promotion came to the Ceylonese officers rather too rapidly. But on the whole they may be said to have risen to their added responsibilities reasonably well.

The government clerical service, as it came to be called, had, of course, always been filled by the people of the country. As the central administration was mainly carried out in the English language, the way to what were coveted posts was through 'English schools', that is, secondary schools where that language was the medium of education. In the early days of the British occupation the bulk of the posts in the clerical service were filled by Burghers, who soon dropped the Dutch and adopted the English language. Later, however, members of the major communities, the Ceylon Tamils in particular, keenly sought these posts. There was little scope for men of education in Jaffna. So when, in the seventies, the 'general clerical service' became organised, and entrance had to be gained through competitive examination, the young educated Tamils, who made good examinees – many of them had the two assets of high mathematical ability and 'photographic memory' – filled the vacant places in numbers altogether out of proportion to the Tamil percentage of the population. This has provoked considerable jealousy on the part of the Sinhalese, which was to have political effects at a later date – a quite recent one.

Certain of the government services, such as the Railway and the Customs departments, had their own clerical services. The pay was in general much better than the young men would have been able to earn in other occupations, except perhaps as mercantile clerks. The government was generally preferred to the mercantile service, owing to greater security and pension rights; it also had a higher status. But there was a certain middle class standard to be kept up, and clerks were rather apt to run into debt, as often as not for such purposes as dowries for their daughters, and costly weddings.

During the period of the British occupation, especially in the present century, the work of the older departments such as Public Works and Medical greatly increased, and a number of new departments were created. The Police Department was of essential importance. Throughout the nineteenth century, however, nearly all the work of policing the country outside the main towns was done by local officers, the headmen – an institution many centuries old. It was not until 1908 that the Ceylon police force was adequately organised, and even then large areas remained unpoliced by it. The Ceylon Police, like many in colonial territories, was a para-military force. The officers, who from 1908 onwards were appointed, in part, by competitive examination, were at first mostly Europeans, with the ranks of Superintendent and Assistant Superintendent – up to the Inspector-General and his deputies. The next grade, the Inspectors, was for some time almost a preserve of the Burgher community; there were also some European police sergeants. The rank and file were Sinhalese and Tamil, with some Muslims. Between the two world wars the force was highly organised by a most devoted and efficient Inspector-General, Sir Herbert Dow-biggin, and developed a strong *esprit-de-corps*. They were prominent in sport, having in some places their own sports grounds and teams, and were smart in drill and in turn-out. Possibly because of all this, but mainly on account of their para-military set-up, the police were highly unpopular with nascent and even with fully-fledged politicians. It has to be remembered that, unlike in most countries, there was little military backing possible in case of outbreaks of rioting. In the later nineteenth century there was a small garrison of British troops stationed in the island, but between the two world wars there was only a battery or two of artillery and a few technical and administrative groups. This was in contrast to the position in the neighbouring sub-continent, which always had a considerable proportion of the British Army stationed there, in addition to the Indian Army. There was in Ceylon a fair sized volunteer force, called the Ceylon Defence Force, which became the nucleus of the Ceylon Army after independence. It included two (later one) exclusively European units. The police force, like the civil service, underwent rapid Ceylonisation in its upper ranks between the world wars. The British, then, may be said to have left a reasonably efficient and well organised police force, at the date of independence almost entirely manned by Ceylonese – from the Inspector-General downwards. Two of these highly placed officers have been in fact drawn from the civil service, though this was done for administrative rather than for political reasons.

Other departments were the Survey and the Irrigation, which developed from the Public Works; the Railway, Post and Tele-graphs, Agriculture, Forests, and Land Settlement. The Medical and the Education departments had their origins quite early in the British occupation.

Ceylon started off her career of independence with a very important asset possessed by few, if any, of the other British colonies, or indeed by India. Partly on account of her small size, and for historical reasons, there was a really adequate system of com-munications, thanks largely to the Public Works Department. Reference has already been made to the Colombo-Kandy road and some of its extensions, and to the construction of the railway. Constant progress was made with road and rail – work on the roads was for many years compulsory. By 1930 Ceylon was excellently roaded. The up-country districts above all were well served, and the improvements made it possible to transport speedily, by motor lorry, the export crops to the nearest railway station, or all the way to the port of Colombo. The roads on the estates were built by their owners with their own estate labour – later on some of them were taken over by the Government, particularly after the Second World War. But quite early on, these main roads ran along the coast from Puttalam, 80 miles north of Colombo to Hambantota, 160 miles to the south-east, and major roads connected Colombo with Jaffna and Mannar in the north and west, and with Trincomalee and Batti-caloa, the east coast ports, as well as a road, crossing seven ferries, connecting these two places – getting across them quickly was always a matter of luck! A number of minor roads, too, were constructed, particularly in the Western Province. All these roads made possible a rapid development of motor traffic between the two world wars.

The layout of the railway system was strategic as well as economic. The principal towns of Ceylon,[1] Kandy, Jaffna, Matara, Kurunegala, Negombo, Ratnapura, Kalutara, and the hill station of Nuwara Eliya were all connected by rail with Colombo before the First World War, and Badulla soon after it by a clever feat of railway engineering. A little later a railway to Trincomalee was constructed, almost entirely for strategic reasons, and against considerable opposition in the Legislative Council. Batticaloa was also connected with the system. The railway mileage was not great – under 1,000 miles in all, but the system was well planned.

The electric telegraph was introduced as early as 1888, and developed steadily in the years preceding the first world war. The telephone, too, was introduced before the end of the century. It has been most useful in the towns. The trunk system left (and still leaves), much to be desired; however, it became widely extended. To complete the story – though going on beyond the limits envisaged for this chapter – wireless was early introduced for external communications and shipping, and before the Second World War a broadcasting station was set up in Colombo.

The work of the Public Works, of the Railway and of the Post and Telegraphs departments had given Ceylon considerable economic advantages. The higher posts in these departments, the P.W.D. in particular, were filled by British engineers and technicians, though the office of Postmaster-General – it is difficult to say why – was held by a Class I civil servant. A certain amount of technical training was available at the Ceylon Technical College, founded in 1893, and gradually Ceylonese, some of whom went or were sent to Britain, became trained civil, railway and postal engineers.

The Survey and Irrigation departments hived off from the Public Works, the former in 1899. But years before this a great and necessary interest had been taken in irrigation by several of the Governors. They could not but be struck by the miserable condition of the district of Nuwara Kalawiya, which covered in area what had once been the very heart of the Rajarata; which had within its borders the ancient capitals – neglected ruins (a book was written entitled 'The *Buried* Cities of Ceylon'). There was hardly a tank that had not been breached, and the inhabitants of the villages were reduced to about 60,000 people, mostly undernourished and stricken by disease – malaria and *parangi* (yaws, a most unpleasant malady) – scratching a bare living from the soil, mostly by *chena*[2] cultivation. When the island revenues of the forties and fifties began

---

[1] See map at end of book.
[2] See Chapter 6, p. 70.

to increase and show a surplus, owing to the success of coffee planting, Sir Henry Ward, Governor from 1855 to 1860, with the approval of the newly started Colonial Office, pushed on with a scheme for repairing the tanks. large and small, and restoring as far as possible the ancient irrigation system. The story of modern irrigation in Ceylon[1] is one which merits study, and research into the Reports (over many years) of the Directors of Public Works and, later, of the Directors of Irrigation. The setting up of Local Irrigation Boards (1889) was a great step forward, and so was the creation of the North Central Province, out of part of the Northern and Eastern Provinces. The results of the irrigation policy were most beneficial, and the villagers of the new province – which had its headquarters at Anuradhapura – were able to grow rice again and, though still very poor, to maintain themselves in any but the really bad seasons when the rain failed. This irrigation policy was steadily pursued, and there came later developments like the foundation of peasant agricultural colonies in the dry zone[2] and the great Gal Oya tank and multi-purpose scheme in the Eastern Province. Doubtless much more could have been done to assuage the deep poverty of the dry zone villagers, but it can fairly be said that the trail was blazed.

In the development of cultivation the Department of Agriculture played an important part. This ought to have been one of the most important of all the departments of government; but for a long time it was something of a Cinderella. It has done admirable work in certain directions. For many years it was principally concerned with high grade botanical work, under the name of the Royal Botanic Gardens at Peradeniya. It had much to do with introduction of both tea and rubber. Some useful research was carried out, affecting the planting industries, especially after tea and rubber growing came in. But it was not until 1912 that a Department of Agriculture proper was formed. Attempts had for a long time been made to encourage better farming by villagers, but their stubborn conservatism rendered the instructors' task very difficult. Agricultural instructors were appointed on a provincial scale, and a School of Agriculture came into being at Peradeniya. It was not really until a Ministry of Agriculture was set up in 1931, with D. S. Senanayake in charge, that rapid progress was made, though it may be claimed that the foundations of an agricultural policy had been laid. But there was little education in agriculture in the rural schools, and none in the University College during the twenty-one years of its existence.

[1] See B. H. Farmer, *Pioneer Peasant Cultivation in Ceylon*, (Oxford University Press).
[2] See Farmer, *op. cit., passim*.

Even today the Faculty of Agriculture in the University of Ceylon, its successor, is neither strong nor popular.

The Medical Department has a very long history, right from the beginning of the British occupation. In the early days its activities were confined mainly to the towns and the planting districts. It must always be remembered that there is in Ceylon, as in other Asian countries, an ancient cult or practice of medicine known as *ayurveda*, to which the people of Ceylon were, and are, strongly attached. The ayurvedic practitioners were men with some medical knowledge, sometimes considerable, more often rudimentary, who possessed a stock of remedies handed down from father to son through many generations. Some of these – they are mainly herbal and quite unpleasant to take! – are without doubt highly effective, always provided that the diagnoses are correct, which is not always the case. Modern medicines – and hospitals too – were looked on with grave suspicion by the villagers. From the seventies onwards medicine seemed to take on a new lease of life, and hospitals were built and staffed. In Colombo there have been for years several first-rate public hospitals, though at times their management has left something to be desired. But the most important development, started by Governor Sir William Gregory, in the seventies, was the setting up on an island-wide scale of small dispensaries, under the general supervision of the district medical officers.

The middle classes of Ceylon took kindly to the study and practice of medicine. A medical college was founded in Colombo nearly a hundred years ago. Here were trained not only the doctors but also the 'apothecaries' who staffed the dispensaries just mentioned; they naturally had a much less thorough course. The medical degree was of high standard (see below, p. 104). The Medical College is now a leading faculty of the University of Ceylon. The Medical Department came to be mainly staffed by Ceylonese doctors and apothecaries at an earlier date than almost any of the other departments, though the post of Director of Medical and Sanitary Services remained in European hands till between the world wars: the post of matron in the leading hospitals was filled by Europeans even longer.

The medical authorities, European and Ceylonese, looked askance at *ayurveda*, regarding it as essentially empirical and un-scientific. This attitude did not change, but since independence the Government has tried very hard to give facilities for the ancient system, and to improve it by imparting some scientific training to entrants to the profession.

The Forests Department, founded in 1889, has done good if

unobtrusive work. The executive posts were largely held by Europeans, partly because the middle class Ceylonese for a long time showed little enthusiasm for entering that department. The fact that the life of a forest officer was usually remote and lonely has sometimes been assigned as the cause for this. But it was not the case with the Survey Department, where officers had similarly to penetrate to the more remote parts of the island and to live in considerable isolation. This was a quite popular department with young Ceylonese, and attracted a type of man who did quite good work.

Another useful department was concerned with Land Settlement. Land laws and tenure in Ceylon are perhaps more complicated than in most countries – which is saying a lot – and the department was founded in 1903, mainly with the aim of carrying out the provisions of the Waste Lands Ordinance of 1897: there was an undoubted need to determine the title of lands as between the Crown and the subject. But this measure has since been virulently attacked, not without justice. This department worked in close touch with that of the Registrar General.

The work of the Education Department will be considered in the next chapter.

Thus there was a reasonably complete administrative organisation by the end of the first world war, covering many governmental activities. The Government Agents and their assistants no longer had the variety of duties carried out by their nineteenth century predecessors, though the civil servants still had their fingers in many pies outside the revenue. It remained necessary for them to work in close co-operation with the technical officers of various departments. Each of these departments had a head, known usually as a Director: most of these heads, though not all, had their headquarters in Colombo. They ranked with the highest civil servants, in Class I or Class II of that service, and had little or nothing to do with political matters – which explains their annoyance at being dragged into them, as they found themselves after 1924. Before that date hardly any Ceylonese had attained to Class I of the civil service, or to the headship of a department.

One other, and a highly significant branch of governmental activity remains to be considered, that of local government. Though little constitutional advance was made in the central government before the First World War, the same is not true of local government. As developed, it became the training ground for middle class politicians. It showed a steady development from the mid-nineteenth century onwards.

What local government there was in the first half of that century

was in the hands of the headmen, chief and minor. The chief headmen were often members of leading families of landowners, particularly in the districts which had formed the Kandyan Kingdom;
though sometimes men in government service were given this office.
The minor headmen performed various governmental functions in
their villages under the control of the chief headmen, and beyond
them of the Government Agents. The headman system had its roots
deep in the past, long before the coming of the Europeans. It was
highly unpopular with the rising politicians, who attacked it
persistently in the new legislatures, and finally got rid of it altogether.

Another ancient feature of local government, the *gansabhawas*,
(village committees) had been, mistakenly, allowed to fade out. This
mistake was rectified in the fifties, when they were revived and given
powers by the Irrigation Ordinance of 1856. Fifteen years later
these powers were increased in the minor judicial sphere as well as
in some of the administrative details of village life, by the creation
of village tribunals. The result was a considerable drop in minor law
cases. Another important development was that district road committees were set up, in which the electoral principle was introduced.

In the towns of Colombo, Kandy and Galle the sixties saw the
creation of municipalities. Here the principle of election was soundly
established, and the elected members outnumbered the nominated
members by one. In Colombo the Chairman of the Municipal
Council (who became known, though not officially, as the Mayor)
was always a senior civil servant; in the other towns the Government Agents were the chairmen. Many of the smaller towns were
given local boards of health, called Sanitary Boards, which carried
out several of the normal functions of local authorities, as well as
health matters.

Without doubt the institutions of local government did what Sir
William Gregory, when the Municipal Councils Ordinance was
proclaimed in 1866, declared to be the intention behind it; that is,
to prepare the ground for political advance, particularly in
habituating the Ceylonese to the practice of voting at elections – a
practice to which they took very readily. But also without any doubt
they were instrumental in effecting genuine improvements in local
matters such as sanitation, water supply, lighting, slaughter houses
and even public transport. Seats on local bodies became an object
of ambition to many middle class Ceylonese, not always from the
highest of motives. The author has a vivid recollection of some
revealing conversations on this topic with a Ceylonese personal
friend who was chairman of one of the local authorities. But cor-

G

ruption in local matters is likely to be found in all countries, to varying degrees, and there is no doubt that local government was a most important factor in the political education of the Ceylonese people.

Taking the outbreak of the First World War, 1914, as the nodal point, it has been shown that Ceylon had a quite well developed administration on bureaucratic lines, under bureaucratic control, but also the embryo of constitutional advance in the Legislative and Municipal Councils.

Chapter 8

Cultural and Social Life

IN this chapter an attempt will be made to frame some estimate of the developments of Western culture and to indicate its effects on all grades of society in Ceylon. It is a continuous story up to the present day, though in recent years it has provoked a reaction of some strength.

The keynote is, of course, education. Under the Dutch and in early British times there had been some attempt to provide education in Sinhalese and Tamil: but the Government under the British showed no great enthusiasm for it, except Governor Brownrigg, who had a number of schools opened. These were missionary schools, and up to 1832 various Protestant missionary societies opened a total of 235 schools with about 10,000 pupils. One of these societies was the American Congregationalist Mission, which from 1816 operated in the Jaffna peninsula and had a continuous history of teaching there. The school they established was up to secondary standard; it ultimately became known as Jaffna College. The Church Missionary Society (Anglican) opened a similar school at Kotte, near Colombo, about the same time.

The Colebrooke Report had strongly recommended education with English as the medium of instruction, and the setting up of a Schools Commission. This, begun in 1834, was mainly under the control of the Anglican clergy to start with, to which the members of other Christian denominations strongly objected. Seven years later the clergy of these denominations and some laymen were given places on the Central Schools Commission, as it was now called. In 1836 a Government secondary school was established in Colombo, the Colombo Academy, which at a later date became known as the Royal College: it is still in existence, the senior government secondary school, and counts many eminent Ceylonese among its former pupils. The Government partly, and the European community generally, regarded these schools as the source from which clerks for government and mercantile offices could be furnished; though the author of this book discovered a letter dated 1835, which threw an unexpected sidelight on this. It was from James Steuart, who was Master Attendant of the Colombo harbour, and also the founder of the old mercantile firm of Geo. Stuart & Co.: he wrote in it that one-fifth of the colony's resources ought to be spent on education – a very unusual point of view for that time. In 1847 the Colebrooke idea was modified, and some government schools teaching through the medium of Sinhalese and Tamil were established for girls as well as boys. The Government was coming to recognise that it had a duty to see that there was education given. But it was content to leave much of it to the Christian missions, to whom grants-in-aid were made for the support of their schools. After the middle of the century the schools went ahead. In 1868 there were 18 government schools with 1,908 pupils teaching through the medium of English, 41 Anglo-vernacular schools, with 1,949 pupils, and 63 vernacular schools with 3,624 pupils. But the mission schools were more numerous. The Society for the Propagation of the Gospel in 1852 founded St. Thomas's College in Colombo, which is still one of the leading secondary schools of Ceylon: and towards the end of the century several big Roman Catholic schools came into existence.

The primary purpose of the mission school was, of course, to convert children to Christianity. In time, however, the Government made it a condition of a grant-in-aid that non-Christian children should not have to attend classes in religious instruction – though doubtless many did. By 1872 there were 402 mission schools with over 25,000 pupils. The parents who sent their sons to the mission 'English' schools were mostly inspired to do so by the desire to get for them an education which would enable them to enter government service, for which it was becoming necessary to pass certain examinations, at various levels. In 1881 the Cambridge Senior examination began to be held in Ceylon, and the next year the London Matriculation. Four years after this the Intermediate Arts examination of London University could be taken in certain subjects. These examinations set the tone for the lower grades of examination and for the school curricula.

In the meantime the Central School Commission came to an end, and in its place was set up the Department of Public Instruction, later becoming the Education Department. This was mainly concerned with the rapidly growing number of 'vernacular' schools. By 1890 government schools had more than doubled in number, though they did not increase as rapidly as the grant-in-aid schools.

The examinations referred to above became very popular, and on the result of the Cambridge Senior a scholarship to a British university was awarded every year. There had been something of a practice before this for young Ceylonese, especially from the Tamil north, to proceed to Indian universities. But from this time onwards the slant was towards the British seats of higher education, and later on a scholarship was awarded on the result of the Intermediate Arts examination. The syllabus for these examinations made no kind of concession to local conditions – that only came many years afterwards. There is no doubt that the schools of Ceylon were far too examination-conscious; and the examinations were British examinations. Some students who took the London Intermediate Arts studied privately, and at a later date, by an arrangement between London University and the Education Department, were able to take the external B.A. degree of that university.

An important result of the grant-in-aid system made itself manifest in the seventies and eighties. There was a revival of both Buddhism and Hinduism, in reaction against the proselytising activities of the Christian missions. Buddhism had sunk to a very low ebb in the sixteenth and seventeenth centuries: but in the latter part of the eighteenth century there was a revival, encouraged by the last kings of Kandy – who were not Sinhalese Buddhists.[1] The ancient *pirivena* schools, which had somehow managed to struggle on, began to revive. The Buddhist bhikkhus were supported in their efforts by some of the laity who had acquired some wealth. In the last quarter of the nineteenth century Buddhism received a 'shot in the arm' from an unexpected source. In the United States of America the Theosophical Society was founded by Madame Blavatsky, a Pole, and Colonel Olcott, an American, with a view to the study of oriental religions. Olcott became strongly attracted to Buddhism, and visited Ceylon, where he helped, in 1880, to found the Buddhist Theosophical Society, of which the primary objective was to establish Buddhist schools. The first of these was started in 1886, as an 'English' secondary school, and after many vicissitudes it became a highly successful institution under the name of Ananda College. Similar activities by members of the Hindu religion in the north of the island resulted in the foundation of Jaffna Hindu College. These schools, however, took a long time before they attained the status of the Christian secondary schools, which were more numerous, had the advantage of getting in earlier, and were, some of them at any rate, partially supported from the funds of their missionary societies or orders.

The activities of the missionary societies and of the indigenous religious bodies were by no means confined to secondary schools, though after the creation of the Department of Public Instruction

[1] See above, Chapter 3, p. 47.

more and more of the primary schools were under its direct control. The primary schools, the great majority conducted in the local languages, had a fairly orderly development. Their problems were the usual kind that have confronted and still confront primary schools in all countries – lack of trained teachers, inadequate school buildings, lack of out-of-school activities, malnutrition of pupils, early leaving, non-attendance, and so on. The general result was that an increasing proportion of the children in town and country learned to read and write, and do sums: other subjects were taught, but it was a long time before the children were taught anything else that would be useful to them in after life, except perhaps in a few schools. There was no agricultural tinge to the curriculum of the rural schools, little or no handwork, no organised games. This was to change later, with the progress of educational theory and practice, and the institution of teachers' training colleges. Anyhow, when the time came for political advance there was a literate substratum in nearly all villages which provided something like a reading public for the vernacular press – to put the educational achievement at its lowest! As time went on, the Education Department made efforts to encourage school gardens, and out-of-school activities, such as physical drill and competitions, in the Sinhalese and Tamil schools. But school premises were for the most part inadequate, and playing space insufficient or completely absent. Teachers' training colleges were started, but the great majority of teachers in primary schools were untrained. The primary schools, and the secondary schools which were developed from them, in which the medium of instruction was one or the other of the local languages, always felt themselves to be – and were – the poor relations of the English schools. This was to have very important consequences later on, as recently as 1956, in the political sphere.[1]

From the point of view of political development it was the English secondary schools which were the operative factor: it was in the few government and the many grant-in-aid schools at this level that the pupils were able to get acquainted with what was going on in Ceylon and in the world at large. But as the goal of the school authorities was apt to be an examination, they were limited. When this examination was, as it was for a long time, the London Matriculation or the Cambridge Senior, the curriculum bore very little relation to the pupils' daily lives and surroundings. For instance, they learned English history, geography from textbooks based on a British outlook, sang English songs and played English games. The higher forms in the schools had to study the Western classics – Latin

[1] See below, Chapter 13.

and Greek. Few schools could afford science laboratories and their equipment, so that science, though its study was begun, was apt to be theoretical rather than practical, thereby losing most of its value. There was hardly any handwork, and agricultural education was almost entirely neglected.

Despite these initial disadvantages, the secondary schools, especially between the two world wars, were developing on something like the same lines as similar schools in England. Most of them were day schools, but some, like Trinity College, Kandy, had a considerable proportion of boarders.[1] They had their sixth forms and their prefects, their organised games and athletic sports, their debating and other societies, in some a house system, and their school songs (in English, of course). Some of them had platoons of cadets, units of the Ceylon Cadet Battalion, with regular parades and an annual camp up-country – to have a platoon of the Cadet Battalion was reckoned a status symbol, highly prized by college principals. (nearly all secondary schools in Ceylon called themselves colleges.) They had their troops of Boy Scouts. Cricket was – and is – the great school game in Ceylon, and the annual match between Royal and St. Thomas's Colleges is a really big occasion in Colombo. They also played both codes of football.

Girls' secondary schools, too, had been established, practically all of them founded and managed by religious bodies. These, too, were run on much the same lines as the corresponding institutions in England. For a considerable time practically all the principals of both boys' and girls' secondary schools were Europeans, in the case of the bigger Roman Catholic schools not infrequently Europeans other than British. It was not until the twenties that any of the missionary societies' schools had any Ceylonese as school principals.

In 1903 a Government Teachers' Training College was started in Colombo. The majority of the trained teachers went to English secondary schools, but later on other training colleges were started for the teachers in schools where the teaching was in Sinhalese or Tamil.

The first two institutions for higher education were the Law College and the Medical College. There had been some qualification for legal practice for forty years before 1873, when a Council of Legal Education was set up and the Law College started: though examinations for both proctors (solicitors) and advocates (barristers) had for a long time been held. By the twenties the qualification for entrance to the Law College was the Intermediate Arts examination of London University. Quite a number of advocates went to

[1] See Chapter 1, p. 23.

England, entered one of the Inns of Court, and became members of the English Bar. The legal profession was undoubtedly overcrowded; but there was plenty of scope – the Ceylonese being extremely litigious – and the rewards at the top of the profession were considerable.

The Medical College was begun in 1870. The degree (L.M.S. Ceylon) of this college came to be recognised by the British Medical Association, which made it possible for young doctors of ability and with the necessary means (or by loans) to proceed to Britain and enter straight away for the higher British medical degrees such as F.R.C.S.

As long ago as 1893 the Government Technical College came into existence: it was really rather a poor relation of the other two. But a certain number of Ceylonese were trained there for technical posts under various departments, and its laboratories made it possible for the Intermediate Science examination of London University, and later the degree examination (B.Sc.) to be studied for and taken.

Higher education in the ordinary sense of the term was a long time in coming. Before the first world war one or two students a year went on scholarship to a British university, and a few of the more wealthy Ceylonese sent their sons (and in later years a few of their daughters) usually to Oxford or Cambridge. While in Britain such young men met other students from overseas, India especially, and were inevitably drawn into the circles of political ferment in which such students inevitably moved. Some of them came back, eager to plunge into national political movements, and several of them became leading figures in these activities.

A movement began soon after the turn of the century whose object was to have an institution of university status in Ceylon. In 1906 a 'Ceylon University Association' came into being. Six years later a committee was set up by the Government to go into the question of providing higher education in the island, and this recommended the foundation of a university college, which was accepted by the Executive Council. The coming of the first world war held up the project, but it was taken up again in 1917, and four years later the Ceylon University College was started with a temporary staff in very temporary quarters in Colombo: laboratories were built, enough to enable students to take the London B.Sc. degree, though the Arts degrees were more popular. A permanent staff was soon built up, many of them Europeans, and after two or three years it became possible to introduce honours courses in most subjects. The institution was in a loose kind of way affiliated to Oxford University – an idea strongly promulgated by Sir Robert Chalmers during his régime as Governor. Oddly enough, he ultimately became Master of one of the Cambridge colleges. But it was for the external degrees of London University that the students worked. The question which bedevilled the institution from the beginning was when it should become a fully fledged university, and, what really attracted public attention, whether this university should be sited in Colombo or elsewhere. The site controversy in the early twenties, when there was, perhaps, something of a shortage of political issues, rent the Western-educated, and the result, as it turned out, was to postpone the coming of a university for twenty years. It was finally decided that it should be sited somewhere near Kandy, and this is where it was eventually built – on a very fine site indeed at Peradeniya, a few miles out of that town.

The two events which held up the transmutation of the University College into the University of Ceylon were, first, the economic depression of the early thirties, and then the Second World War. This meant that the higher education of the young Ceylonese must needs have a very strong Western slant, for there was little effort on the part of London University to make any adjustments in their syllabuses to suit local conditions, except that there was an honours degree course in Oriental Languages, with Sinhalese and Tamil as two of the subjects which could be taken, as well as the classical languages, Sanskrit and Pali.

This course was not taken by many students, however, for one definite reason. The career now open to bright young Ceylonese was the Ceylon Civil Service. The examination came to be held in Colombo at the same time as it took place in London, and the standard was that of a university honours degree. The London University curriculum, especially in Arts, was admirably adapted for this end, and the result was that the brightest students, with very few exceptions, aimed to enter that service. But the course in Oriental Languages was not so well adapted; hence the small number who read for it. It was the institution of the University College which made it possible to supply young Ceylonese with the requisite qualifications not only to the Civil Service, but also to government departments such as the Police and the Survey and, when it came into existence in the early thirties, the Inland Revenue Department. Those who failed to get places in one of these governmental activities – as well as the few who were really interested – entered the schools as graduate teachers, which enabled them to start on as high or even higher salaries than trained teachers.

It is clear from what has so far been outlined in this chapter that students of these institutions for higher education, and the boys and girls who went through the secondary schools, were very greatly affected by Western influences. The result was that the more Western education spread, the wider became the gulf between the Western-educated and the rest of the Ceylonese people, not so much the illiterate as those educated through the medium of Sinhalese or Tamil. And the more Western ideas penetrated, the more did the social life of those exposed to their influence tended to approximate to European standards.

While many of these Western-educated Ceylonese felt a marked dislike for the European community owing to the attitude of most of its members to them – generally unconscious – and some jealousy of their superior type of living, there were others who admired and imitated it. This attitude and style of living, therefore, merit some examination, as without doubt they had political as well as social implications more deep-rooted than would appear on the surface to a visitor from Britain or, indeed, to many of the British residents themselves.

The European community, to adopt the term generally used, took on the appearance of something like a caste. The vast majority were British. For the others there were a few in business firms from continental Europe – a big German firm before the 1914 war, one or two Dutch and Danish firms; a very few Americans, a certain number of individual long-staying visitors for business or pleasure, and, of course, a number of Roman Catholic clergy, many of them French and Belgian, and of nuns; the latter were teachers in convents and devoted nurses in some of the hospitals.

This community was anything but homogenous: it never numbered more than 10,000 and usually rather less – contrast the 77,000 Europeans in Northern Rhodesia, for instance. There were the members of the civil and other government services, whose relations with the Ceylonese were variable. They came into contact with them constantly in the way of their official duties, of course, and more and more with the gradual Ceylonisation of the services. In out-stations where there were few or no Europeans except officials, they naturally saw more of the Ceylonese and got to know them socially – up to a point; it depended, of course, very much on the individual officer and on his wife. But when they were stationed in Colombo, the administrative headquarters, or in one of the planting districts, these officers tended to identify themselves with the social life of members of their own community, so saw little of the Ceylonese outside their official relations with them. There were undoubtedly exceptions. For instance, in the early days of the British occupation, a civil servant, George Turnour, was a scholarly-minded man who became expert in Pali, and undertook the immensely important task of translating the *Mahavamsa*, thereby doing a great service to scholars, especially historians. Sir Emerson Tennent, who was unfortunate enough to be Colonial Secretary at the time when Lord Torrington was Governor – losing his post in consequence – wrote books on Ceylon which showed a profound acquaintance with the history and customs of the people. They are still worth reading and study. In 1845 a Branch of the Royal Asiatic Society was formed, and throughout its century and more of existence both Europeans and Ceylonese mixed freely on its Council and in its meetings, and the former made many contributions of value to the build-up of knowledge about the island's history, archaeology, and customs. Civil servants like Codrington, for instance, who was extremely well versed in the Sinhalese language and who was the first to write a learned work, based on research, which treated the history of Ceylon scientifically,[1] did much to stimulate the Ceylonese in the same field.

The Europeans engaged in the teaching profession and the clergy of various denominations came much more into contact with the Ceylonese, from the nature of their calling. This is also true of the small number of Europeans who were judicial officers; they mostly came from Britain *via* other colonies, and were older and more experienced than officers recruited for the first time to the administrative, technical or educational services. Some of the Europeans who served as judges or school principals were held in the highest esteem by their former colleagues or pupils, and are today received with an affectionate welcome if they get the opportunity of paying a visit to Ceylon.

The European business community was – and still is, though in lesser numbers – mostly concentrated in Colombo, and in general set the tone and standard of social life there, which differed in several respects from the social life of the European community in India. For one thing there were few, if any, who acquired the great wealth possessed by the leading businessmen – the *burra sahibs* – of Calcutta or Bombay. The civil servants of Ceylon had less of the 'heaven-born' touch about them than their counterparts in India, and the military garrison included only a handful of officers. So the typical Colombo European was a business executive, a member of an agency or a brokers' firm, or of a shipping, banking or insurance

[1] H. W. Codrington, *A Short History of Ceylon* (Macmillan's, 1947.)

company. The community was sharply divided into two sections, those just mentioned, on the one hand, and on the other, most of those who worked in establishments such as stores and motor or engineering firms, the other ranks of the services, and the European police sergeants. The executives in the first-mentioned set of firms worked hard in their offices through the day, and in the later afternoon usually went off to their clubs, social or sporting. There were clubs for tennis, golf, sailing, polo, swimming and, for the young and vigorous, cricket, both codes of football, and hockey. Into the social clubs no Ceylonese were admitted as members, and only on the rarest occasions as guests. The same, for that matter, is true of the Europeans in the second section above mentioned, though these had their own clubs which were almost equally exclusive of Ceylonese. The social line was very strictly drawn – and deeply resented by those below it. The two sections met but rarely: only in places of worship with their attendant religious and social activities, in European volunteer units, in freemasonry, in team games like cricket and football, and in circles of arts, music and intellectual pursuits – very infrequent, such circles. This rather ridiculous state of affairs persisted till well into the forties of this century, possibly in some ways it still persists, and was Suburbia at its worst. It was on one occasion reduced to complete absurdity when two brothers, both chartered accountants, came out from Britain, one to an agency firm, the other to a leading store: only the former was eligible to join a certain social club!

This 'mercantile' type of European in general (there were, of course, exceptions) met the educated Ceylonese very little – only in the same ways socially as he met the 'below the line' person of his own community; in the other than European military units and in the spheres of activity indicated in the previous paragraph, of which the field of sport was probably the most effective way in which the races mixed. Though the exclusiveness was, in one sense, quite explicable – people of the same race with the same way of living, in a country far from their home liking to get together – it did without any doubt cause resentment on the part of the Ceylonese, particularly because of the way in which it was done. The situation may be most aptly illustrated by reference to the Colombo Club, the leading European club for men, a club of the type found in the capital cities of most colonies as well as in the big business centres of India. This club occupied just about the finest site in Colombo, near the sea front. It was not possible till during or after the Second World War for a member to invite any Ceylonese to enter the portals of that club as his guest, much less to become a member of it. This one fact was a constant and underlying cause of resentment to the educated Ceylonese.

The two preceding paragraphs may seem petty and personal, hardly perhaps worthy of mention. But the state of affairs indicated had a very real impact. The Europeans would have been wise if they had lifted their objection to Ceylonese as club guests and members much earlier.

The European planting community lived their lives very much to themselves. Those who planted tea in the higher altitudes hardly ever met the educated Ceylonese – only on the rarest occasions. Their social life consisted mainly of dropping in on each other – their neighbours were usually a few miles away – and, a great feature of planters' leisure, visits to their clubs, weekly as a rule, though sometimes more frequently. There were about six or seven big district clubs, and a number of small ones, all of them social and sporting in character – tennis till sunset, and bridge, billiards or bar afterwards. Most of these clubs had one special night a week, when dancing or other entertainment took place and in the contemporary slang, 'a good time was had by all'. Except for a few, the planters' clubs tended to be rather less racially exclusive than those in Colombo, especially in districts where there was a fair sprinkling of Ceylonese planters, such as the rubber districts. With the advent of the motor car and motor cycle, and of the telephone, the lives of planters and their families became much less lonely than formerly, and visits to their clubs could be made more frequently, though they did not become the regular daily routine which prevailed among many of the Colombo or Kandy Europeans. Planters on the whole led hard working but pleasant lives. They were accommodated in – mostly – comfortable bungalows (the usual term in Ceylon for a house) surrounded by small gardens in which, up-country, most of the English flowers could be grown, and as often as not there was a tennis court. Their pay was reasonably adequate and, unless they spent their salaries too freely, as some inevitably did, they were usually able to have their children educated in public boarding schools in their home country, and eventually to retire to it.[1] They looked after their labour forces paternally, and most of them were fluent in Tamil, of the type usually described as 'coolie Tamil'. They did not have much to do with the Sinhalese villagers: though this was not always the case with the rubber planters in mid-and low-country estates, some of whom employed some Sinhalese labour on their estates. This section of the planting community, too, saw more of the Ceylonese

[1] For a description, and defence, of the planter see *Ceylon, Pearl of The East* by Harry Williams, (Robert Hale) Chapter XIII (3).

who had planted some of their ancestral lands with rubber, or acquired land for that purpose, or bought rubber estates, managing these themselves, than the up-country planters.

The social life of the wealthier Western-educated Ceylonese of the upper and middle classes was considerably affected by the kind of life lived by the European community. They had their own clubs, social and sporting, and among the latter cricket flourished exceedingly. The membership of these was entirely Ceylonese, and in the case of some of the cricket clubs in particular, communal – the Sinhalese Sports Club and the Tamil Union, both in Colombo, for instance. This form of communalism was not perhaps very harmful, though some have deprecated it strongly.

Though the landed upper classes of the Kandyan Sinhalese, the chiefs, continued to live on their ancestral lands in a semi-feudal fashion, looked up to by their tenants and the surrounding villagers, round about the turn of the century they began to send their sons to English schools, especially to Trinity College, Kandy, the Principal of which was universally liked and respected.[1] They did this, though it was a Christian missionary school and they themselves were practically all Buddhists, whose privilege it was to take a dignified and prominent part in the procession of the Kandy *Perahera*,[2] wearing their gorgeous traditional dress. On the whole they were not much drawn to politics, though this has today changed somewhat: the present Prime Minister (at the time of writing) is the daughter of a Kandyan chief. A certain number of the wealthier middle-class Ceylonese bought estates – a process which, after the second world war, was to increase rapidly in the case of people mostly from the low-country. These estates were usually coconut or rubber, much more uncommonly tea. To begin with they did not, on the whole, run them very efficiently, being, too often, unwilling to pay their staffs adequately, though there were always exceptions to this, and in more recent years it became rather less the case. A coconut estate does not require anything like the skill in management of a rubber or, *a fortiori*, a tea estate, neither is it necessary to undertake frequent capital expenditure on it, though coconut estate owners who have seen fit to go in for extensive manuring and replanting have found it well worth while. It has been a general and not wholly unjustified criticism of Ceylonese estate owners by the planting community that they have been apt to stint capital expenditure on their estates, with effects likely to be unfortunate in the long run.

In the towns, Colombo in particular, the average middle-class

[1] See Chapter 1, p. 23.
[2] See Chapter 2, p. 30.

Ceylonese lived a family life, and any circle of friends he might have usually consisted of people of the same caste or sub-caste: but many of the Western-educated were likely to extend their circles more widely, particularly when they took interests in social welfare, or in cultural pursuits which impelled them to join societies concerned with the arts or with intellectual matters, or in sporting activities. Between the two world wars their horizons widened considerably. Some of the younger men and women were beginning to break away from the trammels of closely integrated family life. The spread of film theatres was not unconnected with this, and also the sports and games which they learned at school and wished to go on with after leaving. Furthermore, Western dancing, which at one time was held by most Sinhalese and Tamils to be highly improper, was taken up enthusiastically and became popular in upper and middle class circles.

These changes were the more noteworthy inasmuch as they greatly affected the position of women. There was a definite women's movement between the two wars, not indeed of any militancy. Its significance was that the women of Ceylon were beginning to come out of their former obscurity and confinement to the home, and into prominence in social service, in cultural and learned societies, in sport, and even in politics. They were, too, beginning to enter fields of regular employment other than teachers, nurses, and telephone operators. All this was not at all pleasing to the more conservative of the Ceylonese males. Admittedly it had not gone very far when the Second World War broke out – the first time a young Sinhalese woman appeared in the streets of Colombo wearing slacks there was a minor riot, from which she had to take refuge. But the feminist movement had come to stay. To give a light-hearted but not insignificant illustration, the Principal of the University College, having occasion to give a mild reprimand to one of the women students, remarked that he was quite sure it would shock her parents: her reply was that it was the duty of her generation to shock their parents. A reply like this would have been inconceivable twenty years earlier.

Westernisation only affected the upper and middle classes markedly, though of course there were various material developments of which the working classes were able to take advantage. Most significant of these, perhaps, was the advent of the motorbus, which between the two world wars began to run to many villages which the railways did not, and could never reach. The railways themselves had been a factor in beginning to move a hitherto largely immobile society: the motorbus accelerated this very greatly. The villagers could now move out of their villages easily – if they had the money for the fares – and go to a neighbouring town, or even to Colombo for shopping and marketing, or to a cinema. Cinemas were being put up in many of the small towns, or going round in mobile vans; there were very few Sinhalese films, but Indian films in Tamil and even in Hindi became very popular.

The motorbus also enabled all areas, however remote, to get the Sinhalese or Tamil newspapers regularly, and with the spread of education the villagers could either read them or find in the village someone literate to read them aloud.

The spread of literacy immensely enhanced the importance of the press. In early British times, the *Government Gazette* used to publish items other than government notices. In 1831 the Government sponsored the *Colombo Journal*, but this enterprise was frowned upon by the Colonial Office. The first independent newspaper, started in 1834, was *The Observer*, followed twelve years later by *The Times of Ceylon*. Both these evening papers, in English, are still in circulation. Several other dailies have come and gone. *The Observer* in particular was often highly critical of the Government and took up the cause of the Ceylon League (see p. 85) very strongly. It was only a few years later that newspapers began to be published in Sinhalese and Tamil. In 1918 a young Cambridge graduate, D. R. Wijewardene,[1] an enthusiast for political advance, bought a Sinhalese newspaper, *Dinamina*, and soon started a morning paper in English, *The Ceylon Daily News*. Wijewardene made himself into a very capable journalist and a good business man. In 1923 he took over *The Observer*. He founded a company, the 'Associated Newspapers of Ceylon', popularly known as the Lake House Press. *The Daily News* in particular exercised very great influence in the movement for independence, and subsequently – of which more hereafter.

Westernisation had other important effects. It was identified, and for a long period correctly identified, in the minds of the Buddhist *Sangha* and the Hindu priests with Christian proselytism: the reaction against this was referred to earlier. But there was another side, as well as the religious, to this adverse reaction. This took the form of a revival of interest in Ceylon's history and archaeology. The start of this was to a considerable extent due to a few interested Britons. Turnour's translation of the *Mahavamsa* and the founding of the Ceylon Branch of the Royal Asiatic Society have already been mentioned (see p. 107). Much interest was shown in the ruined cities of Anuradhapura and Polonnaruwa, which were found almost

[1] See *The Life and Times of D. R. Wijewardene*, by H. A. J. Hulugalle, Lake House Press, Colombo.

deserted in the eighteen thirties; eventually, in 1908, an Archaeological Department was created. The pioneering work was done by the first Commissioner, H. C. P. Bell, to whom the country owes a real debt of gratitude. He was followed by other distinguished European archaeologists, who carried on his good work. The first Ceylonese Commissioner, Dr. S. Paranavitana, was a very worthy successor. Though he started life as a village schoolmaster, the depth of his knowledge and research and the practical skill he showed in undertaking numerous restorations of ancient monuments, very professionally and artistically carried out, earned him fame in the archaeological world, honorary degrees of foreign universities, and, after his retirement, a professorial chair in the University of Ceylon. Without doubt this reaction, based as it was on solid work in history and archaeology by both Ceylonese and Europeans, has brought, to the Sinhalese in particular, a pride in their past, sometimes accompanied by a disparagement of their present, which has become a part of the national make-up.

With the revived interest in Ceylon's past came also some interest in the traditional music and dancing of the people, though not on anything like so large a scale, even comparatively, as the revival in India. Kandyan dancing, exclusively by men in their traditional and picturesque dress – had never died out, being kept up by a special sub-caste with specially trained teachers. These dancers take a prominent part in the Kandy and other *peraheras*, and of recent years have been much in demand for social occasions, particularly those held in honour of distinguished visitors. The art of drumming also maintained itself, but as far as the other musical instruments are concerned the inspiration has come mostly from India. The arts of painting and sculpture, which flourished in early times, have practically died out. Western influences have been pervasive in music and painting, mainly but not entirely among the Western-educated and, from these, musicians and artists of talent have arisen whose reputations have spread beyond the bounds of the island itself.

It is generally held that the process of Westernisation has gone further and deeper in Ceylon than in any other Asian country. This is probably correct. But to estimate how far, and how deep, is anything but simple. In any case it is too early to make anything like an accurate attempt at estimating whether it is merely a veneer, or whether the effects of four and a half centuries of European, including a century and a half of British influence, will have left an indelible mark on the island's history. There is today a strong reaction against Westernisation, which came to a head as the result

H

of the general election in 1956. In this connexion, the author feels impelled to quote the final words of Dr. G. C. Mendis's thoughtful little book 'Ceylon Today and Yesterday' – 'We must also see that we do not allow our emotions to get the better of facts in making our assessment of the past and minimise the importance of the vast changes that have resulted from the impact of the West, with its science and technology, on our social life, though such changes have not kept pace with those in our political and economic life.'

Chapter 9

Constitutional Development
and the Donoughmore Commission

I T was towards the turn of the century that the new and developing middle class began to feel its feet, and to start an agitation for some measure of political advance. It was pointed out in Chapter seven that the Legislative Council, over the period after 1833, had acquired a few political rights – the introduction of bills and the appropriation of the revenue left over after the fixed civil and military expenditure had been met. It was over the latter, the military expenditure, that the unofficials had clashed head on with the Government in the fifties and sixties, until finally a definite sum was fixed. The objection of the unofficials had been to the cost of Ceylon's defence having to be met out of the colony's revenue, when it should have been an imperial commitment, and they had asked for an unofficial majority in the Council. But the lead was always taken by the European unofficial members, usually backed by the Ceylonese unofficials – they stood together particularly over the question of military expenditure. Once material prosperity seemed assured, however, the demand for an unofficial majority in the Council faded away. The European members no longer took any interest, and the Ceylonese never showed any initiative in this demand. The Government, backed by the Secretary of State, stuck to the point of view as expressed by Governor Ward (see Chapter seven, p. 85), that the Government represented the interests of the mass of the people much better than the representatives of business and planting, or the small Burgher community. This attitude persisted when the Ceylonese middle class began to agitate for political rights, viz. that an incorrupt and impartial bureaucracy would serve the interests of the people at large much better than an oligarchy, whether of Europeans or of Ceylonese. It was certainly the view of the Colonial Office; it now looks oddly shortsighted when contemporary political developments in the home country are taken into consideration. But the point of view had shifted somewhat from the days of Colebrooke. 'The white man's burden' was the angle from which they saw it, and they were convinced that the coloured peoples would never, or at least not for a long time, be really capable of running their own affairs. A benevolent official Government must necessarily do the job of looking after the people far better than a handful of politicians from the upper and middle clases. But this attitude did not really square with the *laissez faire* doctrine of the time. It is conceivable that it might have worked if the idea of the welfare state had then been operative, and before the doctrine that good government is no substitute for self-government began to work powerfully on the minds of men. It is due to this attitude of mind that the protagonists of the early Labour movement in Britain had no use for the colonial Empire. They had suffered from a similar attitude, that the working man was not really fit to exercise the vote: hence the dislike of Labour politicians for the Crown colony system.

The anomaly of a growing democracy at home and bureaucracies in the Colonies may in part be accounted for by the fact that the British public as a whole took remarkably little interest in colonial affairs, and were never greatly affected by the Empire movement, which is typified, in different ways, by Joseph Chamberlain, Lord Milner and Rudyard Kipling. Even today the average British citizen is mildly surprised, though generally quite acquiescent, when he hears a West Indian, quite justifiably, profess himself British.

This imperial idea did not, naturally, appeal to the Ceylonese who was English-educated, and who began to read and to think for himself. He read Burke, and John Stuart Mill 'On Liberty'. He saw the Legislative Council going on as it had gone on for many years. He saw that, whereas constitutionally Ceylon had for many years been in advance of India, this was no longer the case; for Indians were now to be found on Executive Councils both at the centre and in some of the provinces and, moreover, in the Legislative Councils some of the Members were elected. Whereas the Colonial Office looked at the colonial Empire in general, and was nervous of any constitutional advance, the Ceylonese neither knew nor cared about the other colonies; but they did cast their eyes over to their nearest neighbour.

It was in the first decade of the present century that the ideas of political reform really got hold of the leaders of the new middle class, and in 1908 the Ceylon National Association was formed by some prominent Ceylonese. One of these was James Peiris. He was by caste a Karawa. He had been sent to Cambridge University as early as the seventies and had, somewhat surprisingly for that time, been elected President of the Cambridge Union – it was many years before another colonial undergraduate attained to that position.

Another was E. W. Perera, an able lawyer, whose book 'Twentieth Century Impressions of Ceylon', written about that time, sheds much light on the attitude of the leading Ceylonese. Two more leaders were the Tamil brothers, Ponnambalam Ramanathan and Ponnambalam Arunachalam, both of whom had distinguished themselves in the judicial and public services respectively and been knighted. The former in particular was the possessor of a very subtle intellect, and a man of outstanding ability.

By 1906 a Liberal Government had come into power in Britain. The Ceylon National Association, and some other associations which had come into being, sent memoranda to the Secretary of State for the Colonies, judging correctly that these would receive more serious consideration from the Liberal than from the previous Conservative Government. The Governor, Sir Henry McCallum, was averse to this course, but sent forward the memoranda, the best of which was that of the Ceylon National Association, drawn up by James Peiris. The memorandum pointed out that there had been practically no constitutional change since 1833, and asked for territorial representation and the election of some of the Legislative Council Members. The memoranda received attention, but the net result, if small, was significant. In the Legislative Council an extra Member (nominated) was given each to the low-country Sinhalese and to the Tamils. The Europeans and Burghers were allowed to elect their own representatives and a seat known as the 'Educated Ceylonese' seat was created, for which a Ceylonese was to be elected on a very limited franchise. The official majority was still there, but reduced to one. No concession was made in the direction of unofficial representation on the Executive Council. Sir Ponnambalam Ramanathan was elected to fill the Educated Ceylonese seat. Thus a real, if small, step forward was conceded in the direction of constitutional advance, and the Ceylonese politician at last had his foot in the door. Hindsight shows us that full independence was bound to follow; such an idea would have struck horror into the minds of the contemporary British rulers and administrators; it does not seem to have crossed the minds of the contemporary Ceylonese leaders either. What they wanted was a finger in the pie. It is interesting to note that one or two of the Europeans who were entering the civil service about that time were to see the whole gamut of political advance, right up to independence.

It was not, actually, till 1912 that the new constitution, or what may more aptly be described as the slightly revised constitution, became operative. However, the important thing is that the constitution *was* changed, and at the request of the Ceylonese themselves;

and that the elective principle was conceded for a seat for the people of the country – a small number of them. Though this principle had earlier been conceded in India, this was the first time in the colonial Empire that it had come the way of non-Europeans.

Two years later war broke out in Europe, developing into World War I, and in it, as a colony, Ceylon was automatically involved. From the military angle Ceylon was untouched, though not unaffected. To begin with, a number of Europeans and some Ceylonese volunteered for active service: of the latter, some were torpedoed and drowned at sea before they could reach England to join the forces. Many of the Europeans went to Egypt, and thence to the Gallipoli landing, where they suffered heavy casualties. Generous contributions to the war effort were made by members of all races. The German raiding cruiser '*Emden*' was seen near the shores of Ceylon not long before being caught and sunk; and this was the closest thing to enemy action that came anywhere near Ceylon. But the war had important indirect effects, which might be described as psychological. Ten years before, a profound impression had been made on the minds of Asians by the defeat of a major European power, Russia, by an Asian country, Japan. The remarkable rise of Japan, which had always been independent, made Asians, Ceylonese included, wonder whether what the Japanese had achieved they might achieve also. With the outbreak of the 1914 war it seemed at first that the imperial power of Britain was suffering defeat, or only just holding on. However, the feeling was not very apparent. What was apparent was a most unfortunate affair, arising out of a religio-communal conflict between some Sinhalese Buddhists and some Indian Moors, over what seemed a comparatively trifling matter, the playing of music by a Buddhist procession in Gampola, a small town near Kandy, while passing a Muslim mosque. The ensuing riots which broke out in Gampola, and also in Kandy, were suppressed without much difficulty, and indeed most of the trouble was over before the Government took any action. It was unfortunate that the Governor, Sir Robert Chalmers, had been a British Treasury official with no colonial or practical experience of being a Governor. It does not seem that he was well advised, but he certainly lost his head. As a result the small number of regular soldiers in Ceylon were called out, and reinforced by units of the Ceylon Defence Force, including the European Ceylon Planters Rifle Corps. Later, a battalion of the Indian Army was sent. Martial law was proclaimed, which lasted for some months, and a few rioters were shot, more or less out of hand. This created considerable indignation among the Ceylonese. But what was quite inexplicable was the detention of some prominent Ceylonese whose sole fault appears to have been that they were concerned with a Buddhist temperance movement. The authorities seem to have suspected some subversive activity under this cover, possibly German-inspired – the spy mania was not confined to Britain – or perhaps they thought that the Ceylonese leaders might try to seize power if the riots got out of hand. Be that as it may, among those temporarily detained were D. B. Jayatilaka and D. S. Senanayake, who were later to become the most prominent Ceylonese political leaders under a reformed constitution. Both arrests were totally unjustifiable.

The effect of these further severe measures on the minds of the politically conscious Ceylonese was remarkable, as anyone who has ever discussed the matter with any of them, including D. S. Senanayake himself, well knows. Much of the goodwill felt, even unconsciously, towards the British rulers of Ceylon was dissipated by their stupid handling of the affair, and not regained. There was, oddly enough, no resultant resentment between the Sinhalese and the Moors; indeed, there were many public disclaimers of this. The resentment was against the British Government of Ceylon. Chalmers was speedily recalled, and subsequently had a distinguished academic career – much more in his line than governing a colony. An abler successor was appointed, who straightened out the situation as best he could. But the way was now open for political agitation on a much larger scale.

In 1917 the Ceylon Reform League was founded, of which two of the principal leaders were the two Tamil knights referred to earlier,[1] the two brothers, F. R. and D. S. Senanayake, E. W. Perera, Dr. (later) Sir Marcus Fernando, an eminent doctor, James (afterwards Sir James) Peiris, and D. B. (afterwards Sir Baron) Jayatilaka. The next year this body developed into the Ceylon National Congress, which it was hoped would follow the Indian example. The agitation, of a highly constitutional character, was sympathetically regarded in London, and it was decided then to give more political freedom to Ceylon.

There is no doubt that the Montague-Chelmsford Report of 1917 on India influenced both the British Government in London and the new political leaders of Ceylon, particularly the forthright declaration that the intention of the reforms in India was 'with a view to the progress in realisation of responsible government in India as an integral part of the British Empire', and 'the increasing association of Indians in every branch of the administration'. After the 1915 fiasco a delegation of Ceylonese leaders travelled to London

[1] See above, p. 117.

to present a memorandum; they were so nervous about it that
E. W. Perera told the author that he carried it on thin paper in his
shoe. They were sympathetically received in various quarters, and
once the war was over a further measure of reform was considered
and granted. An Order in Council was published in 1920, the effect
of which was to create an unofficial majority in the Legislative
Council – 11 territorially elected members and 6 communally
elected – 2 Europeans, 1 Burgher, 2 Kandyan Sinhalese and 1
Indian: also a member was chosen by the Ceylon Chamber of
Commerce, a European body, and one was to come from the Low-
Country Products Association, which consisted mainly of Ceylonese
coconut and rubber planters, but the members of this Association
were so dissatisfied with the reforms that they declined to elect their
member. Four more, including 1 Muslim, were to be nominated by
the Governor. Though the number of official members was raised to
14, they were now in a minority. But the Governor had the power to
certify any measure as being 'of paramount importance', in which
case it could be passed by the votes of the official members only;
the Governor could also stop proceedings dealing with any measure which he considered would endanger the safety or tranquility
of the country.

The National Congress had asked for a Council of 50 members,
40 to be territorially elected, the rest nominated, or official; they also
demanded an elected Speaker, full financial control, and a wider
franchise. They strongly objected to the retention and intensification
of communal representation, and nearly boycotted the new Council.
On the other hand, the two Tamil knights broke away from the
Congress out of dissatisfaction with the representation of their community, and it became an exclusively Sinhalese organisation –
mainly low-country Sinhalese. However, two big advances had been
made, the concession of the principles of territorial representation,
and of representative government – an unofficial majority (however limited) having been established. As far as the franchise was
concerned, it was on a narrow basis – a fairly high property and
literary qualification for members and a somewhat lower one for
voters. It has been estimated that only 4 per cent of the population
had this franchise. In other words, it was the middle class which had
carried through the agitation, got the vote, and were the representatives in the Legislative Council. A considerable proportion of these
were resident in towns. The villagers were completely unaffected.

The constitution was devised on a system of checks and balances.
The Governor continued to preside over the Legislative Council.
The official monopoly of the Executive Council was ended by the

addition of 4 unofficials; but these could not be members of the Legislative Council. It was not possible, in the latter, for the representative of any one community to swamp the others – the constitution seems to have been designed to this end. Ultimate power was in the hands of the Secretary of State, through the Governor. None the less, 1921 really marks the end of Crown colony government in Ceylon.

Ceylonese leaders did not cease agitating against the insufficiency of the advance conceded by the Order in Council, and it was not long before they secured a further advance. They asked for an elected Speaker, 28 out of 45 members to be elected territorially, and half the Executive Council to be members of the Legislature. By this time the general colonial policy of the British Government was undergoing a pretty rapid change. After all, members of the Empire, free, Indian and colonial, had fought side by side with British soldiers in the world war. Admittedly most emphasis was laid on the volunteers from the dominions, and much on the Indian Army: but this feeling of comradeship and gratitude, however, vague and evanescent, did to some extent stretch out to the colonies. So there was little difficulty in conceding the principle of a further advance, even though, when made, it completely upset the checks and balances of the 1920 constitution.

By the 1923 Order in Council 23 members were to be territorially elected, 11 communally, and 3 were to be nominated by the Governor. The official members were reduced to 12. The communally elected members were: 3 European – Urban, Rural and Commercial; 2 Burghers; 3 Muslims; 2 Indians; and one Tamil seat for the Western Province (this had been the bone of contention between the 2 Tamil knights and the Congress). The property and literacy qualifications for the vote were retained, and the franchise slightly broadened. The Governor kept the powers of certification and of initiating financial proposals as under the 1921 constitution. He was, technically, still the President of the Council, but if he was not present the Council would be presided over by the Vice-President, a member elected by the Council. His power of stopping debates was dropped. He could not himself veto legislation, but could recommend a veto to the Secretary of State for the Colonies. The composition and function of the Executive Council were unaltered – though this body was to lose much of its authority.

Thus there was now an effective unofficial majority, limited only by the Governor's power of certification and by the refusal of the royal assent to legislation (i.e., the veto of the Secretary of State for the Colonies). This really meant that most of the power over finance lay with the Council. All this was deliberately done with the idea of giving the members of the Council political training. The principle of communal representation was kept, and seemed to be firmly implanted in the constitution. This did not apply to the Tamils, who, except for the Tamil member for the Western Province, were territorially elected, but to the smaller communities. The electoral principle ran into some difficulties here – not with the Europeans, for in practice the Chamber of Commerce and the Planters' Association fixed this among themselves. But it was very difficult to define precisely what a Burgher was. The Muslim and Indian communities were both represented by wealthy merchants.

The working of this constitution has been heavily criticised on two counts – power without responsibility, and communal representation.[1] The latter has been generally condemned as likely to exacerbate communal feelings and perpetuate communal differences, and turn the Europeans and Burghers in particular into something like castes.[2] Yet, without it the minority communities felt that they would be completely overridden by the Sinhalese, the majority community. In point of fact this is just what has happened in the last few years. It may be argued that if full territorial representation had been introduced in 1921 the communal spirit would not have been aroused, and the later communal troubles would not have taken place – but this is mere speculation. The view of the Colonial Office was that Ceylon was not yet anything like a nation, and that the first loyalties of the people were to their religion and to their community.[3] Hence undiluted territorial representation could only mean Sinhalese rule, and the authorities felt that if they did this they would be letting down the minorities. On the other hand, some Sinhalese nationalists saw in this merely a cunning scheme of the British Government to keep power in its hands by the policy of 'divide and rule'. The dilemma is inescapable in plural societies, and can only be solved by goodwill. It may be remarked that a solution has a prospect of success in Malaya (the agreement to make society in these parts still more plural by the creation of Malaysia has been signed almost as these words are being written) and the future of the experiment will be well worth watching.

The other problem, power without responsibility, arose out of the fact that the Government must initiate measures, particularly financial measures, but after that control passed into the hands of the Legislature. As it was put by the Donoughmore Commission,

[1] See Report of the Special Commission on the Constitution, Cmd. 3131 (known as the Donoughmore Report) HMSO 1928.
[2] See G. C. Mendis, *Ceylon under the British*, Chapter IX, Sections 1 and 2.
[3] See Sir Charles Jeffries *Ceylon: The Path to Independence* (Pall Mall Press) pp.41–2.

'The official members who are responsible' (i.e. for the conduct of public business) 'are in a permanent minority. The official members owe no allegiance to the Council and are irremovable except by the Governor, in whom all executive authority is vested. The unofficial members, though in complete control in the Council, are denied the prospect of assuming office themselves. Thus, on a counting of heads, those who have the controlling votes in the Council are not called upon to bear the responsibility for their decisions; those who have to bear the responsibility are without the controlling votes.'

In the sphere of finance, this control issued in the composition and functions of a body known as the Finance Committee, which consisted of three of the principal officers of state – the Colonial Secretary, the Controller of Revenue and the Colonial Treasurer, and all the unofficial members of the Legislative Council. It met in private for the purpose of discussing the annual estimates and other financial matters. To assist them, the permanent heads of government departments were called in when matters relating to their departments came up for consideration. This was in a way unfortunate, for it gave the unofficial members a chance, which they had never had before, and in which they revelled, of 'getting at' these hitherto high and mighty personages – in private. The Report (pp. 22–3) gives the picture of what happened:—'It has become the practice for Heads of Departments to be treated as hostile witnesses, against whom it is permissible to apply all the forensic arts of cross-examination. The conciliatory policy of the Government militates against these officers receiving adequate protection from the chair' (the Colonial Secretary was in the chair) 'and the latitude allowed to the Committee places them at a further disadvantage. Questions are rarely confined to the matters at issue, and the Committee are permitted to wander at will over the whole administrative field. Under a constant fire of uninstructed criticism, subjected to grave discourtesy, if not on occasion to personal insult, it is not surprising that these officers find the treatment extended to them painful and humiliating.' To people brought up in the British parliamentary tradition, where a civil servant is screened from parliamentary attack by the doctrine of ministerial responsibility, this was quite horrifying. But, as Sir Herbert Stanley, who was Governor from 1927 to 1931, pointed out, the picture was not as black as it was painted, and the treatment handed out to these officials was apt to vary with the person being interviewed. Up to that time the senior civil servants and the heads of departments were rather like 'little tin gods' in the eyes of the Ceylonese (and occasionally, though not often, in their own); and they were practically all Europeans. It was therefore unfortunate, but not unnatural, and certainly very tempting, for Ceylonese unofficial members – for the first time able to be in a position to do so – to get at them. Iconoclasm can be great fun! The word 'unfortunate' has been deliberately used, because these few years of the 1924 constitution set up a tradition of some hostility as between politicians and government servants which has never quite died down, not even after the 'Westminster model' has been duly followed by the Ceylon Parliament ever since 1947. It was also a factor in the minds of European and even of a few Ceylonese government servants when, a few years later, they had the choice of staying on or retiring on proportionate pension.

The ordinary business of the Legislative Council worked out in a pattern which was to become familiar in other colonies at a later date; though Ceylon, as will be seen, had its own special variation owing to the manner of constitutional advance resulting from the recommendations of the Donoughmore Report. This pattern was of the unofficials (except the European members) ganging up against the Government, so that whenever the Ceylonese members felt like voting together, the Government was bound to be in a minority. The Ceylonese members, however, did not push this to extremes, so as to make government unworkable; but they did sometimes make it difficult to carry on satisfactorily, and having 'power without responsibility', they could – and did – say what they liked, and make extreme and exaggerated statements in Council debates.

The Governors for their part, and their advisers, 'bent over backwards' to maintain good relations with the Councillors, and refrained as much as possible from exercising their power of certification. The Governor from 1925 to 1927 was Sir Hugh Clifford, a big man of outstanding ability. He had been at one time Colonial Secretary in Ceylon. He emphatically disliked the constitution, and just did not want to work it. He was even then showing signs of the mental instability which in the end completely upset the balance of his mind. He got himself transferred to Malaya, but before he went he reported very strongly to the Colonial Office that the constitution was unworkable. Clifford's successor, Sir Herbert Stanley, took a rather better view of its practicability, but the Colonial Office decided to act on Clifford's report, and to send out a Commission 'to visit Ceylon and report on the working of the existing Constitution and . . . to consider any proposals for the revision of the Constitution that may be put forward . . .'

What the Ceylonese who were aiming at political advance wanted was clear. They were not aiming at complete independence, or even at full internal self-government. They wanted a majority of territorially-elected members, with a small amount of communal representation to satisfy the smaller communities; an embryo ministerial system, or at least some of the elected representatives in the Legislative Council having seats in the Executive Council. The franchise might perhaps be somewhat extended. But what they really envisaged was a share of the executive power being put and kept in the hands of the educated middle class, and the gradual Ceylonisation of the administration.

The Commission arrived in Ceylon towards the end of 1927, and stayed for two months. There was much excitement at the time of their visit, but entirely of an orderly kind. The Chairman of the Commission was the Earl of Donoughmore, an experienced politician, and the other members were Sir Matthew Nathan, a former colonial administrator, and two British Members of Parliament, Sir Geoffrey Butler and Dr. (later Sir) Drummond Shiels – one from each political party. The two last seem to have been the most influential.

Their Report, which was presented in June 1928, surveyed the existing constitution and was very severe on its defects, their major point being 'power without responsibility'. To solve the difficulties they put forward an original scheme. It did not meet with the unqualified approval of the Ceylonese leaders, who wanted something nearer the Westminster model: and when the scheme, which seems to have appealed to the Secretary of State for the Colonies, was embodied in an Order in Council, it was adopted only with reluctance by the Legislative Council – a resolution favouring it only got through by two votes.

From the point of view of subsequent history, their two most important recommendations were the abolition of communal representation, and adult franchise. They could see no merit in fixed communal seats, but they recognised the dilemma, and proposed a fair number of seats (twelve) without any definite communal allotment, which could be filled on the Governor's nomination by representatives of the smaller minority communities; the two larger ones would be looked after by the territorial seats. This abolition was important, but still more important was the breath-taking expansion of the franchise. No one had advocated such a step in Ceylon, with one exception. This was A. E. Goonesinghe, who in the twenties had founded the Ceylon Labour Party. He used to hold rallies, and drive round Colombo with a red flag flying from the bonnet of his car. He earned some popularity with the urban proletariat in Colombo: but his ideas got him nowhere with the middle class or, for the matter of that, with the rural workers. The

National Congress was against any extensive broadening of the franchise. The Commission had suggested the minimum age limit for a vote of thirty for women, but the Legislative Council recommended the franchise for women to be exactly the same as for men, and this was accepted; this was somewhat surprising, as the position of women in Ceylon was still very much that of the inferior sex. The Secretary of State readily agreed. It has to be remembered that it was only in that very year, 1928, that the same complete adult franchise was extended to women and men alike in the United Kingdom. The Labour M.P. Drummond Shiels was the most persistent in getting this through – he told the author years afterwards that it was the event of his life of which he was the most proud. There is no doubt that this had the same intention as that which inspired former British Governments in Ceylon, with the backing of the Colonial Office, to oppose the placing of more power in the hands of the middle class, and its representatives in the Legislative Council, since its members would then exercise power as an oligarchy; and, as mentioned earlier, they held that bureaucracy was a better form of government than oligarchy for an illiterate population: they also believed that minorities would be better protected, and that there would be no corruption or nepotism, or to use a picturesque Ceylon expression 'family bandyism', 'bandy' being the old word for coach. Hence the power of the Government must be used to protect the mass of the people. The Commission's solution was to hand over the power to the mass of the people and let them do their own protection – a momentous decision. Sir Geoffrey Butler, in conversation with the author of this book, remarked that as a good Tory he believed in 'dishing the Whigs', as Disraeli had done with his Reform Act of 1876. This particular action did more than anything else to set Ceylon in the forefront of constitutional advance; from this time onwards universal adult suffrage became an essential feature of British colonial policy, and has been elevated into something like a sacred doctrine, or even a dogma, in the minds particularly of African nationalist politicians. In the light of this, the Donoughmore Commissioners' half-apologetic reasons for advocating this extension make interesting reading.

The effects of universal suffrage did not make themselves really manifest on a large scale for another generation, not until the 1956 election. In the first general election, in 1931, a little over half the potential electorate registered and voted; but considerable interest was taken by those who did – and there were nine murders whose cause was attributed to election disputes.

The constitutional solution proper put forward by the Donoughmore Report and mostly adopted by the British Government now appears something of an aberration in the political development of Ceylon: it was not followed in any other part of the colonial Empire. But it is worth a brief examination, since it did have important influence on the nature of the change-over to full independence.

The problem with which the Commissioners found themselves faced was that of the legislative body having power without responsibility, and hence the constant danger of disputes with the executive authority leading to a deadlock which could only be resolved, in the last resort, by strong action on the part of the Governor and the Executive Council. Such action was bound to be unpopular in the country and, in all probability, distasteful to the Colonial Office, and this circumstance had deterred the executive from such action; which in practice meant that the Executive Council exercised very little of its undoubted power, though it remained quite active in non-disputatious matters. It was here that came in the old right won long ago, when the unofficials were European and a minority – the right of appropriating expenditure. This was a right that could not be taken away now that there was a Ceylonese unofficial majority. The Commissioners did not think that executive authority could be completely handed over to the Ceylonese, first, because of their lack of parliamentary experience – the kind of argument which has completely sunk out of sight in the post-war history of the Commonwealth; and secondly, because in their opinion the Ceylonese lacked unity and co-operate spirit, and the 'diverse elements' of which the population was composed suspected and distrusted each other. Fully responsible government, they believed, would inevitably result in the major community imposing its will on the minorities; to quote the Report, 'It is almost true to say that the conception of patriotism in Ceylon is as much racial as national, and that the best interests of the country are at times regarded as synonymous with the welfare of a particular section of its people.'[1]

Having noted that the members of the Legislative Council were primarily interested in administration – hence the activities of the Finance Committee – and having expressed doubts that a party system (the necessity of which they took for granted) could be created in Ceylon so as to make a responsible legislature work properly – hindsight shows a fallacy here, as has since been made manifest in India – the answer seemed to be to give the legislative body some measure of responsibility for the administration, short of full ministerial responsibility. By being enabled to familiarise themselves with the details of administration, the members would be

[1] Report, *op. cit.*, p. 31.

better fitted, ultimately, for fully responsible government. This is not
expressly stated in the Report, but it was certainly in the minds of at
least some of the Commissioners.

The scheme put forward and adopted almost in its entirety was
based partly on the organisation of the League of Nations and partly
on that of the London County Council. The Government Departments were to be divided into ten groups, each of which would be in
charge of a Minister. Of these Ministers, three would be officials:
the Colonial Secretary, henceforward to be known as the Chief
Secretary, in charge of external affairs, defence, and the public
services; the Legal Secretary, in charge of the administration of
justice, and of elections; and the Treasurer, who came to be known
as the Financial Secretary, in charge of finance generally. These
three were to be known as the Officers of State. Each of the remaining seven groups would be under the supervision of an executive
committee, for which purpose the members of the legislature, to be
known as the State Council, were to be divided into seven committees. Each executive committee elected its own chairman.
The three Officers of State and the seven Chairmen of Executive
Committees collectively formed the Board of Ministers who met
frequently for certain purposes. The committees were: Home
Affairs; Agriculture and Lands; Local Administration; Health;
Labour, Industry and Commerce; Education; and Communications
and Works. There were provisions made for the State Council to
meet in executive session, but in fact this very rarely happened.
This, then, was the set-up from the executive angle.

In its legislative aspect the State Council consisted of 50 territorially elected members, 8 nominated, 4 of whom were Europeans,
and the 3 Officers of State (who sat but did not vote) and was
presided over by an elected Speaker. The Chief Secretary was the
Chairman of the Board of Ministers, but the Vice-Chairman, a
Ceylon Minister – D. B. Jayatilaka, Minister for Home Affairs –
was Leader of the House. The procedure was very much on the
Westminster model – three readings of bills, standing committees
(two), question time, formal royal assent, and so on. On the whole
the members got a good training in parliamentary procedure, which
was to come in very useful when the next constitution came into
being sixteen years later – it was in 1931 that the 'Donoughmore
Constitution', as it came to be known, was inaugurated. But there
were no parties. Voting was entirely an individual matter (save for
any 'log-rolling'). The result was that opposition tended either to be
factious or to crystallise against the three Officers of State, as
representing the ultimate governing power of the country.

This was, of course, still in the hands of the Crown as represented by the Governor. His position was by no means an easy one. Theoretically he possessed considerable powers.[1] But these can best be described as reserve powers. If the constitution worked as it was hoped, he would not have to use these powers at all, or at any rate on the rarest occasions. His powers of certification, of declaring any matter to be of paramount importance, and his duty to reserve certain classes of bills for the consideration of the Secretary of State for the Colonies, as well as his ultimate control of the public services, were irritating to those Ceylonese who were desirous of more rapid political advance. But on the whole the hopes were realised.

The protection of the public services was the first of the Governor's reserve powers. It has been suggested that some State Councillors regretted being unable to 'carpet' Heads of Departments, as in the former Finance Committee, a procedure so heavily – perhaps too heavily – reprobated by the Donoughmore Commission. Be that as it may, the position of the higher grade public servants after 1931 was radically altered, in that, if they felt themselves aggrieved, or if they disapproved of the new set-up, or for any other reason, public or private, they were entitled to retire on proportionate pension, with 'compensation for loss of career': the retirement terms were reasonably adequate, but not many Europeans and only a very few Ceylonese public officers took advantage of this right to retire. It would, in the author's opinion, be correct to say that very few European officers retired out of a sense of grievance, and not many more from the fear of future disabilities being imposed upon them.

Another safeguard, proposed in the Donoughmore Report and adopted, was the setting up of a Public Service Commission. This was done, but it was made to consist of the three Officers of State. And this led to difficulties. An unfortunate and unnecessary mistake, not the suggestion of the Commission, was made in giving to the new Executive Committees the power to discuss the higher appointments in the departments which were their concern, and to make recommendations for the filling of vacant posts. But the final decision lay in the hands of the Public Service Commission, who were quite at liberty to disregard any recommendations as to appointments made by the Committees – and did so. This was an additional source of friction between the Officers of State and the members of the State Council. The members sitting in executive committee were extremely interested in appointments. When the appointment to a vacant post was on a Committee's agenda, every member was at the

[1] See *Ceylon*, by Jennings and Tambiah, Stevens and Son, 1952, pp. 86–8, for a list of these as laid down in the (1931) Royal Instructions.

I

meeting on time – which certainly, in the author of this book's personal experience, never happened on other occasions (he only had experience of one Committee, but it would seem that the others did not differ much in this respect). The overruling of a Committee's recommendation by the Public Service Commission undoubtedly led to bad feeling.

The abolition of communal representation did not please the smaller minorities, as it seemed to them that with territorial representation dominance by the Sinhalese was inevitable. But the Commissioners were firmly convinced that it should be terminated. They wrote: 'Communal representation was devised with a view to assisting the development of democratic institutions in countries of different races and religions and in the hope of eliminating the clash of these various interests during elections. It was expected to provide peacefully an effective legislative assembly which would give a fair representation of the different elements in the population. . . . Unfortunately the experiment has not given the desired results. The representatives of the various communities do not trust one another. . . . The minority communities are fearful that any preponderance of governmental powers held by another community will inevitably be used against them.'[1] They thought that the members of various communities mixing together in Executive Committees would enable them to see and understand what a great number of interests they had in common, as compared with those on which there were communal differences.

The constituencies were duly delimited and the registers compiled. This took a long time, and accounts partly for the time lag between the publication of the Donoughmore Report and the start of the new constitution. In the meantime the Report came in for heavy criticism by the Ceylonese. The Sinhalese in particular had an uncomfortable feeling that the country was being made the subject of a doubtful experiment. They wanted a development from the 1924 constitution in the direction of responsible government marching towards the 'Westminster model', and naturally the knowledge that this would make them the all-powerful majority had its attraction. But the matter that considerably disturbed them was the extension of the franchise to the Indian estate population – a perennial trouble from this time onwards. The decision taken finally was to base the franchise on 'domicile', a somewhat vague term. This let in all Ceylonese over the age of twenty-one; there was in addition a literacy and property qualification which let in the Europeans and the Indian merchants; and for the other Indians,

[1] Report, *op. cit.*, pp. 90–91.

estate labourers in particular, there was the alternative of a 'Certificate of Permanent Settlement', of which very few took advantage, or of domicile, depending on five years' residence, of which many did, sometimes in a not altogether regular way.

The Legislative Council turned down various recommendations of the Report one after another; but when it was intimated that it was a matter of all or nothing, they realised that it would actually mean a big step forward politically, and eventually they accepted it, though only by a majority of two votes.

The elections took place in 1931, the first with universal suffrage in the colonial Empire. There was a certain amount of intimidation, and some bribery. The Tamils for more than one reason decided to boycott the election, so that four seats which they would normally have occupied (and subsequently did) remained unfilled. There were 28 low-country and 10 Kandyan Sinhalese elected, 2 Europeans, one an ex-civil servant (see p. 87 above) the other, an up-country planter: 3 Ceylon Tamils, 2 Indian Tamils and 1 Muslim; 4 Europeans, 2 Burghers, 1 Indian Tamil and 1 Muslim were nominated. The members sorted themselves out into Executive Committees, and a Ceylon Tamil and an Indian were among the seven chairmen elected: so that the Board of Ministers included members of these communities.

The outstanding fact that next became manifest, arising from these events, was that Ceylonese leaders of all communities had now in their minds the intention to strive after full internal self government, as early as possible. They had not got as far as the idea of full independence, and they were prepared for the process to go on by degrees, provided it was not too long in coming. What they did dislike was having a constitution thrust upon them not in line with what they had demanded. They did not like the limitations which would be put on Ministers by the Executive Committee system. They decided to make the best of it, but to do what they could to get it altered at the earliest opportunity.

The attitude of the British Government was that the new scheme must be given a fair trial. As it was laid down in the 1931 Royal Instructions to the Governor, the aim was 'the devolution upon the inhabitants of Ceylon of responsibility for the management of the internal affairs of the island'. The Colonial Office still felt uncomfortably responsible for the welfare and interests of the minorities, and could not see a parliamentary system working adequately without the existence of organised political parties – though they could have observed this working very near their own shores, in the Isle of Man and in Jersey! They still had a general feeling of responsibility for the good of colonial peoples – though, as Sir Charles Jeffries asks pertinently in his book *Ceylon: the Path to Independence*, responsible to whom? The answer would seem to be that they were impelled by a sense of duty, sometimes amounting to a sense of mission – a faint echo, perhaps, of 'the white man's burden' of Kipling. The old parallel of mother and children may today be considered as played out, and ridiculed, but the feeling had a resemblance to the duty which most parents feel towards their children, natural affection apart, or that felt by a housemaster at a boarding school to the boys in his house. It was felt in varying degrees by resident Europeans, most of all, perhaps, by educationalists and the more dedicated of the civil service; least by the business community, though with some of them it was not altogether absent: there was always a feeling that certain actions by any of its members 'letting the side down' were strongly to be reprobated.

Chapter 10

The State Council and the World War

THE visitor to Ceylon who comes by sea, on landing at Colombo, finds himself in what is known as 'The Fort', so named as being the site of the former Portuguese, Dutch and early British fortresses; of these few traces remain. But for well over a century the Fort has been the main administrative and business quarter of the country. Near the landing jetty stands a colonnaded building which was for many years the Secretariat and the Legislative Council Chamber. On driving out of the Fort, as he reaches the sea front, he sees on his left a Palladian building which is the House of Representatives, but which many still call 'the State Council building'. Immediately behind it is a very large six or seven storey building known as the Secretariat, which houses most of the ministries and government departments. Both these buildings were erected on a waste piece of land soon after the Donoughmore Report was presented and were completed in time for the State Council to be inaugurated with due ceremony in 1931, and for the ministries to be housed in the building at the rear. The Senate and the Prime Minister's office are still in the old building, which makes the distance between the two Chambers of the Ceylon Parliament further than in any other Commonwealth country. The government departments have long since outgrown even the new Secretariat building, and will probably need another just as large to take them all in, which is symptomatic of the growth of administrative bureaucracy since 1931. The buildings then put up were a sign to the people of Ceylon that a new era had begun.

During the first five years after 1931 the experiment of the Donoughmore Constitution was being worked out. The leaders of the Ceylonese, though they did their best to work it, and in no way attempted to sabotage it, tried from the very beginning to get it altered. As mentioned in the last chapter, it was only a firm stand on the part of the Colonial Office that got the concurrence of the Legislative Council – Sidney Webb, the famous Fabian Socialist, who had become Lord Passfield, Secretary of State for the Colonies, was adamant against any change in the Order in Council which established it. The very next year E. W. Perera, who had been prominent for years in the movement for political advance, moved a resolution in the State Council condemning the constitution on seven counts, six of which were accepted by the Council and formed the basis of a memorandum submitted by the Board of Ministers to the Colonial Secretary: but it was of no avail. The Secretary of State wanted to see how the experiment worked.

The State Council's first act was to elect its Speaker and Mr. A. F. Molamure was chosen. He became a good Speaker, but through some unfortunate events was compelled to resign after a few years, and was succeeded by a Tamil, Sir Vaitialingam Duraiswamy. The procedure was similar to that of the former Legislative Council, and basically to that of the British House of Commons, except as far as finance was concerned – the financial procedure of the House of Commons is unique. The practice in the annual financial debate on the Estimates which grew up was for every item to be gone through in Committee. This was carried on to the Parliament of Ceylon, and is a rather unfortunate heritage, as much time is wasted over minor matters.

The unsatisfactory features of the constitution soon became apparent. The first was that the reference of so many administrative matters to the Executive Committees made for unconscionable delays. The Committees varied in unity and efficiency. The Agriculture and Lands Committee, for example, was extremely well and harmoniously managed by its Chairman, D. S. Senanayake; in it there was little dissension or tension with the permanent heads of departments. But the Minister was very much of a dedicated person, who realised the essentiality of the work that lay before him and his Committee and, being both forceful and knowing how to handle people, was able to get on with his Committee – and with his work. The same could not be said, however, of all the Committees, several of which wasted much time in endless discussions often of trivial matters, which their Chairmen, the Ministers, were unable or unwilling to check. On the whole the Committees had much better relations with the permanent officials than the former Finance Committee. The Chief Secretary or, when financial matters were under discussion, the Financial Secretary, had the right to attend Executive Committee meetings. They did not often exercise that right, and when they did were usually able to make it clear they were present in an advisory capacity, and not to wave the big stick.

The second disadvantage was that the Board of Ministers never quite knew where they were or how they stood. The tendency was towards collective responsibility, but it could not become a real thing, because any Minister might be obliged to put forward something – a policy or some administrative action – with which he was in total disagreement himself, but which had been forced upon him by his Executive Committee; and neither he nor his colleagues on the Board had the power to turn it down.

But the Board of Ministers – that is, the seven elected ones – though far from homogenous in character, had one policy on which they were all agreed, to strive for complete self-government in internal affairs. They were genuinely anxious to improve the living conditions of the people, and to make a beginning in the direction of the welfare state. They also wanted the administration run to an increasing extent by Ceylonese. The University College was now turning out honours graduates who were only too anxious to enter the higher ranks of government service, the civil service in particular; and the Colonial Office gradually gave way in the matter of the proportion of European officers to be recruited.[1] In March 1933 it was agreed that no non-Ceylonese should be appointed to any post in the government service unless there was no Ceylonese capable of filling it, and then only by what came to be known as a 'March Resolution' of the State Council. There were many technical posts for which there were no Ceylonese qualified; but this did not apply to the civil service: the last Europeans to be appointed to this were recruited in 1937.

In 1936 the term of the first State Council came to an end. There were still no formed political parties contesting the elections. But there was a small beginning, with A. E. Goonesinghe's Labour Party.[2] There were, however, several middle class young men from the University College who had gone on to study at English universities, and one of them to America; there they were attracted by the doctrines of Marxism. Two of them, Dr. N. M. Perera and Philip Gunawardana, had worked up the constituencies for which they were candidates, and been elected. They provided an altogether new element among the legislators of Ceylon. On their return from abroad they founded a party which they called the Lanka Sama Samaj Party and, though its organisation was not ready in time for the 1936 elections, it was able to present a programme and to put forward candidates for the next election – for that election did not take place for another eleven years.

[1] See above, Chapter 7, p. 89.
[2] See above, Chapter 9, p. 125.

The 1936 election was very similar to that of 1931. Much the same types of upper and middle class Ceylonese stood and were elected, with the exception of those just mentioned, and one or two others who held rather more extreme views than the majority. However, when it came to the selection of Executive Committees, and the election of their Chairmen, a formula was devised by which all seven Chairmen were Sinhalese. This was worked out by the Professor of Mathematics at the University College, strangely enough himself a Tamil, who subsequently became a Minister and ultimately an extreme communalist. The object of this manoeuvre has been variously explained, but though it does not appear to have been done for strictly communal reasons, it has generally taken to have been such, especially by the Tamil community. One explanation is that it was intended to show the British Government that the Executive Committee system did not necessarily mean that it afforded protection to the minorities by having one or two of them as Ministers, thus knocking the bottom out of one of the arguments for maintaining the Donoughmore constitution.

The new Board of Ministers kept up their opposition to anything but fully responsible government in internal affairs. Their attitude seems to have impressed the Colonial Office, so that when Sir Andrew Caldecott was appointed Governor in 1938 he was instructed to look carefully into the matter. Accordingly, he sent off a despatch to the Secretary of State which condemned the Donoughmore constitution, the Executive Committee system in particular, and reported in favour of something approaching cabinet government on the Westminster model.

The outbreak of the Second World War in 1939 not unnaturally held up further constitutional advance. Though Ceylon was again automatically brought into the war, the leaders of the country, unlike those of India, gave unstinting and ungrudging support to the cause of Britain and her allies. During the 'phoney' war period at the beginning, Ceylon was little affected, though a partial black-out was imposed, and certain other measures taken. Naval activity at Colombo and Trincomalee was considerable. But from the Ministers' point of view there seemed no very strong reasons why constitutional advance could not take place.

The situation was completely changed by the entry of Japan into the war, and her astonishing successes in 1942. With the fall of Burma, Malaya, Singapore and the Dutch East Indies, Ceylon was now in the front line. Active military measures had to be taken. A weak division of the Indian Army was first sent to Ceylon. Then the Australian Government was persuaded to allow an Australian

division on its way home for the defence of Australia to form part of
the garrison until it could be relieved by an Indian Army and an
East African division. Royal Air Force units were sent to the island
in some strength. The Ceylon Defence Force was mobilised and
about doubled in strength. Headquarters, known as the Ceylon
Army Command, were set up in the Colombo Museum, somewhat
to the detriment of the exhibits. Airfields and air strips were hastily
constructed in various parts of the island.

Owing to the pressing danger, the British Government had sent
out Vice-Admiral Sir Geoffrey Layton to be Commander-in-Chief
of the forces in Ceylon, and had given him authority to exercise very
wide powers, superseding the civil authorities, the Governor
included, if it became necessary. As events turned out, he worked
very well with the civil authorities, setting up a War Council which
consisted of the Governor, the Service Chiefs, the Civil Defence
Commissioner, and the members of the Board of Ministers. The post
of Civil Defence Commissioner, to which was later added that of
Food Commissioner, had been given to an able Ceylonese, O. E. D.
Goonetilleke.

But for some time the military position in Ceylon was very weak,
and if the Japanese had seen fit to launch an invasion, or even an
armed raid in strength, either could without much doubt have proved
successful. They did not do so, but they made two air raids, one on
Colombo harbour on Easter Sunday, 1942, and the other on
Trincomalee, a few days later. The attacking aircraft came from
aircraft carriers, and thirty-five of them were brought down by a
squadron of R.A.F. *Hurricanes*. Not much damage was done at
either port, though several British warships which for some reason
put to sea were sunk by bombing from the air. The Japanese did not
attempt anything more, partly perhaps because they had not
succeeded in locating the British Far Eastern fleet, and partly
because it was not in line with their strategy, which stopped them at
the limits of the 'Co-Prosperity Sphere'. It is difficult to understand
why they did not bother to take over Cocos Island, which would
have been a perfectly simple matter.

The loss of Malaya and the Dutch East Indies left Ceylon as the
only considerable producer of natural rubber, a commodity so
essential to the war effort, available to the Allies. Recourse was
therefore had to what was called 'slaughter-tapping', i.e. drawing
from the rubber tree more latex than was healthy for the tree's life,
which would inevitably mean the shortening of the period during
which it could produce rubber in economic quantities. The rubber
companies and the planters willingly co-operated, and in the end

the compensation paid seems to have recouped their losses. Another essential measure was the rationing of rice, much of which had previously been imported from Burma, now in the occupation of the Japanese. This was well planned, and worked well; the credit for this must go to Goonetilleke, for his organisation as Food Commissioner. He never hesitated to cut red tape without scruple when he thought it necessary – for which, later on, he had to face some embittered criticism.

The danger of a Japanese invasion disappeared as the tide of war began to turn against them, with the American naval victories in the Pacific Ocean and the possibility of a land offensive by the Allies, the British in particular.

There were two possible fronts for attack, Burma and Malaya. The Allied troops in Burma were already engaged, and were taking the offensive. It would appear that the main effort in 1945 was to be a grand offensive against Malaya. The headquarters of the South-East Asia Command under Earl Mountbatten as Supreme Commander were sited at Peradeniya, near Kandy – actually in the Royal Botanical Gardens there. The plans for the offensive were worked out and all but ready when the atom bombs fell on Japan, and she surrendered.

The stationing of somewhere about 100,000 soldiers and airmen in Ceylon, in addition to the coming and going of many thousands of naval personnel, had some interesting effects. For defence purposes, small units were tactically disposed all over the island, particularly anti-aircraft gunners and Royal Air Force observers and other detachments. The ordinary people of Ceylon in the places where these were stationed became acquainted with the ordinary type of stay-at-home Briton, clad in uniform. The East African division stayed only a short time in the island, and made no particular impact on the people of Ceylon; they were most of the time stationed at Trincomalee: though there were one or two incidents which gave trouble and caused some indignation in the State Council. In India, in garrison towns and on the frontier, the British regular soldier had been well known. But in Ceylon, the British garrison had for a long time been very small, and confined to Colombo, Trincomalee, and the up-country rest camp of Diyatalawa. Now the amateur soldiers and airmen of Britain were seen by the Ceylonese doing tasks very different to anything they had ever seen Europeans doing before. In actual fact they got on together very well, and the standard of conduct of the British troops was high – there are many ex-soldiers in Britain today with very pleasant memories of the island. But the contacts made meant that after the war the people of Ceylon had a different outlook on the European. There was little anti-British feeling: here and there, perhaps, a feeling of sympathy with Japan, as a partly Buddhist nation, and, as an Asian nation, having made things very hot for the British, at any rate for a time. It may be noted that a number of Ceylonese were able to make unexpected money, contractors, fruit sellers, and unskilled labourers, for instance.

During the earlier part of the war there was some attempt to put the country on a war footing. It became necessary to establish government departments for the control of food and of prices. Several of the young Marxists who spoke against the war as a 'capitalist struggle' found themselves put under detention: they included two State Councillors, Dr. N. M. Perera and Philip Gunawardana, and a few others, such as Dr. Colvin de Silva, who soon after the war became prominent figures in Parliament and in public life; incidentally they succeeded in escaping from detention towards the end of the war. Their doctrines had no particular appeal to the generality of Ceylonese; but the younger generation of the Western-educated, such as were to be found in the University College and the top forms of secondary schools, were greatly taken by them. When the U.S.S.R. came into the war, there was a split in the Marxist ranks: the small number of 'Stalinite' Communists (the Communist Party proper was formed in 1944) supporting the war, the remainder, who dubbed themselves Trotskyists, persisting in their attitude of opposition. The Communists actually tried to join the National Congress, which had maintained a somewhat uneasy existence ever since the coming in of the State Council. But this attempt led to the resignation from that body of D. S. Senanayake, and its resultant collapse. During the twenties it had undoubtedly done much to bring to the people of Ceylon – the educated particularly – the idea of political advance in the direction of self-government. But it never managed to attain in the island a position comparable to that which the Indian National Congress reached and maintained on the mainland.

During the years after the 1936 election political parties began to emerge; as well as the Marxists, three communal parties grew up. It was during this period that the personalities who were to be prominent in the change-over to full independence also emerged.

Stirrings of political consciousness, though faint, began to be found among the estate labourers. The new adult franchise affected them, and about 170,000 became qualified to vote. Politicians soon got busy, and Indians were returned for two of the up-country constituencies. In 1939, soon after the outbreak of war, Mr. Nehru paid a visit to Ceylon, somewhat to the discomfort of the Govern-

ment and, possibly as a result of his visit, a political body known as
the Ceylon Indian Congress was formed. The Ceylon Tamils also
formed a party, the Tamil Congress, of which the leader was an
able lawyer, G. G. Ponnambalam. In 1937 S. W. R. D. Bandaranaike started the *Sinhala Maha Sabha*. The policy of all these three
parties was definitely communal.

Bandaranaike was a clever young man, the only son of Sir
Solomon Dias Bandaranaike, the Maha Mudaliyar, head of the
leading upper-class family in the low-country. The Maha Mudaliyar
was, technically, the 'chief native interpreter', a ceremonial position
of great dignity. In this capacity he was closely connected for formal
and ceremonial purposes with the Governors, and named his son
'West Ridgeway' after one of them. He was in fact a landowner on a
large scale. His autobiography, *Remembered Yesterdays*, throws
much light on the life and ways of thinking of his class. He was a man
highly respected by everyone of all races. He sent his son to Christ
Church College, Oxford, where he read Western classics and
became Junior Treasurer of the Oxford Union, having a natural
gift for speaking. On his return to Ceylon he entered first municipal
and then national politics. The way he was brought up meant that
he had little acquaintance with the Sinhalese language; but he
made himself fluent in that tongue, though he admitted later that
he could neither read nor write the script with any ease. His point
of view differed completely from that of his father, and he became
an enthusiastic nationalist, with emphasis on Sinhalese primacy.
Though brought up as an Anglican Christian, he turned Buddhist,
whether from conviction or for political reasons is a matter of
argument; but he certainly became a convinced Buddhist later on.
Owing to his ability and his high birth he was chosen as a Minister
as soon as he was elected to the State Council, in which he soon
became a prominent figure.

A certain amount of unrest, stimulated by the Ceylon Indian
Congress, had manifested itself among some of the Indian plantation
workers and in 1942 a strike on an estate named Mooloya took place
– a new phenomenon, much to the horror of the planting community.
It resulted in violence, during which a striker was shot and killed by
the police. Inquiries into this 'Mooloya incident' led to a serious
dispute between the Board of Ministers and the Inspector-General
of Police. The Governor supported the latter, a technically correct
action, and the Ceylonese Ministers resigned in a body. However, a
commonsense compromise on both sides was reached, and the affair
blew over. It led, however, to considerable public criticism, and
to the retirement from politics of Sir Baron Jayatilaka: he was

appointed Commissioner to India at New Delhi. He was replaced as Minister for Home Affairs by Mr. (later Sir) Arunachalam Mahadeva, son of Sir Ponnambalam Arunachalam – a Tamil. Jayatilaka's retirement opened the way for the leadership of D. S. Senanayake.

Jayatilaka had come from a humble origin. He made himself eminent as a first class scholar in Sinhalese and was keenly interested in the archaeology and history of his country. He took up the temperance movement and was put in detention for a short time in 1915 – a ridiculous action, but one for which he bore no ill will. He was prominent as a politician in the Legislative Council and was the obvious choice, when elected Minister of Home Affairs, for Vice-Chairman of the Board of Ministers and Leader of the State Council when this body came into existence. He was looked up to as his country's leader in the movement for self-government, and his upright character and pleasant personality made for the general respect in which he was held by all communities, however much his political views were held in suspicion by the minorities.

Don Stephen Senanayake, on the other hand, was a man of wealth, and a considerable landowner, though his wealth came principally from plumbago mining. He was at first uninterested in political affairs, and after leaving school – he attended the top-class Anglican secondary school, St. Thomas's College, as indeed did Bandaranaike, where he distinguished himself at cricket, but not otherwise – took a minor post in government service. But he soon left that and took up agriculture, seriously and scientifically. His elder brother got him interested in the temperance movement and, like Jayatilaka, he was put into detention in 1915 – with no justification whatsoever. For this he never quite forgave the British Government. This stimulated his interest in politics, and on the early death of his able elder brother he took it up keenly: his forceful personality soon brought him to the fore. So when the State Council came into being in 1931, he was the obvious person to become Chairman of the Executive Committee of Agriculture and Lands. As Minister of Agriculture he took long views – and had pretty complete control of his Committee. He was determined that the agriculture of Ceylon must be taken in hand, that the people of the countryside must be induced to grow more food by better than the old traditional methods of cultivation, and that the raising of the standard of living of the rural workers was a task of the very highest importance. He thoroughly understood agricultural matters, and was well aware that neither they nor the rural workers could be hurried, being a practical man with his feet firmly on the ground.

A close relation of his, J. L. Kotelawala, entered the State Council at its inception, and in 1936 was elected Chairman of the Communications and Works Executive Committee. He had been sent to England, where he went to Cambridge University. He had a forceful if boisterous personality, and ran his Committee with success. These three, Senanayake, Bandaranaike and Kotelawala, with one other, were to be the leading figures in the politics of Ceylon for some time to come.

The one other was Sir Oliver Goonetilleke, who was a government servant, and was not a member of the State Council till after the war, when he became Financial Secretary. He was of middle class origin, and a Christian. After some experience in banking and in journalism, during which time he read for, and secured, the external degree in Economics of London University, he entered government service, and rose rapidly, first to the position of Railway Auditor, and then to that of Colonial Auditor, which soon came to be designated Auditor-General. It was with the outbreak of war that he really came to the fore, being appointed Civil Defence Commissioner and then Food Commissioner also. He was a man with a first-class, quick brain and marked organising ability, to whom people instinctively turned in a time of emergency. He never attained the popularity of Senanayake or Bandaranaike, nor did he seek it. But he was immensely skilful in handling people individually, however difficult, and was a first-rate negotiator.

The coming of Japan into the war made no difference to the attitude of the leaders of Ceylon, who continued to support the allied cause wholeheartedly. There may have been a little pro-Japanese feeling here and there, but it was never obvious. Already the British Government, although its energies were fully occupied with the war effort, recognised the urgency of Sir Andrew Caldecott's report of 1938 on the constitution, and Ceylon's unquestioning support of the war effort predisposed them still more in favour of constitutional advance. In September 1941 a promise was given that the question would be taken up as soon as possible after the end of the war.

When the danger from the Japanese ceased to be acute, the Ministers returned to the matter of constitutional reform. They advanced their target from full internal self-government to 'dominion status' (later an unpopular term), now known as 'independence'. The State Council's term was due to expire in 1941, but owing to the emergency its life was prolonged more than once; when an election finally took place, it was to be under quite different conditions. In 1942 a constitutional mission from Britain headed by Sir Stafford

Cripps visited India: the Ceylonese leaders, who requested that he should visit Ceylon for a similar constitutional object, were annoyed when this request was refused on the ground that the matter was one for the Colonial Office. But in 1943 the British Government issued a Declaration of Policy, which restated the promise given in 1941, laying down that the reconsideration of the constitutional position would be directed towards the grant of full internal self-government, but reserving foreign affairs, defence, trade and shipping of any part of the Commonwealth, currency, the rights of British subjects non-resident in Ceylon, and Bills affecting religious or communal interests. They undertook to examine 'by Commission or Conference' any detailed proposals which the Ministers might put forward, provided they had the support of three-fourths of the members of the State Council, excluding the Officers of State and the Speaker. This declaration did not go as far as the Ministers had wanted, but it was an advance, and they were unable to get further clarification of the rather vaguely stated conditions. They therefore decided to formulate their constitutional proposals, embodying them in the form of a draft Order in Council for submission to the Colonial Office. In this they were fortunate in obtaining the assistance of Dr. (later Sir) Ivor Jennings, a well-known writer on constitutional subjects who had in 1941 been appointed Principal of the University College, which the following year became the University of Ceylon, willy-nilly, for it was no longer possible to send back to London University the papers of candidates for their external degrees, as hitherto. Jennings was most helpful in drafting the Order and, presumably, in advising upon it – though he always maintained that the principles were entirely those laid down by D. S. Senanayake.

The draft was got ready with remarkable speed. It was completed by February 1944 and sent to the Colonial Office with the request that it should be considered as soon as possible, and without waiting till the ending of the war. The Secretary of State's reply was that a Commission would be sent out about the end of the year to examine the Ministers' draft and to consult 'various interests including minority communities'. The Ministers were incensed at this, their idea being that it was necessary only to examine their draft scheme. They therefore withdrew it, and decided not to give evidence before the Commission when it came out.

The Ministers' draft may be found in Ceylon Sessional Paper XIV of 1944, which is also printed as appendix to the 'Report of the Commission on Constitutional Reform (1945)' – the 'Soulbury Report'. It suggested a constitution on the lines of the Westminster model, i.e. a Cabinet and a single chamber Parliament, with a

Governor-General who would have powers in the matters of external affairs and defence and a few others. As this draft was the basis both of the recommendations made in the Report of the Soulbury Commission and of the Order in Council which implemented them, a detailed account is not given here. The details appear in Chapter 11, where the independence constitution is discussed.

The Commission was duly appointed. It consisted of three, Lord Soulbury, who had been a Conservative Minister, as Chairman. Mr. (later Sir Frederick) Rees, Vice-Chancellor of the University of Wales, and Mr. (also later Sir Frederick) Burrows, an experienced trade union official. Lord Soulbury was the only politician. They arrived in Ceylon in December 1944, and remained two months, hearing a large number of deputations and of individuals.

Before going into the details of the Commission's proceedings and subsequent Report, the work of the State Council may be briefly reviewed from the point of view of its actual achievements and its effects on subsequent political and economic development. The Donoughmore constitution was something of an aberration from the straight line of constitutional development which the Ceylonese leaders had wanted, and which was that followed by a number of colonies which subsequently obtained full independence; that is, an evolution from an official to an unofficial majority, a gradually widening franchise, more and more ministerial functions entrusted to prominent individuals or party leaders, up to complete or nearly complete internal self-government, and finally full independence as members of the Commonwealth. The pattern of Ceylon was nowhere followed. The Executive Committee system came in for pretty general execration. Yet it is an interesting fact that S. W. R. D. Bandaranaike, after he became Prime Minister of Ceylon, and not long before his death, suggested that the system might be reconsidered, with modifications, when the existing constitution was revised. The suggestion did not find favour, but it was one which he had in mind for a long time, and which he discussed with the author of this book more than once. What appealed to him was the experience of administration which the State Council members had obtained. The things that were wrong with the working were the delays caused in administration by the members of the Committee spending far too much time in rather niggling administrative detail, the difficulty in getting the Board of Ministers to work together as a team, and the absence of anything like a party system. But there is no doubt that Bandaranaike was right in maintaining that the constitution did enable members of the legislature to get some insight into the working of the country's administration, of which members of legislatures are often, perhaps normally, remarkably ignorant, till they become junior Ministers. And it must not be forgotten that it worked well enough to enable the government of Ceylon to be carried on successfully during the immensely difficult period when the greatest of world wars was being waged.

Apart from the political and constitutional aspect, there is no doubt that legislation passed by the State Council enabled notable advances to be made in the spheres particularly of agriculture, health and education. It was unfortunate that it came into being at a time of intense economic depression, and that, when the island was just pulling out of this, it was faced, in 1934, by an outbreak of malaria of fearful severity. Hence, to begin with, finance was a pressing problem, and the situation was met by the institution, for the first time, of an income tax. Previously the revenue of the island was very largely derived from export and import duties, excise, postal revenues, port dues, and such minor items as licences, fees and stamp duties. Income tax affected only a very small proportion of the island's population, but was a fruitful source of revenue.

D. S. Senanayake was determined from the first to do all in his power to improve the country's agriculture. While recognising the basic importance of the three export crops, tea, rubber and coconuts, to the economy of the country, he saw clearly that the essential need was to grow more food, particularly rice, instead of having to import about two-thirds of it: this was no small task, for the villagers were firmly wedded to their traditional methods of rice growing and, moreover, there was far too much fragmentation of holdings, owing to the customary methods of inheritance and the unsatisfactory state of the land laws. There were two main fields in which efforts were to be made, the increase of production per acre in existing paddy lands, and the opening up of new cultivation in the dry zone; to which had to be added the reform of land tenure. These needs had been realized by the British Government, but not a great deal had been done – or perhaps it would be fairer to say that more might have been done, for from the closing years of the nineteenth century onwards, and particularly between 1870 and 1890 much work on the restoration of tanks had been carried out.[1] The policy of the Government with regard to land had been of a very conservative kind. It had been laid down as a principle by the Crown Lands Encroachment Ordinance of 1840 and by the Waste Lands Ordinance of 1897 that all uncultivated land, except that over which an unimpeachable title could be established, was the property of the

[1] For an account of this, see B. H. Farmer, *op. cit.*, Chapters 5 and 6.

K

Crown. This bore hardly on some of the peasants who still kept up
the old practice of *chena* cultivation which, wasteful and minimally
productive as it was, did enable them to keep just outside the margin
of starvation. Some attempt had been made to cope with the
problems raised, by the creation of the Land Settlement Department.
But land was only allowed to be alienated when an adequate return
could fairly be expected. However, in the twenties a more liberal
attitude was adopted, and a Land Commission was set up. This was
partly due to the encouragement of Sir Hugh Clifford and partly to
the efforts of the Senanayake brothers and other leading Ceylonese.
In 1929 this Commission produced a valuable report, which was the
basis of the work which the new Minister of Agriculture undertook.
A far more generous policy towards the alienation of Crown land
was adopted, particularly in the direction of village expansion and
colonisation in the dry zone.[1] The work of the Departments of
Agriculture and of Irrigation was encouraged and developed.

There had been several unsuccessful and rather discouraging
attempts at starting agricultural colonies in the dry zone; but in the
thirties, with the strong backing of the Minister, they began to
succeed. The urgent need for food production in wartime also gave a
considerable stimulus. There were three ways of supplying the
personnel for colonisation: by getting the villagers who lived in the
neighbourhood to give up their small uneconomic holdings and take
up new land; by inducing villagers from overcrowded areas to
migrate to one of the new colonies – possibly even people from urban
areas; and, in a few cases, to allot land in rather larger plots to
middle class colonists.[2] All these were tried by the Minister.

Village expansion was mainly done by grants of Crown land
adjacent to existing villages. In the case of up-country villages
where population was multiplying, this raised some problems,
owing to so much of the land having been alienated in the early days
for plantation: the result was that there had to be some compulsory
purchase of land from estates, much to the annoyance of the
owners. Another development which the Minister, and indeed the
whole State Council, greatly favoured was the promotion of the
co-operative movement,[3] especially in the establishment of better
marketing facilities. The movement was started on the productive,
distributive and marketing sides. The first of these took some time to
establish itself. To the second is due a very large number of co-
operative societies, which have been helpful in reducing the chronic

---

[1] Farmer, *op. cit., passim.*
[2] Middle-class colonisation has not been a success.
[3] See below, Chapter 15, p. 219.

indebtedness of villagers to the 'boutique keeper' (small village shopkeeper) and to the *mudalali* (merchant moneylender). The setting-up of an Agricultural Marketing Department was due to the Minister, and was one of his favourite projects. The co-operative movement was very near to Senanayake's heart: its origin was due to the initiative of the British Government, which sought for expert advice from the Government of India on the matter. But it was taken up and expanded vigorously by the Minister of Agriculture and his Executive Committee. A number of new markets were constructed under government auspices.

Another direction in which there was purposeful advance was public health, on both the preventive and curative sides. For a number of years Ceylon had been well ahead of most other colonies in both these directions. She had a strict quarantine system, which had been effective in preventing all but isolated cases of cholera and plague coming in from the mainland. The quarantine camp in Mandapam in South India, run by the Planters' Association, had proved most valuable for this purpose. But there were other diseases which were endemic, particularly malaria, *parangi* (yaws) and hook-worm (anchylostomiasis). During the malaria epidemic of 1934–35 there were about 50,000 deaths; the incidence of the disease continued to be heavy until after the second world war. The armed services had shown the way to combat malaria by the spraying of stagnant waters with D.D.T. to kill the larvae of the malarial mosquito, and measures were taken to carry this out generally, with marked success. Other measures taken were the development of a schools medical service, and a free daily meal for schoolchildren. Ceylon had, and still has, a long way to go in the sphere of public health; nevertheless the work of the Department of Medical and Sanitary Services has brought the country an appreciable distance on the road to improved public health, and certainly further than almost any other Asian country. A beginning was also made during this period in the direction of improving the system of indigenous medicines – *ayurveda*, but the major part of this development lay in the future.

The State Council paid much attention to education. The economic slump had put off the plan to develop the University College into a fully-fledged university;[1] but when the position improved it was finally decided that the site of the new university would be at Peradeniya, near Kandy. A tea estate there was acquired, which made an extremely fine site. The advent of the war made for more delay, and there was some lack of co-operation

[1] See above, Chapter 8, p. 105.

between the Ministries of Education and of Works. But the services of the distinguished architect and town-planner, Sir Patrick Abercrombie, were secured, and he came out to Ceylon and prepared a site plan and layout for the new buildings. Little could be done, of course, to implement these until the war was over. In 1941 a new Principal of the University College was appointed in the person of Dr. Ivor Jennings, a well known writer on constitutional law, whose particular spheres of study were to prove of much service to the Board of Ministers (see p. 143). He had to turn the University College very hastily into a university the next year, as mentioned earlier (p. 143).

In primary and secondary education advance was also conditioned by financial considerations. The State Council was very anxious to extend educational facilities by having more and better school buildings put up, more teachers' training colleges, particularly for those who gave instruction through the medium of Sinhalese or Tamil, and free school meals, etc. Early in the war years a Special Committee on Education was appointed. One of its members at one meeting suddenly came out with the suggestion that education ought to be free, from nursery school to university: the idea caught on, and eventually was put into effect. But as the primary schools were already free, it did little good except to the poorer members of the middle classes – the tuition fees at the University College, for instance, amounted to only Rs 150 (£11 5s. 0d.) per annum. For them, too, the provision of 50 'Central' schools – government secondary schools – was an advantage: this had the merit, however, of constructing a bridge between the primary and secondary schools which could bring bright children of the poorer people ultimately up into higher education.

The State Council was also anxious to bring in some measure of social welfare after the war. But all that was done was to appoint a Social Services Commission which reported in 1947. Education and health are regarded in Ceylon as social services, and it was on these services that the State Council chiefly concentrated.

There is one more set of developments for which this period is notable. The Ceylonese leaders always resented the fact that the financial structure of the island's economy was almost entirely in the hands of non-Ceylonese. If a Ceylonese wanted to obtain a loan of any size, he either had to apply to a British-controlled bank or to an Indian moneylender: the former were not very forthcoming, the latter were likely to charge excessive rates of interest. A State Mortgage Bank had been started just before the State Council came into being. Soon after this a Banking Commission was appointed, and as a result of its recommendations the state-aided Bank of Ceylon was established in 1935. This competed with the commercial banks, and had the advantage over them of the monopoly of government business. In 1940 an Agricultural and Industrial Credit Corporation was set up, but it did not have much effect during the period under review.

The other field of the economy in which the State Council began to interest itself was industry. The Colonial Development Fund had made to Ceylon an outright grant of Rs100 million ($£7\frac{1}{2}$ million), and several industrial enterprises were planned, including a textile mill and a plywood factory. The outbreak of war gave a boost to the plans tentatively put forward by the Ministry of Labour, Industry and Commerce, owing to the inevitable shortages. But things had to be done in a great hurry. Government factories were started,[1] which included one for making acetic acid – an essential for rubber processes, a steel rolling mill – not at all successful, a drugs factory, a paper mill, and factories for glass, ceramics and leather. These served their wartime purpose, and some of them even showed a profit, for a time. They formed the basis, on the industrial side, of the so-called plan which was about the last act of the Board of Ministers (see p. 168). All of them, except the plywood factory, had in the end to be closed down. But they had shown the way for further plans of industrialisation – though to a considerable extent *exempla horrida!*

In order to make it possible for industries to be practicable and efficient, power was necessary. Ceylon has neither coal nor oil, but a considerable hydro-electric potential. The idea of a hydro-electric power plant was suggested as early as 1922, in the report of an Industrial Commission. But though work on this started in 1924, it fared very badly. A British company offered to take it over, but the Legislative Council would have none of that. In 1931 a Department of Government Electrical Undertakings was established – but it did little more than look after the supply of electric light for the city of Colombo. The project did not really materialise till after the war.

By 1945, then, the Ceylonese, as represented by their middle class leaders, were beginning to take hold of the tasks which confronted them in the political and economic fields. In the former they had got some knowledge of administration, by becoming Ministers, members of Executive Committees, and above all, trained executive officers in high places in the administration. They had had a quite long apprenticeship in the ways of parliamentary democracy, much longer than the colonies which subsequently came to independence.

[1] See also below, Chapter 15, p. 222.

In the latter field their economic ideas were rather on the vague side. They were apt to be carried as far as the blue print stage, but little further. The people as a whole had a fair proportion of literacy and some political education, in local authorities and in two general elections. There was as a basis a good system of transportation and communications, a sizeable revenue, capable of expansion, and a rapidly improving standard of health. Finally, there had come the realisation that it was the intention of the colonial power to hand their country over to them with the minimum of trouble and the maximum of friendly feeling. The omens seemed auspicious for the future of an independent Ceylon.

Chapter 11

The Soulbury Commission
and Full Independence

THE SOULBURY Commission stayed in Ceylon for two months. Its members listened to a large amount of evidence, mainly from the minority communities. A considerable effort was made behind the scenes to get the representatives of these communities to present a united front, or something like it, which would press for a representation in which the total of these communities would equal the total representation of the Sinhalese – 'fifty-fifty', it was called. The Tamil Congress leader, G. G. Ponnambalam, was the prime mover in this, but it failed hopelessly; some of the Burgher and most of the Muslim leaders definitely refused their support.

The real work of the Commission took place in private. The Commissioners had decided to take the draft Order in Council, which the Board of Ministers had withdrawn (see p. 143), into full consideration – they had in fact no other alternative. They had useful discussions in private with D. S. Senanayake and Sir Oliver Goonetilleke, and other leading personalities. When their Report was issued – it was dated July 1945, but did not come out till a few months later – it was obvious that it was based on the Ministers' 1944 draft, with some modifications, particularly the recommendation of a Second Chamber.

Neither the Ministers' draft nor the Commission's Report envisaged full independence, and when the Ceylon Constitution Order in Council was published, in May 1946, this was not conceded. But during the time when the Commission was actually sitting and hearing evidence, the State Council, by an overwhelming majority, passed a resolution in favour of 'dominion status', which implied full independence within the Commonwealth. The resolution was interpreted at the time as a bargaining counter as against the Tamil 'fifty-fifty' claim. But it is now clear that it was an act of much political significance, and that the Ceylonese leaders had set their sights as high as they could go. A similar motion had, in fact, passed the State Council unanimously in 1942, but was not taken seriously by the British authorities.

But now two important events supervened which drastically modified the situation. The first was the result of the 1945 general election in Britain, which brought the substitution of a Labour for the wartime National Government. The declared policy of the Labour Party had for many years been the freeing of colonial peoples and 'anti-imperialism'. The Labour Government of 1929 had been a minority Government, and was in power for so short a time that nothing could be done to put this policy into practice. But Attlee's Government of 1945 had a big working majority, and plenty of time before it. True, there was a tremendous lot of work to be done in clearing up after the war – a herculean task; nevertheless the Government was determined to put its ideas about colonial peoples into practice. The former Government had, on receipt of the Soulbury Commission's Report, invited D. S. Senanayake to London to discuss it with the Colonial Office. The change of government actually took place during his visit, and he was very glad to have the opportunity of consulting with members of a Government whose colonial policy seemed to be more in line with his own ideas.

The other major event was that India was promised dominion status. To the minds of the leaders of Ceylon there seemed to be no reason at all why a similar promise should not be made to them. For whereas the Indian leaders had been actively unco-operative in the war effort of the Allies, and some Indian troops on being captured by the Japanese had actually joined them – to say nothing of the anti-British activities of Subhas Chandra Bose – there had been full and willing co-operation from the Ceylonese people and their leaders. Furthermore, Ceylon had enjoyed something very near full internal self-government ever since 1931, and had made a reasonable success of it. Her leaders claimed that, as far as it fell short of success, this was due to the defects of the Donoughmore constitution. With these circumstances in view they felt that the limitations put on full self-government by the Soulbury Commission's Report[1] should be withdrawn, and Ceylon given full independence.

However, this idea did not appeal to the official mind at the Colonial Office.[2] Ceylon was a small country and a colony. It seemed to the Colonial Office not only that the grant of independence might be a dangerous precedent, but also that it would in any case be wiser to make haste slowly: to try out the constitutional

---

[1] Report of the Commission on Constitutional Reform, Cmd. 6677, HMSO 1945.
[2] For details of the negotiations see *Ceylon: the Path to Independence*, by Sir Charles Jeffries (Pall Mall Press) Chapters XIII and XIV.

experiment set out in the Soulbury Report with a view to the advance to full independence at a later stage. As the Report itself put it: 'The goal of the people of Ceylon is dominion status, and we understand that to be in accordance with the policy of His Majesty's Government. But . . . it is clearly not possible to reach that goal in a single step.' The Labour Government may have felt itself too newly in the saddle to go across the recommendations of the Report and the opinion of the permanent staff of its advisers in the Colonial Office. Hence in October, when the Report was made public, a White Paper was issued which followed pretty closely its recommendations, except that it did not favour the transferring of the control of Ceylon's affairs from the Colonial to the Dominions (now the Commonwealth Relations) Office, nor the raising of the Governor to the status of Governor-General: and, to quote from it, 'The actual length of time occupied by this evolutionary process must depend upon the experience gained under the new constitution by the people of Ceylon.'

To the Board of Ministers, and to Senanayake in particular, this came as a big disappointment, though it did not seem to arouse resentment in the country generally. But Senanayake, with his admirable sense of timing, decided to accept the White Paper, but to make a dignified protest. The motion before the State Council to accept it read: 'This House expresses disappointment that His Majesty's Government have deferred the admission of Ceylon to full Dominion status, but, in view of the assurance contained in the White Paper of October 31, 1945, that His Majesty's Government will co-operate with the people of Ceylon so that such status may be attained by their country in a comparatively short time, this House resolves that the constitution offered in the same White Paper be accepted during the interim period.' The motion received the full sanction of the State Council, only three members (two of them Indians) voting against it.[1] The way was now clear for the machinery to be devised which would put the offered constitution into effect.

The full details of the way in which this was done may be found in Sir Charles Jeffries' book, referred to in the footnote on page 152. Sir Charles was at the time Assistant Under-Secretary of State for the Colonies – he became Deputy Secretary in 1947 – and it was to his able hands that the setting up of the new constitutional machinery was entrusted. Hence nothing could be more authentic than his account; it is also both fair and entertaining.

The drafting was done by the Legal Secretary of Ceylon, Sir

---

[1] Contrast the reception by the Legislative Council of the Donoughmore Report (p. 131).

Barclay Nihill, and in January 1947 he took the draft to the Colonial Office. At this stage emerged two personalities whose actions during the succeeding months were to have very great influence on the course of the negotiations. The first was Arthur Creech Jones, who had been promoted from Parliamentary Under-Secretary to Secretary of State for the Colonies in 1946. He had for many years been keenly interested in colonial questions (at the time of writing he still is) and had written pamphlets for the Fabian Society advocating greater freedom for the British colonies. An eminently reasonable man, and no doctrinaire, he had a grasp of colonial problems, it is fair to say, unusually wide for a Minister holding that office. The other was Sir Oliver Goonetilleke, who had gradually emerged from the background of the government service until, after his achievements during the war period, he was appointed in 1945 to be Financial Secretary, one of the three Officers of State, and the first and only Ceylonese to be so appointed – a significant, and wise, departure from precedent. It would be interesting, if profitless, to wonder what would have happened if all three of the offices had been filled by Ceylonese! Sir Oliver was highly tactful and a skilful negotiator. He worked hand in hand with Senanayake, and when sent to London to represent Ceylon in the negotiations, his handling of them without any doubt had much to do with their successful outcome. Throughout the negotiations he was careful to keep in the closest touch with Senanayake, often by means of the long-distance telephone, then a comparatively novel means of intercommunication

The object of these negotiations was to bring Ceylon to full independence within the Commonwealth in as harmonious a fashion as possible, while preserving the strategic interests of the United Kingdom. Ceylon, from her geographical position, was the nodal strategic point of what was still the British Empire in Asia: this is well illustrated by the fact that the headquarters of the South-East Asia Command were sited in the island in the latter part of the Second World War. As long as naval strategy remained of first class importance, as it did up to the development of the strategy of nuclear warfare, the harbour of Trincomalee mattered very much. Also the airfield at Katunayake was of value in the general scheme of air strategy. Though under the Soulbury constitution, the drawing up of which was the ostensible object of the negotiation, external affairs and defence remained outside the purview of the Ceylon Ministers and Legislature, it was clear that this state of affairs could only last as long as the British Government retained control – and that this could not be very long. Goonetilleke seems to have convinced Creech Jones and the Colonial Office that the sooner dominion status could be conceded, the better.

In 1944 Sir Andrew Caldecott had been succeeded as Governor by Sir Henry Monck-Mason Moore. Strangely enough, he was the only Governor of Ceylon whose early training had been in the Ceylon Civil Service, from which he was promoted in 1919 to be Colonial Secretary of Bermuda, afterwards holding positions of increasing status in the Colonial Service, the last of which was the Governorship of Kenya. A man of great tact and understanding, he realised very early that Britain would be wise to go the whole way to the concession of full independence, and the way in which he handled the situation had much to do with the smooth manner in which the transition went through.

In May 1946 the Ceylon (Constitution) Order in Council had been sanctioned and published. Its provisions were to come into force by steps, but the green light was given for a general election to the first Parliament of Ceylon by this and two later Orders in Council.

The only parties proper in existence were the small Labour Party, entirely dependent on A. E. Goonesinghe, and the Marxist groups. The Lanka Sama Samaj Party, with its Trotskyist basis, was splitting into two sections on some kind of ideological ground. The strengths of these two sections in the country were very much a matter of surmise. They had certainly attracted most of Goonesinghe's likely followers. The other Marxist group, the recently founded Communist Party, had little appeal in any electorate except in a section of the Colombo proletariat.

The Tamil Congress, too, might be described as a party, and as such was putting up candidates for the elections in the north, as was the Ceylon Indian Congress in the up-country constituencies. There was, too, Bandaranaike's *Sinhala Maha Sabha*, but this could scarcely be described as organised. But however weak and unorganised, these parties were in existence and it seemed to the Ceylonese leaders that a party on their own lines must be created. Hence was brought into existence, mainly by D. S. Senanayake and J. L. Kotelawala, the United National Party, with which Bandaranaike agreed to let his party merge. It was to some extent based on the personnel of the defunct National Congress, but it needed and got a quite fresh organisation.

While the election campaign was going on, Goonetilleke spent much of his time in London, trying to iron out the difficulties. The British authorities finally accepted Senanayake's offer of agreements on defence and external affairs. The important agreement was that on defence, by which the British were able to keep their naval base at Trincomalee and their airfield and depot at Katunayake, together with certain facilities for stationing troops in Ceylon should need arise, and for the training of a Ceylon army, navy and air force. It was, as Senanayake was later on constantly to point out, a mutual agreement, a matter of mutual advantage, but one which could be terminated without particular difficulty at any future time. The British Government also wanted, and obtained, an agreement on the future of British officers in the service of the Ceylon Government. The defence agreement evoked the darkest suspicion in the minds of the Marxists, who insisted that behind it there was another undisclosed agreement. This Senanayake always stoutly denied, and when the time came he was seen to have been correct.

This all caused some delay. Another cause, as Sir Charles Jeffries indicates in his book, was the anxiety felt by the British Government about the position of the minorities, and above all about the setting of exactly the right kind of precedent for the future independence of other colonies, for which the coming to independence of India – and Pakistan – gave no help. As events were to develop, the machinery for bringing about the full independence of Ceylon became a most important precedent for that of other colonies. Senanayake and his followers were becoming increasingly nervous about these delays; but finally the Colonial Office had all the complicated machinery for the handing-over completed, and the Governor flew to London to finalise it. The decision to give full independence to Ceylon was announced by him in his speech at the Opening of Ceylon's first Parliament in October 1947.

The constitution as set out in the May 1946 and subsequent Orders in Council followed closely the recommendations of the Soulbury Commission. The Donoughmore experiment of Executive Committees was scrapped, and the Westminster model adopted. No one seemed particularly sorry to see the Executive Committees go.[1] Yet it is only fair to say that the system did not really have a fair chance to prove itself, and that the experience gathered both by Ministers and by Members of the State Council in administrative affairs and in parliamentary procedure was of real value.

The 'Soulbury Constitution' was very similar to the Board of Ministers' draft of 1944, except for the insertion of a second Chamber – the Senate. As far as the Executive was concerned, the Cabinet system was adopted completely. For students of constitutional law

---

[1] By an odd coincidence a copy of the Soulbury Report came into the author's hands, annotated by the late Sir Drummond Shiels, one of the Donoughmore Commissioners. Some of his comments can only be described as blistering!

it is most interesting to see how the unwritten constitution of the United Kingdom was, with the necessary minimum of modification, adapted for the written constitution of Ceylon,[1] which is nearer to the Westminster model than that of any subsequent constitutions of the independent nations of the Commonwealth, and has lasted practically unchanged for sixteen years – though a Select Committee is, at the time of writing, considering the recasting of it so as to turn Ceylon into a republic and probably suggesting other changes.

The Soulbury constitution itself, as such, lasted for so short a time that it is unnecessary to go into the details of the limitations placed on full independence, beyond mentioning that the powers reserved to the Governor were quite small in number. They included external affairs, defence, and amendment of the constitution.

The Senate was to consist of 30 members, 15 elected by the House of Representatives by single transferable vote, the other 15 appointed by the Governor-General, which in practice meant by the Prime Minister. The Order in Council laid down that the Governor-General should 'endeavour to appoint persons who he is satisfied have rendered distinguished public service or are persons of eminence in professional, commercial, industrial or agricultural life including education, law, medicine, science, engineering and banking.' This proved to be only a pious hope. Senators were to be appointed for six years, one third retiring every two years. At the outset, of course, the whole Senate had to be appointed, but provisions were made for one third to be appointed for two, another third for four, and the remainder for the full period of six years: this was determined by lot at the first meeting of the Senate. The prospect of becoming a Senator appealed to quite a number of the Ceylonese, and there was heavy competition for 'first preferences' – somewhat embarrassing to some members of the House of Representatives, the author of this book included! Allegations of 'considerations' on an ample scale for first preferences were bandied about freely at the time. The powers of the Senate were very circumscribed, and rather less than those of the House of Lords in Britain. The Soulbury Commission in its Report expressed the hope that the Senate would obtain 'the services of men upon whom party or communal ties may be expected to rest more lightly'. This hope has not been fulfilled, since from the outset the new Government succeeded in imposing as strict a discipline on the Senators of its party as it did on the members of the House of Representatives. On very few occasions indeed has the Senate, even

[1] For the details of the constitution of independent Ceylon see Ceylon Sessional Paper III of 1948. See also Jennings, *The Constitution of Ceylon*, Oxford University Press, 3rd edition, 1953, and Jennings and Tambiah, *The Dominion of Ceylon*, Stevens, 1952.

with a majority adverse to the Government, shown much independence of judgment or action.

The House of Representatives to begin with had 101 members, one of whom was elected Speaker. Of these, 95 were elected and six were appointed to represent any important interests in the island which might otherwise be unrepresented or inadequately represented.[1] First of all it was necessary to have the constituencies delimited, so as to give 'weightage' to constituencies in rural areas, and the boundaries so drawn as to make it likely that some of the minorities, particularly the Tamils and the Muslims, would have a reasonable quota of representation. In the Ceylon Constitution Order in Council, the Delimitation Commission was empowered, when it appeared to them 'that there is in any area of a Province a substantial concentration of persons united by a community of interest, whether racial, religious or otherwise, but differing in one or more of these respects from the majority of inhabitants of that area' to 'make such division of that Province into electoral districts as may be necessary to render possible the representation of that interest', and accordingly it had power 'to create in any Province one or more electoral districts returning two or more members'. So a few of the constituencies were given two members, and Colombo Central three.

The State Council was formally dissolved in July 1947, and the first general election to the Parliament of Ceylon was held in August-September. The procedure was the same as in the previous election, eleven years earlier. The newly formed United National Party put up a considerable number of candidates, but there was also a very large number indeed of Independents, incurably optimistic and not worrying in the least about the loss of their election deposits. Symbols were used on the voting papers for the benefit of illiterate voters. In the event, the United National Party secured 42 seats, the Lanka Sama Samaj Party 10, the other Trotskyist group (Bolshevist-Leninist) 5, and the Communist Party 3. Of the two communal parties, the Ceylon Tamil Congress got 7 seats and the Ceylon Indian Congress (through the votes of the estate labourers) 6. There were 21 Independents, most of whom eventually supported the United National Party, though two joined the Marxists. The solitary Labour Party member, A. E. Goonesinghe was one of those elected for the three-member Colombo Central constituency, and gave his support to the UNP. Later on he became Minister without Portfolio and Chief Government Whip.

---

[1] Of the six members appointed (in practice by the Prime Minister) in 1947, four were Europeans and two Burghers.

Thus the UNP had no absolute majority, but could usually rely on the votes of a fair proportion of the Independents, and of the appointed members. The House elected as its Speaker A. F. (later Sir Francis) Molamure, who had been the first to hold that office in the State Council, and was thus well acquainted with parliamentary procedure. The new Parliament had for the first four weeks of its existence the benefit of the advice on procedural matters of Mr. E. A. (now Sir Edward) Fellowes, then Clerk Assistant of the British House of Commons.

The layout of the Chamber had been altered from that of the State Council, where members sat in a semi-circle, to that of the British House of Commons – a central aisle and two gangways, with Government and Opposition facing each other, as far as was practicable. It differed, however, from the Westminster model in having fixed places for each member from which he had to speak to be 'in order'. The Chamber still has substantially the same layout, though it has had to be altered so as to take about half as many members again – 155 in all. In formal matters the Westminster model was also followed – a procession of the Speaker in wig and gown, preceded by the Sergeant at Arms with shouldered mace, entering the Chamber, and formally received by the members. A Speaker's chair and a mace were presented to the House of Representatives by a delegation from the British House of Commons, headed by its Deputy Speaker, in 1948.

The Ceylon Independence Act passed through the British Parliament without any difficulty, and an Order in Council fixed the date of formal independence for 4th February 1948. It was decided that there was no necessity for another general election, and that the five years' span of the sitting Parliament should date from its first meeting in October 1947.

D. S. Senanayake was the obvious choice for Prime Minister; he also held the portfolio of Defence and External Affairs. Thirteen other Ministers were appointed, including his son Dudley as Minister of Agriculture. The key ministry of Finance was given to J. R. Jayawardene, an able young lawyer. S. W. R. D. Bandaranaike became Minister of Local Government and Health, and Leader of the House, J. L. Kotelawala Minister of Transport and Works – both these had held similar posts under the State Council régime. There was one Minister without Portfolio, who was also Chief Government Whip. Several of the other Ministers had been State Councillors; of the remainder two were Tamils and one a Muslim.

The independence ceremony was carried out on behalf of King George VI by his brother, the Duke of Gloucester. There was no

hall in Colombo big enough for the ceremony, but a former Royal
Air Force hangar was skilfully converted into a hall and was
beautifully decorated – chiefly by means of paper. This hall was,
for the purposes of the ceremony, the meeting place of Parliament
and His Royal Highness duly opened Parliament on behalf of King
George, now King of Ceylon. The hauling down of the Union Jack
and the elevation of the Sinhalese 'Lion flag' – the official flag of
Ceylon had not yet been decided upon – was greeted with a
terrific roll of drums, which was most impressive.

By and large, the new members of Parliament, especially of the
Government party, were of much the same type, and in a number of
cases some of the same people, as the former State Councillors,
though there was quite an accession of younger men and women
members. They came from the upper and middle class Western-
educated Ceylonese. Parliamentary proceedings were carried out in
the English language; and though members were allowed to speak
in Sinhalese or Tamil if they wished, few of them during this first
Parliament availed themselves of the privilege. This was partly due
to the fact that, if they spoke in either of these languages, their
speeches were reported in the proceedings of Parliament in that
language and printed in that script; and these proceedings were
read mainly by the English-educated, many of whom were unable
to read the script.

Parliamentary proceedings were in general orderly, on both sides
of the House. Dr. N. M. Perera, the Leader of the Lanka Sama
Samaj Party, the largest of the Opposition groups, became Leader
of the Opposition. He had made a close study of parliamentary
procedure for his doctorate, and had become an excellent parliamentarian: his influence did much to keep the Opposition in order.
But there was also a genuine desire that things should be done
'decently and in order' and on the whole this was generally observed.
Some years later a party of Ceylon M.P.s visited the British House of
Commons, and one of them remarked to the author on coming out
that in his opinion the Ceylon House of Representatives was rather
better behaved! This has, regrettably, ceased to be the case.

Parliamentary procedure closely followed that of Westminster,
except for the method of voting; proceedings began with questions
to Ministers, bills had the same readings and could go to Committee of the Whole House, or to one of two Standing Committees;
a Committee of Privileges was appointed – the matter of parliamentary privilege is always complicated and delicate in the Parliaments of newly independent countries. It all worked quite well,
despite the fact that it was never possible to have anything like a

two-party system, with an alternative Government ready to step into the shoes of a Government which had been defeated on a major vote in Parliament, or in a general election. The facilities in the House of Representatives are rather scanty: but it has been possible to find an office for the Government Whip and another for the Leader of the Opposition. It seems probable that, if the number of members increases any more, which is likely to happen unless the present average population per constituency of 75,000 is increased, there will have to be a new Parliament building.

Party organisation was very much in the embryonic stage. The Marxist groups changed round somewhat, but remained three – the only sign of solidarity among them, till very recently, except of course their opposition to most government measures, was the fact that they all appeared at the opening of the first Parliament in October 1947 wearing red ties! The United National Party gradually got itself organised, both within and outside Parliament. A Whip system began to evolve – a certain leading Minister at the beginning of the first Parliament asked the author how this could be run, and received a memorandum on the subject. The Chief Whip had to be a Minister in order to receive a salary! The supporters of the Government, including some Independents and the appointed members, used to meet on the first morning of the parliamentary week to discuss the business of the week and forthcoming legislation – some of these meetings were quite disorderly, and not unamusing. Outside Parliament an organising secretary was appointed; actually he was a Senator, and gradually constituency branches of the party were formed.

The Cabinet system was an essential feature of the new constitution. The Cabinet met regularly, and a highly placed civil servant was appointed as its Secretary. It took some time to accustom the Ministers to the idea of collective responsibility, and the members to the doctrine of ministerial responsibility for all the acts of the departments in his charge. Some of those who had been members of the State Council, and hence of Executive Committees, were rather inclined to regret the loss of opportunities they had enjoyed of getting into direct touch with administrative officers.

A highly important part of the new constitution dealt with the administrative and judicial functions of government. On the administrative side, the most important change, and one laid down in the constitution, was the institution of a Permanent Secretary for each Ministry. These were, in nearly all cases, very senior civil servants, and for a few years some of these posts were held by European officers. When appointed, they became a very special

L

category of public servant, and were the channel of communication between the Minister and the officers of all the departments which came within his orbit – the Minister of Transport and Works, for instance, had the Public Works Department, the Ceylon Government Railway, the Port Commission, Electrical Undertakings, and Civil Aviation in his charge: instead of dealing with the various heads of these departments direct, as formerly, this was done – anyhow in theory – through his Permanent Secretary. It was a basically sound practice.

One of the advantages of the disappearance of the Executive Committees was that members of the legislature no longer had any voice in the appointment to posts in the administration – this had always been an unfortunate weakness. With the disappearance of the three Officers of State, the Public Service Commission was reconstituted, and came to consist of three persons, in the words of the Order in Council 'one at least of whom shall be a person who has not, at any time during the period of five years immediately preceding, held any public or judicial office'. Its members held office for five years, were salaried, and the salaries charged on the new Consolidated Fund. The Commission was given authority over the appointment, transfer, dismissal and disciplinary control of all public officers, except that Permanent Secretaries were appointed by the Governor-General, i.e. by the Prime Minister.

By the constitution, a Judicial Service Commission was also set up, which controlled all judicial appointments except those of the Chief Justice and Puisne Judges of the Supreme Court and the Commissioner of Assize, who were appointed by the Governor-General. The office of Attorney-General was of first-rate importance, and was held for a time by Sir Alan Rose, who subsequently became Chief Justice – the last European to hold these offices in Ceylon. The Judicial Service Commission consisted of the Chief Justice, a Judge of the Supreme Court, and one other person who was a Judge or an ex-Judge of that Court. Heavy penalties were imposed on anyone attempting to influence the decisions of either the Judicial or the Public Service Commission. Both these Commissions seem to have worked well, and their inclusion in the constitution set a valuable precedent for all subsequent constitutions drawn up in the Colonial Office for colonies attaining their full independence.

Under the constitution, the Governor became the Governor-General. Sir Henry Moore was, at Senanayake's special request, appointed Ceylon's first Governor-General, a fitting tribute to the tact and wisdom he had shown in facilitating the smoothness and harmony of the transition to independence. The Governor-General

was now the King's representative with most of the delegated functions and powers of a constitutional Head of State. He received a
salary of £8,000 a year, free of income tax, and charged on the
Consolidated Fund. In the subsequent discussions on the annual
Estimates in the Committee stage of the Appropriation Bill his
salary – and hence his conduct – could not be debated. But a
considerable time was spent, one might say wasted, if often in a
quite amusing fashion, by the Opposition quibbling over his
entourage and the upkeep of his residences.

Sir Henry Moore held the office for about a year, after which he
went on retirement. He was succeeded by Lord Soulbury, who was
now able to see how his Commission's scheme, as modified to secure
full independence, would work out. He held the office from 1949 to
1954, and made himself very well liked by the Ceylonese. The
occasion of his greatest difficulty was on the sudden death of D. S.
Senanayake after a riding accident, of which more will be said in a
later chapter. Lord Soulbury was succeeded by Sir Oliver Goonetilleke, who remained until 1962, when he was succeeded by Mr.
William Gopallawa.

The first three Governor-Generals kept up the tradition of pomp
and ceremony associated with British Governors in all colonies –
full uniform with cocked hat and swords on ceremonial occasions,
such as Independence Day and the Opening of Parliament, three
residences – Colombo, Kandy and Nuwara Eliya, formal dinners
and receptions, and so forth: though Sir Oliver Goonetilleke cut
down considerably on the last of these, partly owing to the disturbed
political situation from 1958 onwards. Mr. Gopallawa, coming in
under a new régime, took up a different attitude, doubtless in
accordance with public opinion, by laying stress on simplicity in
dress and on the minimum of ceremonial. It is quite possible that he
may be the last Governor-General, as there has been for some time
a Select Committee sitting on the revision of the constitution, one of
whose terms of reference is the change-over of Ceylon from a
monarchy to a republic, as has happened in India and in several of
the former colonies, of which Ghana was the first. When Queen
Elizabeth II visited Ceylon, in 1954, she had a rousing reception,
and great emphasis was laid at the time on the fact that she was
Queen of Ceylon.

There are two ways, it may be noted, in which the constitution of
Ceylon differs from that of India – and of several of the more recent
constitutions of Commonwealth countries. The first is that the
Judicial Committee of the Privy Council was retained as the final
court of appeal. Incidentally, one of the members of the Judicial

Committee was a very distinguished Ceylonese legal light, the late L. M. D. de Silva. The other is that there was no attempt to embody in the constitution anything like a declaration of human rights. The only provision resembling this is where it is laid down that any law made by Parliament which 'shall (a) prohibit or restrict the free exercise of any religion, or (b) make persons of any community or religion liable to disabilities or restrictions to which persons of other communities or religions are not made liable, or (c) confer on persons of any community or religion any privilege or advantage which is not conferred on persons of other communities or religions, or (d) alter the constitution of any religious body except with the consent of the governing authority of that body' will be void. The decision on any dispute arising out of this clause of the constitution would presumably be settled by process of law in the Supreme Court, with appeal to the Judicial Committee of the Privy Council. Doubtless both these important aspects of the constitution have been considered by the Select Committee.

The power of altering the constitution is placed in the hands of the Parliament, with the limitation that any alteration must be passed by a two-thirds majority of the whole number of members of the House of Representatives.

Chapter 12

The Rule of the United National Party

FROM 4th February 1948, then, Ceylon was an independent country within the Commonwealth of Nations, and her leaders entirely responsible for the conduct of their country's affairs. During the short session of Parliament from October 1947 to the following February the Ministers were beginning to feel their feet, especially those without even the experience, however limited, acquired during the era of the State Council – five of the seven former Ministers were now in the Cabinet, and formed a nucleus of experience, but the remaining nine were very much 'new boys'.

The main effect of the change from the short-lived Soulbury constitution to full independence fell on the broad shoulders of the Prime Minister, for under the constitution it was his duty to take over the portfolios of Defence and External Affairs. It was freely said at the time that he still wanted to run the Ministry of Agriculture, and that he had therefore appointed his son to that office. Events, however, were to show that Dudley Senanayake was quite capable of taking his own line, and in fact he proved a capable Minister of Agriculture. His father had, of course, during his ministry, laid down the lines on which this, the most essential ministry, except that of Finance, should proceed. But the son did not hesitate to make changes and developments where he thought them desirable.

The new Minister of Finance, J. R. Jayawardene, was fortunate in that he found the country in a reasonably sound financial position. The wartime financial policy of the British Government had resulted in a big rise in the cost of living, but also in the piling up in London of substantial sterling balances, on which it looked as if Ceylon would be able to draw for her capital needs for years to come. The national debt was negligible, and the export crops were reasonably prosperous. The rubber plantations, it is true, had suffered from 'slaughter tapping' to meet the needs of the Allies for that essential commodity sheet rubber; but the compensation made was adequate and the industry gradually recovered. One of the first acts of the Government was to appoint a two-man Commission of experienced and knowledgeable planters, one European and one

Ceylonese, to go into the whole economy of the rubber industry.

The story of the eight years which followed the attainment of independence is in some ways a continuation of the way in which the country was run, especially on the economic side, during the State Council régime. The Prime Minister was not the kind of man to favour sudden and violent change; he never ceased to pursue the aim which had always been in the forefront of his purpose – the rehabilitation of the country's agriculture, the production of more food, and the raising of the rural workers' standard of life. With his increased responsibilities his political stature grew, and he had his team of Ministers well in hand. He was constantly attacked by the Opposition for having accepted what they designated as 'fake independence'; the essence of this attack was on the agreements with the British Government. But the Prime Minister always met this confidently by maintaining they were 'gentlemen's agreements' and that, should necessity arise, they could be ended without difficulty. He was not in fact really worried about the subjects covered by his portfolio, for they were not, during his period of office, especially pressing. Forces for defence, of course, had to be created, and the beginnings of a small army, navy, and later, air force, were gradually put in hand with, in each case, a British officer temporarily in command. From the point of view of external affairs, the two main things to be done were the establishment of a diplomatic service and the recognition of Ceylon as a member of the United Nations. The personnel of the foreign service was drawn to a considerable extent from the ranks of the civil servants; the most important post was that of High Commissioner to the United Kingdom; and for this post he selected Sir Oliver Goonetilleke. The next important post was that to India, to which he appointed a senior civil servant. For political reasons unconnected with Ceylon the U.S.S.R. opposed her entry to the United Nations, much to the encouragement of the Marxist parties, and it was not until the end of 1955 that the Soviet veto was withdrawn. Prior to this, however, Ceylon had been admitted to membership of some of the international agencies such as the World Health Organisation.

One of the earliest and most controversial issues which the Government had to face was that of citizenship. During the previous period it had not really arisen, as all Ceylonese were automatically British subjects, and the members of other Commonwealth countries generally found no difficulty in entering any British colony. The problem arose in its political form over the question of adult franchise. The solution of domicile was not at all satisfactory, and the Ceylonese were resentful of the fact that at the general election of

1947 Indians were returned for no less than six of the constituencies in the Kandyan districts. Just about the same time as this question faced the Government of Ceylon, similar problems were being dealt with by that of the United Kingdom. By the British Nationality Act all Commonwealth nationals were British subjects or, as an alternate designation, Commonwealth citizens. The Ceylon Government were inspired almost entirely by political reasons in the Citizenship Bill. The presence of nearly a million Indians in Ceylon was regarded as a potential danger, if a sizeable percentage of them had the franchise: the six Indian Congress members in the Parliament might at any time have been able to exercise a deciding voice. The first thing the Bill did was to restrict the franchise to citizens of Ceylon. The next was to define citizenship so as to restrict its grant to Indians as strictly as possible. This was effected by making two classes of citizenship, by descent and by registration. Any person born in Ceylon before the coming into operation of the Act (this date was September 1948) was a citizen by descent if he or she could prove that his or her father was born in Ceylon, or failing that the father's father and grandfather. If born after that date, to qualify for citizenship the father must be or be qualified to be a citizen. To become a citizen by registration he or she must be or intend to be 'ordinarily resident in the island'. But this provision was very straitly interpreted. Another Act – the Indian and Pakistani Residents (Citizenship) Act, of 1949, making 'ordinary residence' a period of seven years for married persons with wife and children resident, and ten for unmarried, was passed. There was another provision in the original Act which extended citizenship by registration to not more than twenty-five persons a year on account of having rendered distinguished service to Ceylon, or being eminent in commercial, industrial or agricultural life in the island. This, incidentally, made it possible for the European appointed members to remain members of the Ceylon Parliament.

These Acts, however, were clearly aimed at the Indian resident, primarily the estate labourer. Certain results which they had, and certain ideas which lay behind them, will be considered later on in this book. It may be noted that the provisions of the Act had the effect of excluding practically all the European residents from citizenship. At the time they raised no particular objection to this; but later on, when the question of the period of their residence arose, and they had to obtain 'temporary resident's permits', a rather difficult situation was created for some of them.[1] The immediate object of the Act, however, was entirely successful; Indian representation in

[1] See below, Chapter 15, p. 216.

Parliament came to an end on the dissolution of Parliament, and in most of the up-country constituencies in the 1952 election which had returned Indians as members the number of registered voters was reduced to a few thousands, whereas the ideal number aimed at by the Delimitation Commission was 75,000. There is no doubt that the Citizenship Acts met with the warm approval of the Sinhalese people generally. The Opposition groups in Parliament combined against it. The Tamil members objected to discrimination against members of basically the same race, the Marxists on general grounds of principle, but perhaps in practice because they saw in the estate workers a potential field for the spread of their political ideologies; they already had some influence in small trade unions which had been formed among the estate workers, though the union to which most of these belonged was controlled by the leaders of the Ceylon Indian Congress. The stand which the Marxists took against the Citizenship Act probably reacted against any effective increase of their following among the major community.

The greatest insistence was laid by the Marxist opposition on the need to bring about a transition from a colonial to a modern national economy. To their minds this could only be done by the nationalisation (without compensation) of all estates, whether owned by 'white or brown capitalists', and the immediate development of industrialisation on a large scale. These, they maintained, were impossible until a 'true' was substituted for a 'fake' independence. The policy of the Government did not comprehend nationalisation, but was in favour of a better balanced economy. They felt that Ceylon's economic position was too dependent upon the three export crops, which were so dependent on world markets and the terms of trade, and upon imported foodstuffs, especially rice. Hence the first consideration should be an increased production of foodstuffs, and the next, some measure of industrialisation. These two would help to reduce the quantity of imports, and should afford more employment; if successful, they would also provide funds for more social welfare.

This policy was not new. In 1946 the Board of Ministers had, as one of its last acts, produced 'Post-war Development Proposals' which indicated that some kind of planning was desirable. They could hardly be described as a plan, since they were little more than a hotch-potch of schemes drawn up by heads of departments in each ministry for the development of activities concerned with their particular departments, and lacking any overall co-ordination. There was always a good deal of talk about planning, but the Prime Minister, an essentially practical man, had no use for theoretical schemes. He preferred to tackle at the outset problems which seemed to him should be dealt with as early as possible; and of these food production had the first priority. Speaking to a meeting of his party in January 1948, he said that he fully recognised that for a long time to come the economy of the country would depend on the export crops, so that interference with the three industries producing them should be as small as possible.

The Minister of Finance, in his 1948 Budget statement, gave an outline of a six-year plan, based primarily on several large scale agricultural schemes, of which the principal one was the construction of a vast tank at Gal Oya in the southern part of the Eastern Province, the estimates for which had been submitted a month or so before, the expansion of colonisation in the dry zone, and the improvement of agricultural methods to increase crop yields in the already cultivated areas; these were to be buttressed by an embryonic scheme of industrialisation. Marketing facilities needed improvement, and he foreshadowed 'a higher percentage of participation by the nationals of the country in trade, commerce and industrial activities as regards management, labour and finance, by means of the Ceylon Citizenship Bill and further legislation arising from it'. Though he described rubber as 'a wasting asset', he recognised, like the Prime Minister, that the country depended and would depend for some time to come on the three export crops.

This speech gave the key to the economic policy of the Government of Ceylon from that time onwards, however developed and modified subsequently. During the next five years two events which were to influence its development considerably were the starting of the Colombo Plan in 1951, and the visit and Report of a Mission from the International Bank for Reconstruction and Development in the following year.

On the political side the Prime Minister's task presented no very great difficulties. The Opposition was nothing more than a number of small groups, communal and ideological. On the Government side the Prime Minister did not confine himself to the United National Party or to the Sinhalese for his Ministers and Parliamentary Secretaries. He appointed two Tamils, one as Minister of Commerce and Trade and the other as Minister of Posts and Telecommunications, and a Muslim (Malay) as Minister of Labour. The Minister of Commerce and Trade, C. Suntharalingam, did not last very long: he was very much of an individualist, and fell out with the Government mainly on the question of citizenship. He went into strong opposition, but as an independent, and very much of a lone wolf. He was succeeded by a Karawa Sinhalese, Henry

Amarasuriya, who had gone in for planting with a considerable degree of success, and had acquired a number of estates. About the same time the leader of the Tamil Congress Party, G. G. Ponnambalam, who had never been anything but uneasy on the Opposition benches, came over to the Government and was appointed to the vacant portfolio of Minister of Industries and Fisheries. All but two of his party members came with him; but one of them, S. J. V. Chelvanayakam, was never satisfied with the general set-up from the point of view of the Ceylon Tamil community; he eventually, as will be seen, started the Tamil Federal Party and carried most of his community with him. This action of Ponnambalam's ensured a safe majority for the Government, with the aid of those Independents who habitually gave the Government their support, and of the six appointed members. It also gave the Government a more comprehensively national complexion.

For the time being the Prime Minister was on the crest of the wave. He was immensely popular in the country, as the man who had been mainly instrumental in securing Ceylon's independence. He made an excellent impression at the Conference of Commonwealth Prime Ministers which he attended in London. The European business and planting communities felt that they were getting and would get a fair deal from him, and had great respect for what everyone called his 'horse sense'. But it was from within his own party that the trouble was to arise. Senanayake was not old – he was in his late sixties – but he had lived a strenuous life and was a sufferer from diabetes. The question therefore as to who should be designated to succeed him was bound to come up. The Leader of the House was Bandaranaike. He had come in as the leader of the communal party which he had founded, the *Sinhala Maha Sabha*;[1] but this had not, in accordance with the Prime Minister's policy, prevented him from joining the United National Party. His background has been outlined earlier (see p. 140). Some time after he returned from Oxford University and entered politics, he seems to have realised what few, if any, of his fellow politicians perceived, that ultimately there was likely to be a strong reaction against the Western-educated, and an increase of Sinhalese communal, or as the Sinhalese would prefer to have it styled, national, feeling. If he took up this kind of line, his chances of rising to the top, which was his ambition, would be greatly enhanced. He was anything but a revolutionary. His position as the son and heir of a big landowner of 'the upper crust' was an advantage to him, for it meant that he had, without asking for it, the respect of the ordinary conservative-

[1] See above, p. 155.

minded villager, especially in the Western Province, where his family property lay. Being able to take this for granted, he set himself to make an appeal to the lower middle class Sinhalese, the leading men in the villages, such as the smaller landed proprietors, the Sinhalese-educated schoolteachers, and the ayurvedic physicians. To bring this about, he took several carefully thought-out steps. He gave up wearing European dress in public, and took to what has come to be known as 'national dress', consisting of a cloth to the ankles, a collarless shirt worn outside it, a narrow stole round the neck, and sandals. This dress was in fact invented by a well known schoolmaster, P. de S. Kularatne, the principal of the chief Buddhist secondary school in Colombo. It is usually of white cotton. He refrained from making any visits to Europe. He showed no desire to become a knight like his father, though doubtless he could have done this without difficulty. Most important of all, as mentioned earlier, he gave up Anglican Christianity and became a Buddhist. He made himself fluent in Sinhalese, taking particular care to be the first member of Parliament to address the House of Representatives in that language – though in fact, like so many of the Western-educated, English had been the language he used mostly at home and among his family circle and friends. As Minister for Local Administration and Health in the State Council, portfolios which he continued to hold after independence, he had excellent opportunities of getting to know the personnel of local authorities, and of making himself popular with them – a course of action which was to serve him well later on. As a Minister he was fairly successful, though he was apt to let his duties slide for a time and then work desperately hard till he caught up with them. His personality was pleasant, but he was inclined to lose his temper rather quickly.

When he became a Cabinet Minister, he seems to have thought that he must necessarily be the next in succession to D. S. Senanayake, expecially as he was made Leader of the House. He pressed every now and then to be appointed Deputy Prime Minister, but Senanayake was never willing to do this. Bandaranaike was outside the Senanayake family circle – some wits used to interpret the initials UNP as 'Uncle-Nephew Party' – unlike Dudley Senanayake, Sir John Kotelawala and J. R. Jayawardene. Kotelawala, who was knighted in 1948, was the next senior to Bandaranaike, and the relations between them could hardly be described as cordial. Kotelawala was very much at the centre of the party organisation.

The Prime Minister kept his own counsel about his successor. Rumour had it, not without reason, that his relations with Bandaranaike were those of growing mutual distrust and that he did not want him as his successor; politically, Bandaranaike was well to the left of the Prime Minister. Be that as it may, Bandaranaike made up his mind to strike out on his own, and on the morning of Budget day, July 1951, he ostentatiously crossed the floor of the House. It would seem that he expected a number of members to follow him, but in fact there were only six. But that day the position seemed to the Prime Minister himself distinctly precarious. However, the smallness of the number who supported Bandaranaike did not endanger the Government majority, and for the time being merely created another opposition splinter group. Bandaranaike renamed his party, which was based on the former *Sinhala Maha Sabha*, the Sri Lanka Freedom Party. Sri Lanka literally means 'Holy Ceylon' and is the ancient name for the island. He published a party programme which was to be the basis of his later policy. Kotelawala succeeded him as Leader of the House.

Before all this happened, Senanayake's Cabinet received an accession of strength in the person of Sir Oliver Goonetilleke, who, on his return from the post of High Commissioner to the United Kingdom, was appointed to a vacancy in the Senate, and given the portfolio of Home Affairs.

The only other change of any significance in the parliamentary set-up was among the Marxists. What had been known as the Bolshevist-Leninist group, led by Dr. Colvin de Silva, threw in its lot with the Lanka Sama Samaj Party. This, however, was not to the liking of Philip Gunawardana, who apparently had some personal grievance against de Silva; so he and a few followers broke off relations with N. M. Perera, calling his group the Viplakari (Revolutionary) LSSP, while Perera's group became known as the Nava (new) LSSP. Within themselves these groups were closely organised, probably better than any other party or group; but in spite of the considerable respect in which both Perera and de Silva were held, inside and outside Parliament, they never seemed to have made much headway in the country beyond what they held at the beginning of independence.

The British Government decided in 1949 to hold a meeting of Commonwealth Foreign Ministers in Colombo; this took place early in 1950. It was attended, among others, by Ernest Bevin, the British Foreign Secretary and by Jawaharlal Nehru, who as Prime Minister of India also held the portfolio of External Affairs, which included Commonwealth Relations. At one of the meetings the Australian Foreign Minister, P. C. Spender, made the first suggestion of organised aid to the underdeveloped countries of Asia; J. R. Jayawardene also had something to do with this suggestion. It was taken up with enthusiasm, and out of it arose the Colombo Plan, which came into being the following year, with its headquarters in Colombo itself. This looked as if it might be of great assistance to Ceylon in carrying out some of the schemes envisaged by the Six-Year Plan: and so it turned out to be.

This Six-Year Plan, never very concrete, was due to come to its end in 1953. The Government, possibly not too optimistic as to its success, decided to request the International Bank for Reconstruction and Development to send a Mission to Ceylon 'to survey the development of the country', with reference to specified fields of economic activity, covering the whole economy of the island. The Mission was headed by Sir Sydney Caine, a high ranking and able official of the British Treasury, but with much wider experience than most of such officials – subsequently he became Vice-Chancellor of the University of Malaya and then Director of the London School of Economics – and aided by representatives of two other international agencies, the Food and Agricultural Organisation and the World Health Organisation. The Mission arrived in Ceylon in October 1951 and stayed about two months. Its Report was sent to Ceylon in 1952. The two volumes are full of interest, and many, though by no means all of its recommendations have since been adopted.

In March 1952 the Prime Minister met with a riding accident from which he did not recover. This was most unfortunate, for he had succeeded in establishing himself as the undisputed leader of the Government and indeed of the country, an outstanding statesman and an international figure of note. He had done a very fine work in steering Ceylon to independence with the minimum of trouble, and in stablilising his country's position and status in the Commonwealth and in the world at large. As Prime Minister his political stature grew with his responsibility. As Lord Soulbury once observed, his sense of timing was remarkable. His loss was a severe blow to his country, and he was universally mourned.

It so happened that at the time of his death the Governor-General was away in England on short leave, and the Chief Justice, Sir Alan Rose, had been left in charge – a very awkward situation for him. Some very complicated manoeuvring went on, the object of which was to put the late Prime Minister's son Dudley into the vacant premiership. The logical successor (Bandaranaike having departed) would seem to have been Sir John Kotelawala, the Leader of the House, the Chairman of the UNP, and a very experienced Minister. But it was understood that Senanayake had expressed the wish that his son should succeed him, and opinion in the party and in the country turned in his favour. The only obstacle was the reluctance of Dudley Senanayake to accept the office. Lord Soulbury, who flew back to Ceylon immediately, exercised his discretion as Governor-General, which constitutionally he was entitled to do, and pronounced in his favour. It took over a day to persuade Dudley, but in the end he gave way to pressure from a number of quarters. Kotelawala was naturally much chagrined at being passed over. He never forgave either Lord Soulbury or his cousin Dudley.[1]

The new Prime Minister decided to go to the country; the general election was in any case due that year. He came back with a substantial majority. He was without doubt personally popular in the country, but he was carried to power in a great wave of sympathy and respect for the memory of his father. The 54 seats won by his party gave him a clear majority in the House of Representatives. Bandaranaike's party, the SLFP, though it polled about 300,000 votes, did not much increase the number of members who had crossed the floor of the House with him, winning only 9 seats. Dr. Perera's party, the VLSSP, went down to 9, and the Communist Party, with whom Philip Gunawardana had made an alliance, for electoral purposes, secured 4. The Tamil Congress also had 4 members. Owing to the citizenship laws there were no Indian members, but the new Prime Minister selected one Indian as an appointed member. The Cabinet was much the same as it had been at the end of the last Parliament, except that J. R. Jayawardene took on the Ministry of Home Affairs and was succeeded as Finance Minister by a young economist of the same name, M. D. H. Jayawardana. Goonetilleke became Minister of Agriculture.

The young Prime Minister – he was only forty-two – had been an excellent Minister of Agriculture. But he seemed to find the responsibility of his new office weigh heavily upon him. He was sincere and conscientious, but had not yet developed powers of leadership: moreover, his health was not at the time really up to the strain. He attended the Commonwealth Prime Ministers' Conference in 1952, where he created a favourable impression: he was also present at Queen Elizabeth's Coronation.

But in 1953 he came across a problem which was to be, and still is, a source of perennial trouble. During the war years the supply of rice from Burma, previously Ceylon's main source, was cut off. A strict system of rationing had to be imposed, and strenuous efforts had to be made to expand the production of paddy – in any case one of the main objectives of the Government's policy. The Government

[1] For Sir John Kotelawala's account of these happenings, see his book *An Asian Prime Minister's Story* (Harrap), 1956.

took over the entire import of rice, and also its distribution under a rationing system, fixing the price. They also gave a guaranteed price for their rice to paddygrowers. This was, of course, essential to prevent speculation and to ensure that all the people got their fair share of food; also to keep down the cost of living as much as possible – it increased rapidly during the war. This meant a certain amount, though not at first very much, in the way of rice subsidies. The scheme was continued after the war, keeping the price of rice stable, despite considerable variations in the world price. D. S. Senanayake, who disliked controls (as he once said specifically to the author, in private) yet saw no alternative to maintaining the rice subsidy, except, of course, the long-term plan of expanded production in the island. But in 1952 the situation became serious. The war in Korea had involved an upset of the world market in rice, and the following year the price rose steeply, which made the rice subsidy into a heavy burden on the revenue, accounting for no less than 20 per cent of it. The International Bank Mission had strongly recommended the reduction of subsidies,[1] pointing out that 'by concealing the real level of food prices and the real cost of production, they destroy the producer's initiative or need to achieve higher productivity. At the same time they tend to confirm the widespread belief that any further rise in food prices is to be compensated automatically by higher subsidies'. It seemed to the Government that it was absolutely necessary to reduce the rice subsidy, which meant an increase in the price of rationed rice. This step produced great public dissatisfaction, of which the Marxist parties were not slow to take advantage and to stir up trouble by organising demonstrations. Through the trade unions, over which they exercised much influence, a *hartal* (general stoppage of work) was organised in August 1953, particularly in Colombo and the south-west. This got out of hand, and the Government felt constrained to take repressive measures, declaring a partial state of emergency. The army was called out, and in one or two places the police had to fire on the demonstrators. As a result there were ten deaths. These incidents greatly upset the young Prime Minister, whose health had deteriorated, and he finally decided to resign. Sir John Kotelawala was Leader of the House, and it was obvious that he could not be passed over again. Accordingly, in October 1953, he became Prime Minister, a post which he held till 1956.

Kotelawala was a forceful character, and prided himself on getting things done. This was justified, but he did not always go

[1] See *The Economic Development of Ceylon* (the Report of the Mission) Part II, pp. 34–5.

about it in the most tactful way, and made for himself many .
enemies. However, he held his party together, though there is no
doubt that it lost some popularity by the retirement of Dudley
Senanayake, for a time, from public life, and by his quarrel with
R. G. Senanayake, the son of D. S. Senanayake's elder brother
(see p. 141) whom his cousin Dudley had appointed Minister of
Commerce and Trade, and who had made a barter deal with the
Government of Communist China of Ceylon rubber for Chinese
rice.

It had previously been arranged that Queen Elizabeth would
visit Ceylon in 1954, on her way to Australia and New Zealand.
There was some talk of cancelling the visit, but the new Prime
Minister strongly urged that it should take place. Queen Elizabeth
and her husband accordingly reached Colombo in April – an
unpleasantly hot time of the year – and formally opened Parliament. They also visited Kandy, where a special *perahera* was
arranged. Certainly the visit was very popular, and the royal
visitors received a most enthusiastic welcome from vast crowds –
the Ceylonese always enjoy a spectacle.

Later on in the year Lord Soulbury's tenure of office as Governor-
General came to an end, and it was decided to replace him by a
Ceylonese. To the Prime Minister Sir Oliver Goonetilleke seemed
to be eminently the right man for the post, and he remained
Governor-General for eight years.

The Prime Minister interested himself considerably in external
affairs, which will be dealt with later on in this book. He decided
in pursuance of this to pay a number of visits abroad, which
certainly had the effect of 'putting Ceylon on the world map',
though it did not increase his popularity at home; he was attacked
on account of the cost of his journeys, and it was freely said that he
undertook them to satisfy his vanity and increase his personal
prestige. In 1955 the U.S.S.R. finally withdrew its objection to
Ceylon being a member country of the United Nations, and this
was well received in the island. Kotelawala also entered into a
series of negotiations with Nehru, the Indian Prime Minister, in an
endeavour to settle the difficult problems which the citizenship laws
of both countries had raised. A certain quantum of agreement was
reached, but the problems were by no means finally solved, and the
difficulties still subsist.

The life of the Parliament was due to expire in 1957. But Kotelawala decided, against a considerable amount of advice to the
contrary, to go to the country in 1956. Now that year marked a
great event in the history of Buddhism, for it was to be celebrated

as the 2,500th anniversary of the enlightenment (*Nibbana*) of Gautama Buddha, and known as the *Buddha Jayanti*. The grand celebration was to be on *Wesak* day, in May of that year. The date decided for the general election was April.

Here without doubt the Prime Minister made a bad tactical blunder. He was, it is true, a Buddhist, but his Westernisation had gone very far, and it would hardly be accurate to describe him as devout – unlike his predecessor, Dudley Senanayake. In the words of an American observer,[1] 'He cared little for the conventions of puritanical Eastern society, but had made his own the secular, uninhibited worldly life of a Western urban society'. He does not seem to have had any idea of how unpopular the United National Party had become in the country. It was accused of corruption, nepotism – 'family bandyism' – and indifference to the welfare of the common man, and to the Buddhist religion. There is no doubt that the party had got very badly out of touch with the general trend of feeling and opinion in the country without realising it.

This the results of the election were to show. But no one, including Bandaranaike himself, had expected anything like the electoral landslide which took place. Bandaranaike looked round for allies and, rather surprisingly, found one in Philip Gunawardana. For the previous election Gunawardana had had a working agreement with the Communist Party. But he was a firm supporter of the 'Sinhala only' policy; moreover, he seems to have thought that the SLFP's leader had a bias towards socialism, of which he might take advantage, though his brand of Marxist socialism had little in common with the somewhat vague and academic socialism of Bandaranaike. Another ally was W. Dahanayake, who had quitted N. M. Perera's group to form a small party of his own based on the language issue. The three groups, joined together for electoral purposes, called themselves the *Mahajana Eksath Peramuna* (People's United Front). Some independent candidates also joined this party, and between them they were able to contest sixty seats. Furthermore, a no-contest pact was made with the two Marxist groups, on no other basis than a common desire to throw out the UNP. That party put up seventy-six candidates. It is interesting to note that two of these, both members of the House of Representatives, had quitted the SLFP not long before the election: one of them had even been the Secretary of the Party. Another interesting fact is that R. G. Senanayake, who had been appointed Minister of Commerce and Trade by his cousin Dudley, but had fallen out with the next

---

[1] W. H. Wriggins in *Ceylon, Dilemmas of a New Nation*, (Princeton University Press), 1960.

M

Prime Minister, contested the seat held by J. R. Jayawardene, and in the upshot was successful.

The UNP succeeded in polling a total of just under 740,000 votes. But this was utterly insufficient. The MEP polled over a million. This, however, gave them a gain of no less than 40 seats, winning 51 in all. All the UNP Ministers save two, one of whom was Kotelawala, lost their seats, and in the end they succeeded in winning only 8 seats in all, less than the LSSP who won 14, a gain of 4, or the Tamil Federal Party, who won 10, making an almost clean sweep of what may be described as the Tamil constituencies. The Communists had 4 seats, a gain of 1, and there were 8 Independents. The percentage of electors who voted was as high as 70.

The result came as a surprise to everyone and, of course, a stunning shock to the UNP. The more deep seated causes of Bandaranaike's victory and their defeat will be considered in the next chapter.

Chapter 13

The 'Revolution' of 1956 and its Results

T HE result of the general election of 1956 has been hailed as a turning point in the history of independent Ceylon, and has even been described as a revolution.[1] Though it took place seven years ago, at the time of writing, it is perhaps still a little early to say definitely how far this appellation is deserved. Bagehot, writing of the British constitution in the nineteenth century, made the famous aphorism that it was not true that Britain had no revolutions, she was always having them, every general election. The next general election is due in Ceylon in 1965 – though of course it may take place earlier, even before this book is published. The result of that election may quite possibly determine whether the 1956 election was just a revolution in Bagehot's sense, or something more deserving of the appellation.

The outstanding feature of the 1956 election is that it marked the strong reaction of the voters educated through the medium of Sinhalese against the Western-educated who had been running the country, and against the kind of government which the United National Party had given its people. This, however, was no accident, but was the result of the clever and foreseeing tactics on the part of S. W. R. D. Bandaranaike and his Sri Lanka Freedom Party. The political ideas which induced him to break away from the UNP in 1951 have already been outlined (see chapter 12, p. 171). Since that time he had been very carefully building up his party, and preparing in a limited number of constituencies for a long and ably conceived electoral campaign. The programme which he had put forward in 1951, however, was modified in an essential respect. He had laid it down that the *Swabasha*, that is, the languages of the country, Sinhalese and Tamil, should replace English as the official languages. But owing to the course of events as he foresaw them, he changed this to the intention that the official language should be Sinhalese only, due consideration being given to the use of Tamil and of English both officially and in the sphere of education. It was

---

[1] See G. C. Mendis's *Ceylon Today and Yesterday*, Chapter 13.

this which made a very special appeal to the Sinhalese-speaking electorate.

He had seen clearly the ever widening gap between the Western-educated and the *Swabasha*-educated. In particular, those who had passed the English Schools Certificate examinations were eligible for posts in government service and elsewhere for which the Sinhalese-educated had no chance. The Tamils had taken to English rather more thoroughly, in the Northern Province and elsewhere, and had obtained posts in the government service far in excess of their proportion of the population; it has often been jestingly said that government service was the principal industry of Jaffna. In every Sinhalese village there were three persons who were capable of exercising considerable influence, the village headman, the schoolteacher, and the ayurvedic physician: to these must be added the Buddhist bhikkhus dwelling in the neighbourhood. The influence of the headman, once all-powerful, was declining. The ages-old 'headman system' of local administration, made use of by all three of the occupying European powers, was the target of constant attack in Parliament, especially by the Marxists, and in the Sinhalese press. The chief headmen had been already done away with and replaced by District Revenue Officers, and the centres of provincial administration, the 'kachcheris', at the time of writing have just been replaced by District Councils. The other two, the schoolteacher and the ayurvedic practitioner, were apt to be disgruntled. The latter felt himself being gradually ousted by the practitioners of Western medicine and the increased use of hospitals by the people, and that the whole organisation of the Department of Medical and Sanitary Services was against him. The common people had long remained faithful to their indigenous medical system, but seemed to be turning more to the Western system, and crowding the hospitals when sick. The schoolteacher was well aware that his scale of pay and opportunities for promotion were greatly inferior to those of the teacher in English schools, and that his pupils had far less incentives than the pupils in the English schools. The Sri Lanka Freedom Party paid special attention to these two classes in their propaganda and their campaigning, and obtained the hearty support of many of them.

The Buddhist bhikkhus in general preferred to keep out of politics and to lead the life of contemplation which their religion demanded of them. But there was growing among some of the younger bhikkhus, and a section of the Buddhist laity, a movement which was greatly stimulated by the coming of Ceylon to independence. Various attempts had been made under the UNP Government to have a commission set up to investigate the state of the Buddhist religion, but without success. However in 1954, with the advent of the *Buddha Jayanti* year in 1956 (see p. 177) an unofficial Committee of prominent Buddhist laymen was formed to enquire into the state of Buddhism in the country. The idea was not favoured by the two senior chapters of the leading 'Siamese' sect, but nevertheless the Committee met and produced a Report, of which a summarised English translation was published under the title *The Betrayal of Buddhism*. This Report had a wide circulation. It bitterly attacked the British Government for its favouring of Christians – the Roman Catholics were the particular target of its quite venomous attack – and the neglect of Buddhism, against the undertaking given in the Kandy Convention of 1815: and the UNP Government was blamed for lack of action. The younger bhikkhus formed a political body named *Eksath Bhikkhu Peramuna*, which worked very hard for Bandaranaike's cause,[1] and were undoubtedly a strong factor in its success. The bhikkhus too, on the whole, objected to a general election being held in the sacred Jayanti year, and Kotelawala certainly made a tactical error of judgment here.

There was throughout the country a strong reaction against the United National Party. The author was told by a Minister of the present Government that if the UNP had won the election there would have been real danger of 'a bloody revolution'. The UNP had become increasingly unpopular. Its former leader, Dudley Senanayake, was still in political retirement, and it was thought at one time that he might possibly take the vows of a bhikkhu. Sir John Kotelawala, though returned to Parliament, was to all intents and purposes retired: he rarely visited the House of Representatives, and spent quite a proportion of his time in looking after a farm which he had bought in England. J. R. Jayawardene had been defeated in the election by R. G. Senanayake, the first Prime Minister's nephew, who joined the SLFP, and M. D. H. Jayawardana, the Finance Minister, was also defeated. The remnant of the UNP in the House of Representatives, 8 in all, were led by M. D. Banda, the only UNP Minister, except Kotelawala, who did not suffer defeat. He did this very well.

Bandaranaike's first task was to form a Cabinet. Though in fact his immediate followers of the SLFP. were in the majority, he was faithful to his electoral allies, and gave the portfolios of Agricul-

[1] For a detailed examination of the electoral campaign and these Buddhist activities, see Wriggins, *op. cit.* Mr. Wriggins, an American, spent two years in the late fifties studying conditions in Ceylon, a period which included the general election. In 1960 he published the results of his study, which are most illuminating. The quotation on p. 177 is by permission taken from this book.

ture and Food, and of Industry, to Philip Gunawardana and one of his followers. The portfolio of Commerce and Trade went to R. G. Senanayake. These two, Gunawardana and Senanayake, were very far apart in their political ideas. A woman M.P., Mrs Wijewardena, was the first woman in Ceylon to attain Cabinet rank, as Minister of Health. The material for Ministers was thin, and the average ability shown by them was in consequence not very high. The personnel of the House of Representatives showed changes, for though many of the English-educated remained, a number had come up through the channel of local government, some of them entirely Sinhalese-speaking, and few with much understanding of the nuances of parliamentary procedure.

The new Prime Minister was a well-meaning man, with considerable knowledge of administration and of the needs of his country. He was aware of the growing economic difficulties. But he was, in a sense, a captive of his own success. He had to carry out the items of his political platform which had been mainly responsible for bringing him to power. Possibly if he had been a man of strong and determined personality he might have been able to tackle the most urgent economic problems which faced him. But as it was he was bound to go with the tide, so his first action was to tackle the language question. To him and his Cabinet their first duty was to make Sinhalese the official language, while allowing for the reasonable use of Tamil.

So in June 1956 the 'Sinhala only' bill went through Parliament, making Sinhalese the sole official language. Under Kotelawala's premiership the question had been under consideration, but his policy seems to have been rather vague and undecided. He was reported as having said, on a visit to Jaffna, that both Sinhalese and Tamil would be the official languages: but his party decided to follow the 'Sinhala only' policy. This grievously offended the Tamils, so that in the 1956 election those Tamil members who had cooperated with the UNP were all defeated at the polls by the Tamil Federal Party, led by S. J. V. Chelvanayakam, an experienced parliamentarian. The only Tamil Congress member who was returned was their leader, G. G. Ponnambalam, former Minister of Industries: but after this he took comparatively little part in politics. The new Prime Minister tried to reassure the Tamils, speaking rather vaguely of this 'reasonable use of Tamil'. But nothing specific was put forward, and the harm was done.

Bandaranaike had always expressed himself in favour of socialistic ideas in domestic and neutralism in foreign affairs. The author well remembers a long argument with him a long time before he became

Prime Minister, in which he envisaged Ceylon as a kind of Asian Switzerland. This was in the days before the idea of non-alignment had become specific and, too, before the strategy of total nuclear warfare had been developed. The counter-argument used was that Ceylon's strategic situation geographically rendered this out of the question. The foreign policy of Ceylon after independence will be dealt with in a later chapter: but his neutralist policy issued in the termination of Senanayake's defence agreement with Britain. This was carried through quite harmoniously. As far as the British Government was concerned, the change in its world strategy made Ceylon far less important, though the former arrangement would still have been helpful. However, the harbour at Trincomalee ceased to be a potential British naval base, and the airfield and the Royal Air Force depot at Katunayake, which had been constructed during the war and maintained and developed afterwards was handed over to the Government of Ceylon. The airfield became the principal civil airfield, the runway of the earlier one being too short for modern aircraft, and the depot became the headquarters of the Royal Ceylon Air Force, still in a somewhat embryonic state: a British R.A.F. officer remained as its commandant for several years. Some attempt has been made to utilise the harbour at Trincomalee as a civil port, to help relieve the congestion at Colombo, and for a time half the tea exported came through this port; but its geographical position prevents this from being very effective; transport costs are higher than those to Colombo.

Two important schemes of nationalisation were carried through by the Bandaranaike Government, motorbus transport and the port of Colombo. The bus services had grown up in a most haphazard fashion before and during the war. All kinds of vehicles, many of them at first of doubtful roadworthiness, were used, and some bus operators became wealthy very quickly. Rivalry between some of them led to violent crime. Some of the biggest companies were efficient, but the same cannot be said about the smaller ones. The UNP Government started to take the matter in hand, and improvements were made in safety regulations. A Motor Traffic Bill was passed in Parliament to regularise and improve the bus services, and to restrict their competition with the railways. The wealthy bus owners, very much the 'new rich', were constantly attacked by the Opposition for, they alleged, helping to finance the UNP. Accordingly, in 1958 the bus services were nationalised, and put under a Ceylon Transport Board. This in its turn has since been attacked for not providing better services or showing anything but a loss on its working.

The port of Colombo has always been revenue earning, but various private companies for lighterage, etc., had always operated. Considerable improvements were made to Colombo harbour when Kotelawala was Minister of Transport, especially the making of several alongside shipping berths, instead of having to transfer passengers ashore by launches or even rowing boats and to unload cargo into lighters. Oil bunkering facilities were also improved. Ever since the war there had been considerable labour unrest among the port workers, partly because of the activities of rival trade unions led by different brands of Marxists. European business opinion had long favoured the establishment of a Port Authority, but this idea never appealed to the Ceylonese. In 1958 Bandaranaike decided to nationalise the whole working of the port, and this certainly had the effect, though only for a time, of cooling down labour troubles. These had seriously damaged the reputation of the port in international shipping circles, and this of course meant the danger of a drop in revenue accruing from harbour dues, etc., which could be considerable when the port was in full working order.

A measure which aroused considerable attention was the Paddy Lands Bill introduced by the Minister of Agriculture and Food, Philip Gunawardana, in 1958. The measure was well-intentioned and designed to give the villager greater security of tenure and better conditions, and to bring about more effective methods of cultivation. But some of its provisions provoked opposition inside the Cabinet itself, to whom it looked too much like collective farming on the Soviet model. A further measure, the Rural Credit Bill, intensified this dissension, and this resulted in the resignation of the two Marxist Ministers, and they and their followers quitting the coalition. They hung on to the name *Mahajana Eksath Peramuna*, while the Government now consisted almost entirely of the Sri Lanka Freedom Party and reverted to that name. The Government was now in a distinctly shaky state, though it still had a majority in the House of Representatives.

The main preoccupation during the years following the election, however, centred in the dispute arising out of the 'Sinhala only' Act. The Tamils were thoroughly provoked, and indeed scared. They fought the Bill tenaciously in Parliament, where they had the support of the two Marxist Opposition groups – which, incidentally earned the latter a distinct loss of popularity among the Sinhalese. The Tamils felt themselves driven into a corner, and reacted by putting forward as the central object of their policy an idea which, before, had been on the tentative side. This was to change the constitution by making Ceylon a federal state. Some of the more extreme Tamil racialists did more than hint that if this were not granted they would have to consider the possibility of an autonomous Tamil state. The Sinhalese in their turn found cause for alarm in this, for they are perpetually nervous of the 50 millions of Tamils on the adjacent mainland, as well as the 1 million on the estates. The solution offered by the Government was an increased regionalism, and after considerable negotiation Bandaranaike and Chelvanayakam between them came to an agreement in July 1957. The Tamils wanted their language to be used officially in the two mainly Tamil-speaking provinces, the Northern and the Eastern, and also as the medium of instruction in the schools there. Some kind of arrangement was reached – it is by no means clear just what it was – but it did not really satisfy the Tamils, and greatly angered the more extreme Sinhalese racialists.

Before this, however, and shortly after the bill had passed through Parliament and become the law of the land, the Tamil Federal Party decided to make a public protest in the form of *satyagraha* (passive civil disobedience), a sitting down in some public place and refusing to move. This had been employed with some success in India as a method of agitation against British rule. It was at first intended to stage it on the steps of the House of Representatives; but when this was prohibited, they held it on the Galle Face Green, a strip of public land along the sea coast adjacent to the House, where a number of meetings are held. Unfortunately this provoked violence on the part of a big crowd of Sinhalese, and some members of the Tamil Federal Party were assaulted. Worse rioting took place in the district round Gal Oya, where land was being opened up irrigated by the great Gal Oya tank. It was in the Eastern Province, and the Tamils there resented the planting of Sinhalese in an agricultural colony. A number of deaths resulted – 150 is the number given; the situation might have been much worse had it not been for the prompt and decisive action of the police.

Thus communal antagonism was increasing, stimulated by extremists on both sides. The only possible solution was a considerable amount of regionalism in the Tamil provinces, and a precise definition of the 'reasonable use of Tamil' which would go some way to satisfying the more moderate elements on both sides. How far the Bandaranaike-Chelvanayakam pact would have achieved this cannot be known, for in April 1958 Bandaranaike, who had been subjected to strong pressure from Sinhalese extremists, including some of the more militant bhikkhus, repudiated the pact, on the grounds that the Tamils were still pressing for a federal form of government.

The Tamil leaders, not surprisingly, were highly incensed by what they considered a breach of faith, and shortly afterwards a match was applied to this keg of gunpowder. It began in a small way, by the Tamils in the Northern Province objecting to the placing of Sinhalese characters on the number plates of public transport, and showing their displeasure by tarring them over. Reprisals came quickly, and it looked very much as if they were the result of organisation. All over the Sinhalese districts everything written up in Tamil characters, on notice boards, shop signs and so forth was obliterated with tar, even on the Prime Minister's car.[1] How far this was the work of organised gangs of what in Ceylon are described as *goondas*, usually translated into English as 'thugs', and how far it was due to an outbreak of racial feeling among the Sinhalese is not clear – the information given to the author from several quarters indicated the former. It was probably a mixture of both.

During the two years (nearly) after the passing of the 'Sinhala only' bill, the enforcement of law and order sadly deteriorated. To take an instance, in several residential districts of Colombo shanties were erected and inhabited by squatters in thoroughly insanitary conditions, quite illegally, but no attempt was made to remove them. Again, in 1957 a procession of United National Party supporters, led by J. R. Jayawardene, was attacked, but no action ensued. Then, during a strike, probably communist-inspired, a riot broke out in Colombo, and damage was done; but no punitive action was taken. Many very disorderly strikes took place too.

In May 1958 the Tamil Federal Party arranged a party convention at Vavuniya, in the Northern Province. On the 22nd a train travelling in that direction was wrecked by a gang at Polonnaruwa; but the passengers, having been warned, had left it. The station at that place was damaged, and during the next few days rioting took place in which some Tamil people were assaulted and murdered. The Government Agent of the North-Central Province barely escaped with his life after doing his best, with inadequate police protection, to quell the disturbances. Some troops who had been called out had to fire on the rioters, killing several of them. The Prime Minister was requested to declare a state of emergency, but refused. On the 27th and 28th the rioting spread to other places, including Colombo, and many atrocities, some of a horrible kind, were committed against Tamils. In the Eastern Province some Tamil thugs took reprisals against the Sinhalese, killing some and damaging Sinhalese property.

---

[1] See *Emergency '58* by Tarzie Wittachi (André Deutsch), for a vivid account of the racial riots.

On 27th May a state of emergency was at last, possibly at the insistence of the Governor-General, proclaimed, and the army and naval personnel were called out. The situation in Colombo had got completely out of hand, and severe measures had to be taken by the services, who, acting with promptitude and decision, succeeded in putting down the riots. When trouble broke out in the Northern Province, during which a famous Buddhist *vihare* was destroyed, the army was sent there, and occupied the town of Jaffna.

From all quarters of the island refugees made for Colombo, Tamils from many Sinhalese districts, and Sinhalese from Jaffna. There were about 12,000 Tamils in the refugee camp, and many of these were sent to Jaffna by sea, for which purpose ships were requisitioned by the Government. By the end of the month the fires had died down. The putting down of the riots had been directed by the Governor-General, who took charge as soon as the state of emergency was declared. He imposed a very strict censorship, and maintained the state of emergency which lasted for over nine months. Many Sinhalese people formed the impression that the Government had interfered unnecessarily on behalf of the Tamils, so that there was always a danger of trouble breaking out afresh.

The Prime Minister on 27th May proscribed the Tamil Federal Party and, a week later, an extremist Sinhalese organisation led by a member of Parliament. On 4th June prominent Tamils of the party, including their leader, Chelvanayakam, were put under house arrest, as was the Sinhalese M.P. just mentioned.

The number of deaths and the cost of damage to property have never been accurately determined. The official estimate of the number of deaths was 159, but the general impression in Ceylon was that there were many more – allegations have been made that one thousand was a conservative estimate.

The rift between the Sinhalese and the Tamils, always to some extent present but dormant, had come to the surface in a surprising and shocking manner. How deep and unbridgeable it is cannot really be estimated. But most of the Tamils who left their places of abode in Sinhalese districts seem to have returned, and to be settling down with at least some degree of amity. It can only be hoped that this is a good omen for the future, though the situation has several times since been quite tense. Any solution, one fears, is likely to take a long time.[1]

[1] For a review of the situation by an outside observer, but with considerable knowledge of and interest in the island, see B. H. Farmer, *Ceylon: A Divided Island*, (Oxford University Press), 1963.

In August 1958 the bill for the reasonable use of Tamil passed through Parliament and became law under the title of *The Tamil Language (Special Provisions) Act*. Provision was made for the use of Tamil in official matters for prescribed administrative purposes, and as a medium of instruction in secondary and higher education. But these only went part of the way to meet the demands of the Tamils generally. The use of Sinhalese as the sole official language has borne very hardly on Tamils in government service: many have felt compelled to retire, and it seems likely that under the regulations which have been made many more will have to do the same. The opportunities of promotion for Tamils in the government departments and the judicial service seem likely to be jeopardised. The Tamils are very resentful over this and fear that their culture will be relegated to a secondary place. Some able Tamil professional men and administrators have taken posts in Africa and other parts of the Commonwealth. As Chelvanayakam put it 'The "Sinhala only" principle . . . means the reduction of people whose mother tongue is Tamil to an inferior status in the country'. So the Federal Party is continuing its policy of resistance, though not in an active manner outside the law. It did, however, threaten to re-start a campaign of *satyagraha* in October 1963.

The Government was now finding itself in financial straits. Not only was there the constant burden of the rice subsidy, which they had restored, but the various commitments in which nationalisation, planning and increased social welfare had involved them had to be met. The Financial Minister's 1958–59 Budget therefore produced a number of new taxation expedients, based on schemes devised by Nicholas Kaldor, an economist from Cambridge University, but not completely followed. The problems of finance will receive further consideration in a later chapter, but it may be noted that the new taxes had the effect of stimulating a flight of capital from Ceylon and of making the tea companies in particular nervous of ploughing back their profits into the tea estates which they controlled. This was also due in part to the utterances of the militant section of the MEP Cabinet, and partly to the fact that the nationalisation of all foreign-owned estates (with compensation) had been on Bandaranaike's electoral programme – if low down on the list. The Prime Minister soon realised that such a measure was financially impracticable, and gave assurances that no steps would be taken to nationalise estates under his Government. Nevertheless, as the Marxist section of his Cabinet was saying exactly the opposite, his assurances were looked upon with a certain amount of dubiety.

In more ways than one the Government was losing the popularity which had swept it into power. The Marxist section of the Cabinet had resigned, breaking the MEP coalition. The Marxist part of the Opposition – and Dr. N. M. Perera was the official leader of the Opposition – had hoped for a greater degree of socialisation. When Parliament first met after the election the Marxists were so delighted with the downfall of the UNP, to which they had to some extent contributed by not putting up candidates against the MEP in a number of constituencies, that they almost fawned on the new Government. But they gradually cooled off. The extremist Sinhalese wing of the MEP was greatly annoyed over the pact with the Tamils, maintaining that the 'Sinhala only' policy had not gone nearly far enough. Also, as is so frequently the case after an electoral landslide, many of those who had supported the MEP thought that very much more could have been done for their particular interests. The MEP's electoral programme had perhaps been rather on the rash side – it may be remembered that the party had not really expected to win – and it was no easy matter for the Prime Minister, with a very divided Cabinet, to make good all his undertakings so as to satisfy the various groups inside as well as outside his Cabinet. Added to all this were the heavy new taxes, which bore hardly on those in the upper and middle income brackets. The press, an important section of which was in the hands of Ceylon Associated Newspapers, on the whole took up a hostile attitude – which was to lead to complications later. The general impression was that the Government was in a very tottery state. Dudley Senanayake came out of his retirement, having recovered his health, and took up again the leadership of the United National Party, which had now high hopes of regaining at least some of the ground lost in the 1956 election at the next one, which was due in 1961, but might well come earlier.

At this juncture the situation was radically changed by a terrible and tragic event – the assassination of the Prime Minister in September 1959. The deed itself was perpetrated by a bhikkhu who had failed to get the advancement he had hoped for in a college for the study of ayurvedic medicine. But behind him was the sinister figure of another bhikkhu, the head of the most ancient and important Buddhist *vihare* in Colombo, and a man of most unsaintly character, named Buddharakkita. He had been prominent in the MEP electoral campaign; and he was closely associated with the only woman member of the Cabinet. After the murder he, together with the assassin and several others, were brought to trial. The woman Minister was exculpated, but the actual assassin was condemned to death and Buddharakkita was given a very long term of imprison-

ment. The death penalty had actually been abolished by the Government, but was hastily reimposed and made retrospective: so that,
when after a long time the trial was over, that penalty could be and
was exacted.

Solomon Bandaranaike faced death with supreme courage, even
requesting mercy for his murderer. Almost with his last breath he
gave the Governor-General his necessary consent for the proclamation of a state of emergency. The whole country stood aghast, and
for a time popular feeling ran high against the bhikkhus – quite
unfairly. It was not necessary to keep up the emergency for long.
But politically a confused period ensued. The Governor-General
called upon W. Dahanayake, the Minister of Education, to fill the
murdered Prime Minister's place. Dahanayake was a very experienced politician. He had been a member of the State Council,
where he once delivered a speech lasting for about thirteen hours.
He was elected to the first Parliament after independence, and joined
the Trotskyist party, though actually he was no Marxist. In opposition he was very active, and being possessed of a delightful sense of
humour, made some telling speeches – though not of the same length.
At the 1956 election he was the leader of a small party which threw
in its lot with the MEP. When he became Prime Minister he showed
himself very strongly anti-communist. But he had no real following,
and he fell out with and got rid of Ministers, one after another. It
was not long before his Government was defeated. A general election
was called for March 1960.

Dahanayake formed his own party, having broken away from
what was left of the SLFP, which seemed to be in a state of confusion.
Its leader, C. P. de Silva, a former member of the civil service, was
in poor health, and it was really only Bandaranaike's personal
influence and experience which had kept the party together: even
at that, before his death, it seemed to be in danger of breaking up
under him.

At this juncture the party was rescued in a remarkable way. The
SLFP leaders tried to persuade the murdered Prime Minister's
widow to take over the leadership of the party. She was the daughter
of a Kandyan chief – very blue blooded. She had taken little part in
politics, and then only as a Prime Minister's wife might be expected
to participate – on social and ceremonial occasions, mostly. She
declined to stand for Parliament, although she would not have had
the faintest difficulty in being returned for her late husband's
constituency. She would not at first agree to take the leadership,
though she gave her unstinted support to its electoral campaign.

The murder had aroused an immense wave of sympathy all

through the country for the widow and her children, and had the effect of elevating Bandaranaike to the status of something like a martyr. A big memorial was built near his stately home, to which pilgrimages were made by thousands of ordinary Sinhalese folk. Tremendous, even fulsome, emphasis was everywhere, in and out of Parliament, laid on what he had done for the Sinhalese people. Nevertheless the party had little time to reorganise itself, unlike the UNP, which under Dudley Senanayake had undergone a pretty thorough rehabilitation. Had it not been for the feelings aroused by the murder, and the effect of Mrs. Bandaranaike's support of the SLFP, the UNP might well have romped home, even though the party still lacked popularity in some of the Sinhalese districts. The UNP have professed themselves keen supporters of the 'Sinhala only' policy, and put forward a policy not very dissimilar to that of their principal opponents. The Marxist parties had lost popularity from their opposition to 'Sinhala only', except for Philip Guna-wardana's group. They remained influential in some towns, and in their home constituencies, where their support was mainly on personal grounds.

The result of the March election was that the UNP did not do as well as it had hoped. It secured only a slight advantage over the SLFP, 50 seats as against 46: although this meant that they had regained 42 seats, this was not enough. The Tamil Federal Party swept the board in the Tamil Provinces, winning 19 seats: but they were bitterly opposed to the UNP for supporting the 'Sinhala only' policy. Of the other parties, Philip Gunawardana, still calling his followers MEP, got 10 seats. Dr. N. M. Perera, whose party was once more the Lanka Sama Samaj Party, could command only 10 seats (losing 4), and the Communist Party got 3. Dahanayake's own little party was blotted out, and he himself lost his seat for the town of Galle, in which he had been immensely popular for years.[1] At this election there was a surprisingly high percentage of the electorate voting, no less than 81·5.

The Governor-General called on Senanayake to form a Government, which he did. But almost at once it became obvious that he could not possibly command a majority. The very day Parliament met, the UNP candidate for the Speakership of the House of Representatives, Sir Albert Peries, who had been an excellent Speaker during much of the first two Parliaments after independence,[2] was defeated on a vote of the House. After this reverse, an

---

[1] He was more fortunate in the July election, and was returned again.
[2] In 1951 his predecessor, Sir Francis Molamure, was taken ill while in his chair in the House of Representatives, and died almost immediately.

adverse vote on the Opening Address meant the defeat of the UNP Government, and Senanayake resigned.

It was at this stage that Mrs. Bandaranaike agreed to assume the leadership of her late husband's party. She refused to contest a constituency for the House of Representatives, but let it be known that she was prepared to form a Government if her party was successful. The Marxist groups were anxious above all things that the UNP should not get back, and, except for the MEP rump, arranged a no-contest pact with the SLFP. This certainly had some effect, but the decisive factor was undoubtedly the personality of the murdered Prime Minister's widow. A wave of emotionalism swept through the electorate; though, to do her justice, Mrs. Bandaranaike did not exploit it as much as she could have done. The platform she put forward was the determination to carry on her late husband's policy, which in the circumstances had a strong appeal. However, it was the decisive factor, and though the UNP actually polled a larger total of votes than her party, the voters in most of the rural constituencies backed her up solidly, so that her party won 75 seats to the 30 which returned UNP candidates. The LSSP were represented by 12 members, the Communist Party by 4, while Gunawardana's remnant, which had secured 10 votes at the March election, went down to 3; and there were 15 independents, most of whom were willing to support the Government.

Chapter 14

A Woman Prime Minister

M RS. SIRIMAVO BANDARANAIKE, having won a complete victory in the election, was called upon by the Governor-General to form a Government; and thus she became the first woman Prime Minister in history. This success she achieved partly because she was the widow of the murdered Prime Minister, but to a very considerable extent by her own personality and status. She had given little indication in her earlier career of what she was to become. To anyone who met her casually she was a Sinhalese lady of the upper class, quiet and well mannered, with not very much to say for herself, no apparent talents or brilliance; just a good wife and mother, who happened to be brought into the public eye because she had married the man who, somewhat unexpectedly, became Prime Minister. But the leading men of her late husband's party seem to have had no doubt that she was possessed of the capacity to lead them, and showed no hesitation in putting themselves under the command of one who was not only almost devoid of practical political experience, but also a woman. Her reluctance to take the position is easily understood; the remarkable thing is that she had the moral courage to do it. At the time of writing she has held power for over three years, is personally popular, especially with the rural masses and the women voters, has made for herself a position in the international politics of Asia, and is well in control of her Cabinet.

Politically she was in a strong position for, with the votes of the appointed members, which could generally be relied upon, she had an overall majority in the House of Representatives, and the Opposition was very divided; furthermore, it was reasonably certain that she would have the support of at least some of the independent members. She herself took a vacant seat in the Senate, from which Chamber she appointed three more Ministers, an unusually high proportion for a second Chamber. The previous leader of her party, C. P. de Silva, Minister of Agriculture, Lands, Irrigation and Power, became Leader of the House of Representatives. The key post of Minister of Finance she gave to a new member, a young advocate named Felix Dias Bandaranaike, a close relative of her late husband. This young man also held the post of Parliamentary Secretary to the Ministry of External Affairs and Defence, which meant that he spoke for the Prime Minister in the House, since by virtue of her office, under the constitution, she held that portfolio; it was an odd arrangement, unique in the Commonwealth, for a man to be at the same time a Minister and a Parliamentary Secretary. The Opposition, of which Dudley Senanayake was now the Leader, raised objection to the Prime Minister not being a member of the House of Representatives, but Mrs. Bandaranaike decided to stay where she was, leaving the two Ministers just mentioned as the principal figures on the Government side in that House.

At the time of writing Mrs. Bandaranaike's Government is still in office, and it has another possible two years to run. She has, in fact, announced her intention of letting it run its full course. Right from the start of her electoral campaign she made a big point of her intention to follow closely the lines of policy laid down by her husband – the encouragement of the Sinhalese language and culture, and of the Buddhist religion, a socialistic approach to economic problems, and what was described as 'dynamic neutralism' in foreign affairs.

The first official announcement of her policy, in the Governor-General's speech at the Opening of Parliament in August 1960, however, set forth a policy which her husband had never definitely put forward – the taking over by the State of the denominational schools. The former Prime Minister, W. Dahanayake, speaking against the measure which introduced this, averred that such had never been the former Cabinet's intention – and he had been the Minister of Education in Bandaranaike's Government. The avowed objective was the setting up of a 'truly national' system of education.

Some account of the system of education in Ceylon up to the fifties was given in Chapter 8 of this book. To sum up briefly its salient points, higher education was imparted exclusively through the medium of English at the Law College and at the University, now well established up-country at Peradeniya, which had absorbed the Medical College as its Faculty of Medicine; this, however, remained in Colombo, as did the Faculty of Science. The University was an autonomous body, but owing to all education having become free, its cost was borne entirely (except for one or two very small endowments) by a block grant from the Government. The majority of the secondary schools were denominational, Christian (Protestant and Roman Catholic), Buddhist, Hindu and Muslim (one or two only of the last), all teaching through the medium of English. Following the recommendations of the Special Commission on Education (see Chapter 10, p. 148) all education was free in government and grant-aided schools, except for boarding and games fees. Only a very few schools stood out against this, and remained private, fee-charging institutions; for these schools, incidentally, there have been ever since long waiting lists for admission; they included some of the leading schools for both boys and girls. For all the other schools a beginning had been made, at the most junior standard, of teaching through the medium of the *Swabasha* (mother tongue of the pupil), except in certain specified subjects, such as science; this went up annually, a standard at a time, till by 1959 the medium throughout the whole school became the *Swabasha*. This arrangement raised practical teaching difficulties for some schools, especially in the larger towns, where the mother tongues of children in the same class could easily be Sinhalese or Tamil or English (the Burgher community's home language is English). In all these schools, however, English was taught as a compulsory second language. For some time – and the time is yet hardly over – there was a dearth of suitable school text books in the two languages. This difficulty, of course, multiplies itself the higher the standard or level of education; for now the Government is insisting on the use of Sinhalese at the University level, despite the almost united opposition of the university authorities, who maintain that the time is not yet ripe for this.

With the advent of Mrs. Bandaranaike's Government, all the assisted schools were taken over, Grade III schools without exception; Grades I and II schools (denominational) could continue as before, but were not allowed to charge any fees or to take in any but children of parents who were of the same religion and even the same denomination as the school. This was, of course, in practice next to an impossibility, as grants-in-aid ceased. But religious instruction was made compulsory in all schools.

This legislation provoked great indignation, especially in the Christian community, whose members thought, not without justification, that it was specially aimed at them, and in particular at the Roman Catholics. The fact that their schools had been built at the expense of the missions, in many cases, and were being taken over without compensation, was especially galling. Angry demonstrations, some approaching rioting, by the indignant parents of Roman Catholic schoolchildren took place, until their bishops managed to stop them. So the schools had to give way. They had done a great service to Ceylon, for without them, considering the historical circumstances and environment of the time, it is highly probable that both the quantity and the quality of education in the Ceylon of the nineteenth, and maybe the twentieth century too, would have been very low. The conversions which the missionaries in schools had effected were probably comparatively small in number, certainly in the later years. But the Buddhists were always highly nervous of proselytism and it was pressure from them which brought about this change. It meant a big take-over, for in June 1960 there were 3,470 of these assisted schools as compared with 4,400 government schools. In May 1959 (the latest date for which figures are available) the government schools had 987,462 pupils and 29,543 teachers, the comparable figures for the assisted schools being 775,527 and 25,024.

The number of *pirivena* schools (these were left out of the scope of this legislation) was 187. Of these, two were in 1959 raised to the status of universities. They were the Vidyodaya and the Vidyalankara *pirivenas*. Their medium of instruction is Sinhalese, but courses can be given in English to non-Ceylonese students. 'Science' is one of the subjects included in the curriculum. In 1960 they had between them nearly 1,500 internal and, one of them, over 6,000 external students, a fair proportion of them being bhikkhus. A scheme is under preparation for a university to be established at Jaffna, called the Ramanathan University (after Sir Ponnambalam Ramanathan), where the medium of instruction will presumably be Tamil – an idea at which S. W. R. D. Bandaranaike once publicly shuddered. In August 1963 a Universities Commission recommended the closing of the two *pirivena* universities, and that there should be only three universities, at Colombo, Peradeniya and Jaffna; there should be a separate university for bhikkhus.

The other main lines of policy laid down in the 1960 Governor-General's speech were the removal of the press from private hands into those of a public corporation established for the purpose, and responsible to a Minister, the nationalisation of life insurance, and the establishment of a republic. At the time of writing only the second of these has been implemented.

The proposals concerning the press had considerable repercussions all over the newspaper world, and incurred general condemnation. The reasons were that, during the two election campaigns, rather unpleasant attacks had been made on Mrs. Bandaranaike, as 'the weeping widow' and, more important, that the two leading newspapers, but especially the Associated Press – 'Lake House' – were pro-UNP. Bills to control the press have several times been brought in (one caused a major row inside the Cabinet, and even outside it, between Ministers), but nothing has yet been effected. The daily press has considerably changed its tune; it has, on more than one occasion, had to submit to censorship.

The problems which the new Government had to face were multifarious and difficult. It is clear that, despite the encomiums that were showered on the memory of the murdered Prime Minister, he had in his three years of office coped with hardly any of the major difficulties which beset his Government; though, considering the circumstances under which he came to power, it would perhaps be unfair to condemn him unduly for this. Obviously he had no alternative but to fulfil, or try to fulfil, the main promises of his electoral programme, which lay at the very root of his party's policy, and were largely responsible for his success. They may be summed up as follows. During the rule of the British, and to some extent of the United National Party, the true interests of the Sinhalese people had been neglected, first of all for 'colonial' interests and then for those of the Western-educated Ceylonese and the 'brown capitalists' who had come to power. The Buddhist religion had been elbowed aside, and the UNP had done nothing active to correct this. Therefore the tasks were to save and to revivify the Sinhalese language and culture, to put Buddhism back to its proper place as the religion of the majority, and to raise the standard of living of the masses of the inhabitants of the island by measures of a socialistic character. But in order to achieve these aims, and particularly the last, what was needed was a clear line of policy carried out by a strong leader with a united Government behind him; and these prerequisites were unfortunately not there. Bandaranaike was a well meaning and liberal-minded man, but apt to be irresolute and to find difficulty in making up his mind. His Cabinet was hopelessly divided, and contained few Ministers of even average ability. He had on his hands two sets of communal extremists, one Sinhalese and one Tamil, whose activities were intensified by his policy and the way he handled it; so that a communal explosion of unprecedented violence was precipitated, with which he found himself unable to cope – it had to be done by the Governor-General. One set of these extremists was responsible for his assassination.

The problems which his widow had to face, therefore, were the restoration and maintenance of law and order; the immensely difficult task of coping with the embittered and recalcitrant Tamil community; the perennial problems inherent in the presence of a million Indian estate labourers on whose work the economic stability of the country to a considerable degree depended, and further by illegal immigration, very hard to prevent, and by difficulties with the Government of India over citizenship; relations with foreign countries, which were matters that came under her ministry; the revision of the constitution and the establishment of a republic; the crying need for the increased production of food and the improvement of agriculture; the establishment of a balanced economy through a measure of industrialisation; and increasing unemployment and underemployment. These were alarming enough. But more fundamentally important than any of them were the deterioration of the island's financial and economic situation, which was causing a serious run-down of Ceylon's sterling assets, and, underlying everything else, the phenomenal increase of the population.

These, then, were the problems up to which this inexperienced woman had to face. To have a woman as Prime Minister in an Asian country was in any case a remarkable political happening. It was freely stated, to begin with, that she was little more than a figurehead, used by the politicians of her party to get back into power on a strong wave of emotion which only she could inspire; and that the real leadership was in the hands of the young Finance Minister, her relative by marriage. Events, however, have shown this to be anything but the case. For in 1962 Dias Bandaranaike resigned his portfolio. In his Budget statement he proposed to cut the rice ration by half a measure per person per week, which was excellent sense economically, but so politically inexpedient that his Cabinet colleagues flatly refused to support him. Without doubt the Prime Minister placed great reliance on him. This is clear from the fact that she kept him on as her Parliamentary Secretary, and brought him back after a few months – first as Minister without Portfolio and then as Minister of Agriculture, Food and Co-operatives. Nevertheless it would seem that she is in full control of her Cabinet, and is facing her problems not only with great courage but also with remarkable ability. With an overall majority in Parliament, she had the prospect of five years of power in which to tackle the knotty problems just specified; three of these years have already passed.

The problems listed above will now be examined in the context of their development since independence, or if necessary before it. Though they are being taken in order, many of them are closely interconnected; this is always the politician's headache, and under present day conditions, as always in history, it takes a statesman to get anywhere near solving it, usually one individual, a Prime Minister – or a dictator.

The first problem, the maintenance of order, was made difficult in two ways, one expected and the other unexpected. It was expected that the Tamil Federal Party would give trouble, for it was determined not to accept 'Sinhala only', and to go on pressing for a federal constitution. This seems to lie more within the category of the second than of the first problem listed, but it comes under the first because of the adoption of *satyagraha*, non-violent civil disobedience, as a method of agitation. This will be discussed under the whole problem of the Tamils, though the maintenance of order, as events were to show, was bound up with it.

The unexpected denouement was an attempted *coup d'état*, in January 1962, by some army and police officers, which was only just nipped in the bud. It miscarried, apparently, through inadequate preparation, and the failure of these officers to carry the armed forces and the police with them. Also – somebody talked. The leaders were arrested and put under detention, and at the time of writing (August 1963) are only now being tried in court. Two trials have been started, but the first failed on account of a judicial objection, well justified, to the appointment of a tribunal by the Executive: the second owing to a technical objection to one of the judges, on the now properly constituted tribunal. The abortive *coup d'état* seems to have been engineered by a section of the Western-educated among the army and police to overthrow the existing Government, to arrest the leaders of the Marxists, and, for the time being, to put the Government into the capable hands of the Governor-General, if he would take it: he himself was quite innocent of any share in the matter, and this was officially stated. However, shortly afterwards Sir Oliver Goonetilleke's tenure of office, now about three years over the normal span of five, was very abruptly terminated. Mr. William Gopallawa, a relative of the Prime Minister, was his successor. The new Governor-General has had considerable experience of local government, and a short spell as his country's ambassador to the United States of America. Goonetilleke had rendered yeoman service to Ceylon from the period of the war onwards, though some of his less scrupulous actions, however necessary – as they usually were under the circumstances – had not always been appreciated by his fellow countrymen: without any doubt Ceylon owes him much. Kotelawala and Dudley Senanayake, whose names some people tried to associate with the *coup d'état* also, entirely disassociated themselves from it. According to a newspaper report, Kotelawala said, very characteristically, that if he and Sir Oliver had had anything to do with it, they would have made a success of it! A state of emergency was declared after the movers had been arrested, and has been prolonged from time to time. Only quite recently has it been terminated.

The prolongation was not due to the unsuccessful coup. The Tamil Federal Party renewed its campaign against 'Sinhala only', and the Government, apprehensive lest bad trouble might recur, ordered the detention of its leaders; only threats of similar treatment to the leaders of the big Indian trade union of the estate workers prevented an extensive strike on the estates, in sympathy. The continuance of the state of emergency has tended rather to create an impression, and not only in Ceylon, that the Government was moving away from democracy and in the direction of an authoritarian régime. Many people at the time in Ceylon were certainly nervous of expressing their opinions in public, or even aloud.

The story of Sinhalese-Tamil relations in early days was outlined in the first few chapters of this book, and was designed to show the historical basis on which they rest. Under the Portuguese and Dutch, the two peoples had been almost completely apart, politically by reasons of having a different administration, and geographically by being separated from the Sinhalese by a wide belt of scrub jungle, the Wanni, much of which had in ancient times been a part of the flourishing Sinhalese kingdom of the *Rajarata*. With the unification of Ceylon by the British, and the rehabilitation of what is now the North-Central province, the two communities came into touch again.[1] Owing to missionary efforts, the Tamils had good educational opportunities at hand; and they took to English education rather more readily than the Sinhalese. The prospects of young men with any ambition were not very bright in the Jaffna peninsula. Owing to the presence of underground water there it had always been possible for the thrifty and hard working Tamil peasants to wring a livelihood from the arid-looking soil – they get up at all hours of the night to take their turn at drawing water from the wells. Hence many of the educated Tamils left Jaffna to better their prospects. The education they had received in the missionary schools, and their facility of studying for and passing examinations, particularly in mathematics, for which branch of learning they have a really remarkable capacity, enabled them to get into the government and other services in a larger proportion to their numbers than the Sinhalese. In many parts of the island, in many walks of life, Tamils were to be found occupying comparatively well-paid posts and exercising the authority which their positions gave them. But they always kept in touch with their homes in the north, which is why the Western-educated Tamils never got so far out of touch with

[1] See B. H. Farmer, *Ceylon: A Divided Nation* (Oxford University Press), 1963.

the rest of their community as did the Western-educated Sinhalese with theirs. To the ordinary Sinhalese man, then, there was always a feeling of some resentment against these descendants of the race which had ruined their ancient cities, wrecked their wonderfu systems of irrigation, and even occupied part of their own island: and who now came, exercising authority over them; this feeling was more to be found among the uneducated who kept up the ancient legends of Ceylon's past in their memories than the middle class, who knew more about Henry VIII than about Vijayabahu I. But these middle class people resented the way in which the Tamils had insinuated themselves into well-paid jobs; they always alleged that the Tamils did all in their power to favour and push forward their own people, especially in certain government departments and sub-departments. To a certain extent the Tamils mingled with the Sinhalese socially, but even among the Western-educated there was little intermarriage: their religion, their social customs and their language tended to keep them apart. Yet in some ways their religions mingled, for in many Buddhist vihares there was a *kovil* (Hindu temple), where the Sinhalese villagers were quite willing to pay their worship to Hindu deities.

During the British occupation there was nothing to stop what may be called the expatriate Tamils – expatriate from Jaffna – from prospering. When independence came, the concept of a Ceylonese nation was one very close to the heart of D. S. Senanayake. He had lived through a period of close co-operation with Tamil leaders like the brothers Ramanathan and Arunachalam in forming the Ceylon National Congress – though it may be remembered that these two broke away from Congress on a communal issue.[1] The Tamils were always nervous of what might happen to their community when the governing hand of the British was withdrawn, fearing Sinhalese dominance; which is why they always agitated for built-in constitutional safeguards for minorities. Yet, in the middle of the 'fifty-fifty' agitation, when the Soulbury Commission was listening to evidence (see above p. 151), the author vividly remembers the leader of that movement, G. G. Ponnambalam, saying – in private – that he would gladly call off 'fifty-fifty' if there was a real chance of *purna swaraj* – full independence. When this came, he certainly did his best to co-operate with Senanayake's Government. But, as events were to prove, he could not take his community with him. There was always a hard core of Tamil communalists who did not believe they were going to get a square deal -- as they saw it – from the Sinhalese. So that when Bandaranaike brought in his 'Sinhala

[1] See Chapter 9, p. 120.

only' policy, and the United National Party took it up too, this convinced them that they had been right: and they carried the bulk of their community with them.

With the coming of 'Sinhala only', the Tamils in government service saw any prospect of their advancement slipping away from them. Under the changed circumstances they had, some of them quite late in life, to try to make themselves reasonably well acquainted with the Sinhalese language, if they hoped to get any further; and if they did not try, they were in danger of losing their posts altogether. One leading Tamil bitterly remarked to the author of this book that no one stood any chance in present-day Ceylon unless he was of Goigama caste and a Buddhist. Not only did they see no prospects for themselves, but they saw none for their children either.

The Sinhalese point of view – not that of the Sinhalese extremists, who want 'Ceylon for the Sinhalese' – is that, being the majority community, their language, religion and culture ought to have preference. They see no reason why the Tamils should not learn Sinhalese as they learned English – in the past. In the world there are some 7 million Sinhalese, practically all of them in Ceylon, with their own culture which, under the British, was being steadily eroded and in danger of disappearing altogether, along with their language. But there is no such danger for the Tamils, for a short way off, on the mainland, are 50 million Tamil people to keep their language and culture going. To the minds of the Sinhalese this constitutes a danger. As recently as 1945, Nehru put forward the suggestion that Ceylon might be well advised to consider carefully becoming one of the States of India – though he subsequently retracted the suggestion. But there might be in the not very distant future a definite attempt to create *Tamil-nad*, a state comprising all lands where Tamils dwell. Conceivably, this might happen if the Indian Union were to disintegrate; though it does not seem at all likely. However, the term *Tamil-nad* is sometimes heard in South India, and even, occasionally, from the mouths of the more extreme Tamil communalists in Ceylon. There is no doubt that the fear of it constantly lurks in the minds of many Sinhalese.

Every plural society inevitably has its problems, which often seem incapable of solution. But solutions are by no means impossible. In Malaya, for instance, a solution seems to be working out between the Malays and the Chinese, who differ radically from each other – though there is no centuries-old tradition of hostility between them, as there is between the Sinhalese and the Tamils. Possibly if the two latter were two races rather than two communities the issue might be clearer and the solution more simple; possibly, too, if both communities were less politically minded.

The tragic events of May 1958 did incalculable harm, though one can only hope, not irretrievable. The cold fact to be faced is that, somehow, upwards of seven million Sinhalese have got to coexist with one million Ceylon Tamils, if the country is to go forward to the prosperous future that can be hers. But this is scarcely possible if that million are permanently dissatisfied and resentful. It is obvious that the Sinhalese, being the great majority, will not, and should not, give up the priority of their language and culture, nor agree to the extreme constitutional expedient of a federation. But something in the nature of an extended regionalism should be possible. Can the Sinhalese put behind them the memory that the Tamils are the descendants of invaders who did their forefathers so much harm – but centuries ago? Can the Tamils forgive and forget the events of May 1958? Will they learn Sinhalese, as a second language, as the Bretons have learned French? Can agreements be hammered out which will turn away for ever from Sinhalese minds the fear that the Tamils will come again from India and take over their island? In short, can both communities find enough common ground to begin thinking of themselves as Ceylonese first and Sinhalese or Tamils after, and grow into a nation in which the cultures of both can be harmonised without being absorbed the one by the other?

Only a strong and tolerant Government, or succession of such Governments, can help to provide the answers to these questions. Bandaranaike was obviously anxious to go some way in this direction, as witness the pact he tried to make with Chelvanayakam. But witness also his inability to carry it out – his irresolution. If these questions are going to be answered, if the problems are even going to begin to be solved, there will have to be unprecedented give and take on both sides. This would certainly bring the most violent protests from both sets of extremists; and unfortunately in Ceylon the tail is too often found wagging the dog. To create a Ceylonese nation requires statesmanship. D. S. Senanayake had made a beginning, with his idea of Ceylon as a nation, and he might have done more if he had lived. Bandaranaike, possibly, could have, had he been let, had he been strong enough to resist the pressures applied to him to go back on the pact, and had he survived.

The problem of the Ceylon Tamils may be capable of a long-term solution – so all the friends of Ceylon hope. But in the island there are not only a million Ceylon Tamils, but a million Indian Tamils too, all of them of the working class, labourers on the estates. With them the Ceylon Tamils have had comparatively little contact, so far. The solution which the Sinhalese would like to see is a gradual repatriation of these people back to their homeland. A sum of half a million rupees for this purpose is in the 1963/64 estimates. But here arises the difficulty that, anyhow for some time to come, the economy of the island is to a considerable extent based on the work of these Indian Tamils on the tea estates. The first facet of the problem is whether, if these Indians go, the Sinhalese will be willing to take their place. The Kandyan villages, with their growing population, are swelling to bursting point. The villagers in the nineteenth century lost much land, even if then quite unproductive, to the plantations; and this has always been a grievance,[1] operating against the British Government, the European planters, and the Indian estate labourers. But the quality tea, for the most part, if not quite exclusively, grows on land at high altitudes, which was cleared of heavy jungle, where no one, or scarcely anyone, then dwelt; and it is on this high-grown tea that the reputation of Ceylon tea in the world market depends. But it is at these altitudes that the climate can be cold and wet for fairly long periods of the year, in the time of the south-west monsoon; and it is definitely disliked by the Sinhalese. The question is whether economic necessity, the prevalence of unemployment, due to the phenomenal growth of the population, will be strong enough to overcome this dislike. Of this population growth more will be said in the next chapter.

But the problem is not even as simple as this. Its second fact is that many of the workers on the estates cannot go back to India, because according to the constitution of that country they are not Indian citizens; and according to the constitution of Ceylon they are not citizens of Ceylon either. So at least a sizeable proportion of them have to be 'stateless'. An increasing number are of the third and fourth generations born in Ceylon. Many of them are certainly eligible for citizenship; but the authorities have been somewhat chary of admitting them as such. The question is, can these ever be brought to think of themselves as Ceylonese? The author of this book recently had a talk with a young Sinhalese Member of Parliament who thought they could. If the Government takes over the estate schools, which for so many years were run and paid for – often somewhat unwillingly – by planters and their employers, and the chilrden are taught Sinhalese as a second language, something might be achieved. On some estates, though not usually those up-country, there has of recent years been more mixing of the two

---

[1] For a full if prejudiced account of this, see the *Report of the Kandyan Peasantry Commission*, Ceylon Sessional Paper XVIII of 1951.

races – the word is used advisedly here. So there may be some possibility of this.

The problem of the Indian estate workers is one which has for a number of years bedevilled Indo-Ceylon relations, certainly well before the independence of the two countries. Various efforts have been made to effect a basis of agreement between them. So far the nearest thing to a workable agreement was that come to between Nehru and Kotelawala in 1954; but this was not final. Bandaranaike entered into some negotiations, but they never got very far. The present position may best be illustrated by a quotation from the English edition of the Governor-General's speech delivered at the Opening of Parliament in July 1963. 'My Prime Minister and the Prime Minister of India agreed that discussions regarding the settlement of the problems of persons of Indian origin should continue between officials of the two countries. . . . My Prime Minister proposes to take up the question direct with the Prime Minister of India. . . . My Government . . . will seek a solution to satisfy national aspirations.'

The author of this book in 1961 attended a debate in the Senate of Ceylon when a vote of censure was being moved by the Opposition. Neither of the Ministers present were willing to reply to it; but the Prime Minister entered the Chamber and took up the cudgels for the Government. When she sat down, an Opposition Senator jumped up and thanked her for speaking, remarking that obviously she was the only man on the Government benches. Perhaps she will be the only statesman.

Some body is given to this hope by the fact that a field of policy with which she has recently entered with some determination is that of international affairs, a subject for which she is responsible by virtue of holding, as Prime Minister, the portfolio of Defence and External Affairs. She had previously described her foreign policy as one of 'dynamic neutralism', but it is only very recently that it began to show any signs of dynamism. Neither of the Senanayakes had concerned themselves much with foreign policy. Ceylon was in no danger from any foreign country. The agreement with Britain was harmless, and might at any time be useful and even beneficial. Britain, too, was far and away the best customer for Ceylon's tea – she still is – and the links binding the two countries remained close. It seemed most desirable for Ceylon to be a member of the Commonwealth. By the comprehensive system of intra-Commonwealth consultation and the passing on thereby of information on world affairs, the Government of Ceylon was able to be kept, in the easiest way, in touch with the cross currents sweeping around the world –

and she was not yet a member of the United Nations. To those
Ceylonese to whom it appeared that the only possible menace to
Ceylon's security or even independence could come from India, it
was obvious that this would be reduced or even removed as long as
they were fellow-members of the Commonwealth. Moreover, while
Ceylon's diplomatic service was in the process of being formed,
Britain was perfectly ready to let her diplomats look after Ceylon's
interests in any countries until Ceylon's own representatives were
appointed. To the United National Party it appeared that the
communist countries, while not for the time being a menace, might
perhaps become so in the future. The U.S.S.R. had vetoed Ceylon's
application for membership of the United Nations: and anyhow, as
the Marxist Opposition was for the communist countries, the UNP
would be against them. This anti-communist feeling was taken a
step further by Kotelawala when he became Prime Minister. He was
far more actively interested in world politics than his two predecessors. He strongly favoured the Commonwealth connexion – he had
been for a time Vice-Chairman of the Commonwealth Parliamentary Association – and was a convinced anti-communist. However, he was also attracted by what is sometimes called 'Asianism'.
He conceived the idea of a conference of five Prime Ministers of
newly independent Asian States – India, Pakistan, Burma, Indonesia and Ceylon – which met at Colombo in 1954.[1] This conference
was something of a forerunner of the much bigger and more
publicised conference at Bandung the following year, at which
conference an attack by him on Russian colonialism for a time 'put
the cat among the pigeons'.

Bandaranaike's ideas on foreign affairs followed very closely those
of Nehru. At one time he was against Ceylon remaining in the
Commonwealth, as he saw no particular purpose in it. The author
of this book well remembers a conversation with him on this matter
– at his request – the very day on which he crossed the floor of the
House, when he said that if he became Prime Minister he would be
inclined to take Ceylon out of the Commonwealth, but that he was
not anti-British at all; in fact, his very first action on becoming
Prime Minister would be 'to make an alliance with England'. Later
on he changed his point of view and came to favour the Commonwealth connexion, though not with any great enthusiasm. His policy
was one of neutralism rather than non-alignment, which was very
much in line with his favourite doctrine of 'the middle of the road',
and his notion of Ceylon as 'an Asian Switzerland'.

In the first year of Dudley Senanayake's premiership, 1952, the

[1] See Kotelawala, *op. cit.*, Chapter 15.

rubber industry was in a bad way, largely as the aftermath of the war in Korea; also it was very difficult to buy rice on the world market. Negotiations on these difficulties were opened with the U.S.A. to help meet the situation, but were not successful. So R. G. Senanayake, the Minister of Commerce and Trade, negotiated a bilateral agreement with Communist China, already to some extent a buyer of Ceylon rubber, to exchange 30,000 tons of rubber for 270,000 tons of rice, at agreed prices. This annoyed the Americans, who went so far as to prohibit the export of sulphur to Ceylon: this sulphur is used to spray rubber trees against the pest of *oidium*. This action caused some bad feeling in Ceylon against the U.S.A. The rice-rubber deal has been kept up ever since, though not always to Ceylon's advantage when the rice market recovered. It was not popular with the Kotelawala Government, which was one cause of the Minister's resignation from the Government and ultimately from the party, since he favoured an intensification of trade with China.

This was really the beginning of relations with communist countries. When Bandaranaike came into power, his policy of 'friendliness to all countries' made him sheer away from the predilection of his predecessors for Britain and the U.S.A. Diplomatic relations were opened with the U.S.S.R. and the People's Republic of China, who established embassies in Colombo, with large staffs, in 1956. Both these countries were willing to offer a certain amount of economic aid and, though this did not total anything like as much as Ceylon received from the Colombo Plan and other aid from the West, it was far more heavily publicised. Both these countries have done all they can to attract visitors from Ceylon, and the Government has willingly encouraged this. Bandaranaike's foreign policy planted Ceylon firmly inside the Afro-Asian block in the United Nations, of which Ceylon had become a member, and there Ceylon generally followed India's lead.

What brought Mrs. Bandaranaike into the field of international politics was the border dispute, breaking out into open warfare, between India and China, consequent upon the latter's aggression: the situation was not an easy one for her, since relations with China were now of comparatively long standing, owing to the rice-rubber deal. On the other hand, friendly relations with India were of the utmost importance, and public opinion in India was disappointed with the Ceylon Government for not giving India more definite moral support. Mrs. Bandaranaike's object, therefore, following her husband's policy of friendliness to all nations, was to deplore the breach between the two greatest Asian countries and to see what could be done to close it. She took the initiative, immediately after the rather surprising cease-fire by China, in getting certain countries not directly affected by the dispute together – Burma, Indonesia, Ghana, the United Arab Republic and Cambodia. She invited their representatives to Colombo for a conference, where they drew up a plan for peace, and sent it to both China and India. She followed this up by travelling herself to New Delhi and to Peking to see if she could persuade both parties to agree to the plan. She met with some success in these missions, as both countries accepted the plan, though the Chinese Government made some reservations – which in the end were to make the whole plan look like being fruitless. Whatever may be the outcome of this immensely significant conflict, there is no doubt that Mrs. Bandaranaike achieved prestige for herself and her country by the lead she took in this matter; though an unkind critic has stigmatised it as a 'diplomatic charade'.

With the U.S.A. relations have deteriorated. As mentioned earlier, the stopping of the sulphur supply, though temporary, created some ill feeling. But relations improved with the massive aid which the U.S.A. was willing to give, both as part of the Colombo Plan and in other ways. However, in 1962 the Ceylon Government was looking in all directions for ways of conserving foreign exchange, of which she was – and still is – lamentably short. The then Minister of Commerce and Trade, Ilangaratne, brought forward a measure for setting up a Petroleum Corporation which would buy oil from Russia and sell it at a lower price than that charged by the two American and one British oil companies, which had previously had the sole rights of importing and selling. When they objected, he announced the take-over of a proportion of the petrol-distributing stations owned and managed by these companies, which would be run in competition with the installations they were permitted to keep. This was done, much to the annoyance of the companies and their representatives. Compensation was promised, but was not forthcoming in time, nor were the companies satisfied with the amount, which they alleged was unilaterally determined and not according to customary international practice. The American Government took a hand in the matter and protested strongly to the Government of Ceylon. The protest was without avail, so the Americans took the extreme step of cutting off altogether the aid which they had been giving to Ceylon. This was a quite serious blow to the economy of the island. The Ceylon Government retaliated by taking over all the installations except oil bunkering and aviation fuel, so that the Ceylon Petroleum Corporation now has the monopoly of both import and distribution for all other purposes.

Relations with Britain, though nothing like as close as they had been under the Senanayakes, remained in some sense of a special nature, on account of close economic links and, of course, previous history. The powerful Shell Company is, naturally, annoyed at the arbitrary take-over of their installations in Ceylon, and diplomatic representations have been made on their behalf by the British Government. No such steps, however, have been taken as those taken by the U.S.A. Tea interests, too, which have many millions invested in Ceylon, are nervous about the recurrent threats of nationalisation.

The Government of Ceylon has appointed High Commissioners to most of the Commonwealth countries, and ambassadors to others, particularly the U.S.A., the U.S.S.R. and the Chinese Republic, the neighbouring countries of Burma and Indonesia, and others, like Japan, the United Arab Republic, France, Germany and Holland, with whom trade relations are already or prospectively important. There were in 1961 thirty-nine countries diplomatically represented in Ceylon, though twelve of these had their interests in the island looked after by their representatives in Delhi.

The revision of the constitution is an item which has been on the programme of all the parties for quite some time. All seem to be agreed that Ceylon should be a republic. Incidentally, when this happens it will be the end of by far the most ancient monarchy in the world for, by the Kandyan convention of 1815, King George III took over directly from the deposed King of Kandy, and that monarchy dated back to Devanampiya-Tissa at the latest, say a few centuries over two thousand years. The change to a republic can be done quite easily: but none of the parties seem to be agreed on what should follow. In order to change the constitution, embodied as it is in British documents – an Act of Parliament and some Orders in Council – the House of Representatives will have to agree to what will presumably be an entirely new document, by a two-thirds majority of its total membership, which comes to 102 favourable votes. If the two parties, the SLFP and the UNP were to agree on this issue, accepting the report of the Select Committee on the reform of the constitution, perhaps with agreed modifications, they could get it through the House: and they would presumably have in addition the support of the appointed members – though in voting for it, these could be sounding their death knell, for the Committee is likely to regard them as an anachronism. The Marxist Opposition would probably like more drastic changes than the others, and the Tamils want a federation. It may be this which has for so long held up any alteration at all. The position of the Senate is one matter on which there are differences of opinion.

O

One point on which the 1948 constitution has been criticised is the absence of any provisions on fundamental rights, such as are found in the constitutions of India and of all the British colonies which have since that date obtained their independence, beginning with Ghana. How far the incorporation of something like a bill of rights with a constitution does really safeguard individual liberties is a matter of opinion, which the future will decide. But it will probably find a place in the next constitution of Ceylon.

This problem is the least difficult, as it is certainly the least urgent, of all the Prime Minister has to face.

Chapter 15

Ceylon's Crucial Problems, 1

I N Chapter 7 a factual statement and an appraisement were given of the economic situation of Ceylon at the end of the period during which there was complete, or nearly complete, European control of the economy. At that time, say about the end of the first world war, this position seems to have been accepted without much question by the great majority of Ceylonese. The landowning classes carried on their lives in much the same way as they had done, save that they had the benefits of the increased amenities which Western civilisation had brought in its train – the motor car and the telephone, for instance.

No great changes, either, were to be found among the rural workers – peasant proprietors, tenants, or landless agricultural labourers. They carried on their agriculture in much the same manner as their forefathers had done, and most of them seemed impervious to change, despite the efforts of the Department of Agriculture. They had benefited, in the dry zone, immensely by the restoration of tanks and the work of the Irrigation Department. They were, of course, free from the wars and raids of former centuries. They appreciated the even-handed justice that was available when things went wrong between individuals, and felt that they would probably though not necessarily get a square deal any time it became desirable for them to appeal to the powers that be. They had certain facilities of which they could make use: for instance, schooling for their children, not always wanted; medical treatment at dispensaries and in hospitals – but they generally preferred *ayurveda*; and public transport when they could afford it.

The Buddhist *sangha* was never quite content. The bhikkhus resented the prominent position taken in the affairs of the country by the Christians, both clergy and laity, especially in education. They were willing, on the whole, to support, if guardedly, the setting up of Buddhist secondary schools teaching through the medium of English. They were convinced that their religion had been elbowed aside, or at least left too much to itself, when the terms of the

Kandyan Convention of 1815 had laid down more support for Buddhism than the Government ever gave them.

These three sections of the people, however, generally acquiesced without much question in the state of society into which they had been born, though they doubtless had, if only in their subconscious minds, the feeling that they were being ruled by foreigners, however beneficent and well-meaning, and however used to this they had become. They did not greatly interest themselves in the political activities of the rising middle class, whose leaders were the spearhead of nationalist feeling. The activities of these were primarily political. But after a time there arose among them some who began to regard affairs from the economic point of view also, and to examine the character of the island's economy. The existing state of affairs came under the heaviest criticism from the young men who, having become attracted by the theories of Karl Marx and drawn into the communist fold in the twenties while they were studying abroad, when they returned to Ceylon in the thirties found what seemed to them imperialist and capitalist exploitation at its worst. Their attacks on this undoubtedly influenced other people's thinking to some extent, or at any rate made moderate people who had not thought much before about economic matters start to consider them. In the late twenties, a Ceylon Economic Society was started, and papers on economic subjects were read and published. In this Sir Marcus Fernando, a prominent political leader of considerable ability, played a conspicuous part.

To such moderate people it was clear that it was the plantation industries that had made possible the development of Ceylon from a static semi-feudal towards a progressing modern economy, and that, for better or for worse, this economy depended almost entirely on the export cash crops.[1] They altogether rejected the Marxist demand for nationalisation of foreign-owned estates – some of them were estate owners themselves, and one never knew whither that kind of idea might extend. But they were not satisfied with the economy as it stood.

The point of view of the strong Ceylonese nationalist in the thirties and forties, and indeed beyond, was somewhat on the following lines. The plantation industries had turned the island's economic development the wrong way round. The process had been started by the British Government in Ceylon treating all non-cultivated lands as Crown land, and alienating it at absurdly low rates to Europeans for the cultivation of coffee. A by-product of this was that the Kandyan peasantry had been unfairly deprived of some of their

[1] For statistics of this, see Appendix A.

ancient customary rights, and penned within a small area of land around their villages and paddy fields. Another result was serious soil erosion due to the haphazard and extensive clearing of high forest and the unscientific planting first of coffee and then of tea. It must fairly be admitted, it may be interpolated here, that there is much to be said for this point of view; though it has been argued that worse erosion has been caused by the villagers themselves in burning the grass of the *patnas* (grassy downland) for pasture, and by *chena* cultivation; and that contour planting[1] has now provided the remedy. The next result was the bringing in of a large foreign influx, of Indian Tamils, endangering the health of the country and importing an undesirable alien element, which kept in such close touch with its original homeland that it was not and never could be absorbed into the life of the country. All the management had been kept by Europeans in their own closed circle, so arranged as to keep any Ceylonese from rising to any position of importance in a business firm or in a managerial capacity on an estate. (The same thing was true of the Indians in the retail and importing trades). Hence, as far as the major part of Ceylon's principal industries was concerned, tea in particular, it was being run on foreign capital by foreign management using foreign labour: and the people of the country were systematically kept out. Furthermore, the large profits accruing were sent out of the country, when they should have gone to benefit its people. Even the greater part of the rail and road mileage had been designed primarily for the benefit of the European planters, and only incidentally for the benefit of the people of the country. Banking, too, had been entirely in the hands of the big European-controlled commercial banks, and one or two run by Indians; and these were chary of accommodating Ceylonese. Owing to Ceylon being part of the British Empire, any British subjects could enter the country, whether the people wanted them or not. Hence the undesirable element of Indian moneylenders, always at hand to lend money on low security at exorbitant rates of interest to Ceylonese who wanted to buy land (which they often could not afford to work) or for unremunerative expenditure, such as big dowries and weddings (which was frequently done for purposes of social prestige).

The effect on Ceylon's economy of being almost entirely a plantation economy, they maintained, was to make it quite un-balanced, and altogether too dependent on the vagaries of world markets for the export crops. If the world prices of both tea and

---

[1] 'Contour planting' means planting tea bushes along the contours of slopes instead of vertically up and down them, thus preventing the full flow of water down the slopes carrying the topsoil with it.

rubber slumped simultaneously, the whole economy was imperilled. With the extension of tea planting to other countries, such as the East African colonies, with synthetic rubber, and the far bigger natural rubber industries of Malaya and Indonesia as competitors, this might quite conceivably happen.

Finally, owing to the economy being geared to the production of export cash crops, the production of food had been neglected. The British Government had been quite content to see two-thirds of the total rice consumed imported from abroad, fully confident that it would be paid for by the proceeds of the export crops. If these should fail, the country's food supply would be endangered, and no funds would be available for the nascent social services, such as health and education.

This case against the plantation economy and its concomitants has been put at its strongest, short of Marxist ideas.[1] The error into which extreme nationalists are apt to fall is in attributing to the British Government a purposeful repression of the interests of Ceylon in order to benefit the capitalist interests of their country; which neglects the historical aspect of the matter. The growing of coffee, tea and rubber was the result of the kind of individual enterprise favoured and practised universally in the nineteenth century, and encouraged by the Government in order to increase the revenue. Without the development of the plantation industries it is doubtful if much economic progress could have taken place at all, and Ceylon might for a considerable period have remained with a peasant economy, in the same state of general poverty, from the Government downwards, as during the first thirty years of the British occupation.

But there is enough in the indictment to have influenced the thinking of moderate men! The fact is beyond doubt that dependence on these three export crops, directly and indirectly, for most of the revenue, and to pay for at least one half of the country's food, which has to be imported, is an unstable economic position. This has profoundly influenced, in different degrees, all the Governments which have been in power since the coming of full independence, and the desire for a better balanced economy has been expressed in a number of policy statements and debates in the Ceylon Parliament.

Up to 1956 the attitude of the Governments was that the existing economy had to be recognised for what it was, but that measures must be taken to diversify it so as to make it better balanced. The

---

[1] The extreme case is stated in a little book published in Ceylon entitled *Freedom: What Then?* by H. Corea, a Marxist writer, about the end of 1959. For a more impartial view see H. M. Oliver, *Economic Policy and Opinion in Ceylon* (Duke University Press, Durham, North Carolina, U.S.A.) 1957. Mr. Oliver spent a year at the University of Ceylon as Lecturer in Economics.

plantation industries must be encouraged in order to maintain and improve the island's prosperity. For this reason British interests must not be scared, lest they take out of the country their capital and their expertise. But it was quite wrong that they should monopolise the country's trade, so therefore measures must be taken to introduce Ceylonese into various businesses and into the management of estates: and Ceylonese must be encouraged to go into firms, or with government help to start their own firms, instead of concentrating on frenzied efforts to scramble into the various government services and the professions. Hence were introduced a series of measures which insisted on a gradually increasing proportion of Ceylonisation in the executives of all non-national firms and businesses and a limitation of the entry of non-nationals to replace those who had gone on retirement or died. A similar limitation was applied to superintendents and assistant superintendents of estates owned by European companies. The more enlightened heads of firms, agency houses and banks in Colombo saw the red light early, and sought to recruit the most capable young Ceylonese they could get hold of to take into their offices, or to train as assistant superintendents on estates. They also looked to their existing office staffs to select any of them suitable for promotion to executive grades – the office staffs were apt to resent Ceylonese newcomers as potential executives, though they did not show the same objection to young Europeans. The head of an agency firm once remarked to the author of this book that he was perfectly ready to take a Ceylonese as a junior executive into his firm, provided that he believed the young man would at some future date be capable of occupying satisfactorily the position held by himself. On the other hand, some heads of firms were apt to express grave doubts that the Ceylonese would show the required business integrity that they demanded from their executive staffs. However, there came to be but little choice in the matter, for the measures introduced by the Government, referred to above, laid down that any non-Ceylonese who wished to take up an appointment in Ceylon must apply, or the firm which wanted his services must apply for him, for a 'temporary resident's permit'. This would only be granted if the Government authorities were satisfied either that a certain proportion of Ceylonese were already employed on the executive or administrative side of the firm, or that there were no Ceylonese available with the qualifications requisite for the post. In consequence of this a number of young Ceylonese went abroad, mostly to Britain, to undergo courses in management, in accounting, and in economics. Another expedient was to encourage Ceylonese to start their own businesses, particularly import and export, and to create facilities for loans from Government institutions to assist them in doing so. When trade with Germany and Japan was revived, after the end of the second world war, the UNP Government restricted it to Ceylonese nationals, individuals or firms. All trading involved in the rice-rubber deal with China was similarly restricted.

This policy of Ceylonisation was pushed much further by the post-1956 Governments. Measures were taken to compel non-national firms to have a Ceylonese director, or directors, on their boards, or Ceylonese as partners in partnership firms, as several of the agency firms were. The issue of temporary resident's permits had under the UNP Governments been made to apply to all non-nationals, except Indian estate labourers; this varied somewhat in strictness of application, but some Europeans resident in Ceylon all their lives, and retired there, were distinctly annoyed at being compelled to apply for these permits: some of these retired people, however, applied for and were granted Ceylon citizenship under a special clause of the Citizenship Act (see p. 167 above). In 1963 it was announced that all import business would be restricted either to the State, in respect of certain commodities, or to Ceylonese firms or individuals. The State is to have the monopoly of certain classes of imports, controlled by a State Trading Corporation set up for this purpose. To rice and sugar, the import of which had been government-controlled for some years, are added subsidiary foodstuffs, drugs, textiles, fertilisers and cement. The import of all other foods (except potatoes and chillies), tobacco, chemicals, agricultural machinery, transport equipment, electrical apparatus and appliances, and paper packing materials and containers are reserved to Ceylonese importers. All directors and partners of Ceylonese import firms must be citizens of Ceylon, except that one managing director or manager in each firm may be a non-national. Of the capital of these firms, 51 per cent must be in Ceylonese hands. For foreign firms closing down, the repatriation of assets must be spread over a number of years. It is laid down that 75 per cent of the executive or administrative staff of those firms must be Ceylonese. The reason for all these precautions is the fear that some so-called 'Ceylonese' firms are really being run by non-nationals with Ceylonese as figureheads. Other measures are that no Ceylonese will be allowed to open an account in a foreign-controlled bank, and that no non-Ceylonese will be allowed to engage in pawnbroking or moneylending.

The most notable instance of this policy is the taking over of the oil installations of American and British companies by the State Petroleum Corporation, as mentioned in the last chapter (see p. 208). In 1960 the Government decided to nationalise life insurance, and a

Government Insurance Corporation was set up for the purpose. For many years insurance was entirely in the hands of non-nationals, mostly of large companies like the Sun Life of Canada, which had its own branch office in Colombo, and others which had their agencies in European firms. Shortly after independence several Ceylonese companies entered the insurance field; some of these were sound enterprises, but there were also some very unstable 'mushroom companies'. Just about the time of writing the Ceylon Government has unexpectedly announced its intention of taking over, on 1st January 1964, all forms of insurance business, although the insurance companies had been previously informed that only life insurance would be nationalised. Banking will be dealt with later on in this chapter.

To the UNP Government the first and best way of trying to balance the economy was by increasing the home production of food, especially the growing of the staple food, rice. This was begun in real earnest by D. S. Senanayake when he became Minister of Agriculture and Lands in 1931, and carried on with equal enthusiasm by his son after 1947. What had to be done was obvious. More land, eventually up to the limit of what was cultivable, had to be opened up for the growing of paddy and other food crops. This could only be achieved in the dry zone; in the wet zone there was little if any more land that could be cultivated. Opening up land in the dry zone was largely a matter of irrigation. Once there was a prospect of this, grants of Crown land could be made to those willing to take it up by leaving their own overcrowded and probably fragmented holdings and moving to a peasant colony.[1] The process was expensive. First of all the necessary irrigation facilities had to be provided. This could only be done by restoring old tanks or by constructing new ones. Various irrigation schemes were set on foot, the biggest of them being the construction of the great reservoir at Gal Oya, to which earlier references have been made. The Gal Oya (*oya* means river, or stream) flows eastwards for about sixty miles through the dry zone in the southern part of the Eastern Province. A great dam was constructed, by an American company, and completed in 1951, by which was formed one of the largest artificial lakes in the world, 250,000 acre-feet of water. It is now known as the *Senanayake 'Samudra'* (sea) in honour of the man chiefly responsible for the project – though the scheme originated in the brain of a former British Director of Irrigation. It is a multi-purpose scheme, not only for irrigation of up to 70,000 acres, but also for generating electricity and for flood protection. This scheme has undoubtedly

[1] See B. H. Farmer, *Pioneer Peasant Colonisation in Ceylon*.

been successful, and other schemes on a lesser scale have been started. One of them, on the Walawe Ganga (river), has recently been completed to irrigate 50,000 acres. Since the Gal Oya colony was founded, 8,694 families have been settled, over 45,000 acres alienated and asweddumized,[1] and 7,500 acres are under other crops, including sugar.

When the irrigation facilities are completed – tank and irrigation channels – the land, which has previously been surveyed, has to be cleared, possibly of dense jungle, and divided into plots, on each of which quarters for the incoming colonist have to be put up. Then he must be provided with the necessary agricultural equipment. In some cases the whole or part of the equipment has been furnished by the colonists themselves on a co-operative basis, as for instance by the co-operative purchase of a combine harvester. Then the land for rice growing has to be asweddumized, and facilities for the colony to be provided, such as medical attention, hospitals and dispensaries, wells, schools, and retail stores, preferably co-operative; also, if practicable, community centres. The figures quoted in the Ceylon Year Book for 1961 give, at the end of 1960, 37,908 colonists holding 115,824 acres of paddy land and 68,280 acres of high land (i.e. non-irrigated land under gardens, pasture, and other crops). Whatever the changes in the complexion of Governments, these schemes have steadily continued. But it has to be remembered that there is, even in the dry zone, a limit to the extent of cultivable land.

In lands already under cultivation, efforts have been made to improve agricultural methods, so as to increase the average yield per acre. The best examples are the efforts to introduce the Japanese method of transplanting, the provision of good strains of seed paddy and the encouragement by various means of the use of fertilisers. The yield per acre in Ceylon is low, averaging 38 bushels per acre as compared with 90 in Japan. The Finance Minister in his 1963 Budget statement said with some pride that the yield had increased from 32 to 38 bushels; but it has a long way to go yet: it is hoped in ten years' time to increase it to 48.

Ancillary to all this are improvements in the marketing of food products. These were essential in order to cut down as much as possible the undue profits of middlemen. The paddy grower has a price guaranteed, a measure which was brought in during the world war to stimulate production, and kept up ever since. It has its dangers to the economy. To improve marketing facilities the

---

[1] 'Asweddumized' means prepared for the growing of rice, by suitable terracing and channelling to ensure that the roots of the rice plants are kept covered with water. It is the only word in English derived from the Sinhalese language.

Government set up Agricultural Marketing Boards, and has had new markets put up in various places.

One of the most striking developments has been that of the Co-operative Movement. This was started on the initiative of the British Government as long ago as 1912, and in its early stages was concerned almost exclusively with rural credit. In 1921 the movement was further developed. The Government got down a special adviser from India to make recommendations. A Government Department was started, with a Registrar of Co-operative Societies at the head of it. From this time onwards, for several years, the main activity was in consumers' co-operatives. During the Second World War considerable progress was effected, and the societies were made use of by the Government particularly in the distribution of rice. In 1921 there were 154 co-operative societies; by 1941 they had gone up to 1,852. In the next ten years their number quadrupled, and in another ten had risen to nearly 14,000, and the movement spread to cover all phases of rural life, including small craft industries. A very useful development under the SLFP Government has been the integration of a number of small societies into multi-purpose societies. In 1943 the Co-operative Wholesale Establishment was founded mainly to serve the numerous consumer stores. This was at first under the Government, but later became an autonomous body. There have been some very severe public criticims of its working; but if it can be properly and incorruptly managed, it should be of the greatest value. For the financing of the movement a Co-operative Federal Bank has been established, with 15 Provincial and District Banks. In 1961 it was merged into the People's Bank with other rural credit institutions. One of the most useful of the multifarious types of societies has been the Agricultural Production and Sales Society, though by the end of 1960 there were only 256 of them, compared with 3,886 of the consumer type: however, many of the former must have been absorbed into the multi-purpose societies, as in 1957 there were nearly a thousand of them.[1]

Another activity, started in 1947, was Rural Development. A number of societies for this object have been formed, including women's societies for self-help, and in 1960 there were 7,387 of the former and about 3,800 of the latter.

It was desirable not only to encourage the growing of rice, but also of other food crops, such as maize, sorghum, kurukkan, chillies, pepper and various vegetables like red onions. In most of these Ceylon could be self-sufficing if agricultural workers were willing to make a real effort: at present far too many of these products are

[1] For statistics see Appendix B.

still imported from India. Efforts are being made to grow sugar, particularly around Gal Oya, but have not yet been very productive. Cotton is another crop which the Government is anxious to encourage, to supply the textile mills.

Another source of food supply which is being encouraged is fishing. For centuries the methods of fishing were unchanged, and fishermen put to sea in the same kind of craft, mainly catamarans, which had been used from time immemorial. When the first Senanayake Government was formed, Industry, Industrial Research and Fisheries was one of its ministries: but now fisheries come in, rather more appropriately, with Agriculture and Lands. Numerous attempts have been made to improve the fishing industry. The Department bought some trawlers, which have had some good catches; in 1960 these amounted to over two million pounds weight. Japanese experts have come to Ceylon to advise, and improvements have resulted. Some fishing boats have been mechanised, and others towed out to sea far distances, and back, by motor boats. A useful innovation has been the construction of cold storage plants near some of the landing places; new fishing harbours have been constructed and old ones improved. Efforts are being made to increase the curing of fish: previously nearly all the dried fish was imported from the Maldive Islands, which, incidentally, are no longer a dependency of Ceylon, as in colonial days.[1] Efforts are being made to encourage the co-operative movement among the fishing population, with doubtful success and, a very desirable improvement, to build for fishermen some decent quarters instead of the miserable shacks on the shore in which they previously had to exist.

Ceylon is always reckoned to be deficient in mineral resources, except for graphite, owing to the geological formation. However, a geological survey has recently been set on foot. It is certain that there is no coal, and doubtful if there is any oil, though there has been tentative boring. It has been known for a long time that there were deposits of iron here and there, but in very recent years two places have been found where there are considerable iron ore deposits, estimated at some six million tons, which may possibly be worth mining on a commercial scale. There are certain mineral sands from which can be derived monazite and ilmenite; there is also some radio-active thorianite; for these three there might be a world market and the possibilities are being examined. The gemming industry for which Ceylon has always been famed goes on in the immemorial way, as it always has. Salt is a valuable mineral, and is

[1] They have the unique distinction, for the present day, of having experienced a revolution which put a monarch on the throne to replace a republic.

obtained by the evaporation of sea water in large shallow depressions in the earth, known as *lewayas*. Salt is a government monopoly, and is now under the control of a National Salt Corporation, whose management has come in for considerable criticism.

The absence of coal and oil means that, where power is required, it must be got from other sources. Here Ceylon is fortunate in having a large potential water power. Hydroelectric schemes were started in the twenties, quite unsuccessfully (see above, p. 149) but the credit for the first successful one must go to J. L. Kotelawala, when Minister of Transport and Works. An elaborate scheme in several stages has been devised, and is in progress, and also a grid system to work in conjunction with the electrical power generated by the big multi-purpose irrigation dams, especially Gal Oya.

In the above ways attempts have been and are being made to increase the food supply and develop the natural resources of the island. Some of them should go some way towards a better balancing of the economy; but much more will have to be done before it can be substantially corrected. The most essential need remains the increased production of rice, which must of necessity be a slow and gradual build-up. Simplification of the laws about land tenure, the extension of the Paddy Lands Act (promised for the 1963-4 session of Parliament), more rural credit, and improved methods of farming will all be helpful.

The three export crops, of course, remain the essential pillars of Ceylon's economy. The production of tea has been increased. On the whole, the tea industry still mainly looks after itself. The majority of the tea estates are still owned by British companies, though ever since independence Ceylonese have been buying tea estates, and coming on the boards of rupee companies as directors.[1] The Tea Research Institute, founded in 1925, which has done sterling service to the industry, is still maintained by a small cess on all tea exported. It has been particularly successful in fighting a very dangerous disease of the tea bush known as blister blight, and its experiments on contour planting,[2] when followed by tea planters replanting their fields, had excellent effects in checking soil erosion. In 1961 the Government decided to set up a State Plantations Corporation, the idea of which was to compete with non-national estates and to set an example to Ceylonese ambitious to go in for tea planting themselves. It is potentially an instrument whose scope could be extended to take over many or all estates, if the threat of nationalisation which figured, though low on the list, of Bandara-

[1] For figures on the ownership of tea estates, see Appendix C.
[2] See above, p. 213 (footnote).

naike's original programme at any future time became a reality. This, of course, would be a tremendously expensive operation, unless the Marxist threat of nationalisation without compensation was adopted – an action which would have serious political repercussions. But Mrs. Bandaranaike's Government has explicitly disclaimed any intention of undertaking the nationalisation of foreign-owned estates. The State Plantations Corporation has so far taken over one or two estates, but it will probably be expanded.

For the rubber and coconut plantations big schemes of rehabilitation and replanting, specially necessary for the latter, which were started in 1953 and 1956, are continuing, and should result in higher yields. These are being subsidised by the Government, and in the short term constitute a considerable drain on the revenue. There are Research Institutes for these products also, which have done very useful work indeed. The Rubber Research Institute is financed in a similar way to the Tea Research Institute, but has had rather more help from the Government. The Coconut Research Institute was started in 1929, and comes rather more directly under Government control. Most of the staff of the three Research Institutes are young Ceylonese scientists who have passed through the University.

The favourite device of politicians to achieve the desired balance is the development of secondary industries. Here Ceylon is up against the same difficulties that face most of the newly independent countries the world over – the lack of capital, of experience, and of trained technical personnel, the competition of advanced industrial countries, and the unwillingness of the consumers to make do with inferior products. Industrialisation has long been the favourite panacea of the Marxists for Ceylon's economic disabilities – for a better balanced economy, for unemployment, and for rectifying the balance of payments.

In 1947 a separate Ministry for Industries and Industrial Research was set up (Fisheries rather oddly added). Under the State Council régime the Ministry had been Labour, Industry and Commerce. During the second world war, owing to the shortage of shipping and the necessity for the manufacture of war material, it had perforce to make efforts at the manufacture in Ceylon of some articles that had previously always been imported, the raw materials being those readily obtainable in the island.[1] Government factories were hastily run up for such products as plywood (for tea chests), acetic acid (essential to the processing of latex for sheet rubber), ceramics (there are deposits of kaolin), leather (from local hides),

[1] See above, Chapter 10, p. 149.

paper (from a grass called *illuk*, and other materials), glass and rolled steel (from scrap iron). These for the most part did little more than meet, with varying efficiency, some of the temporary shortages in the home market. There was, naturally, a grievous lack of technical know-how; though some experts were hastily secured, and some Ceylonese sent to get technical training, there was an absence of skilled labour. It is quite remarkable that these improvised factories were able to produce with any success at all. The steel rolling mill was an utter failure: the plywood factory was some time before it was able to turn out tea chests up to standard.

After the war the Government did its best, by an 'Industrial Products Act' to force the articles manufactured in these factories on an unwilling public. In the end nearly all of them had to be closed down. Nevertheless the idea of industrialisation was planted. But it was realised that for it to succeed there must be a plan. The story of planning under D. S. Senanayake's Government, and of the Report of the International Bank Mission's Report was related in Chapter 12 (see p. 173). The Commission went carefully into the matter of industries. They recommended against the government management of factories, but in favour of aiming at 'the promotion of initially small industries which will contribute to the spread of industrial techniques and know-how as a basis for later growth, rather than at the undertaking of single large projects making heavy demands on the still restricted capital, technical and managerial resources available'; in other words, learn to walk before trying to run. They suggested the setting up of public corporations managed by 'competent managers chosen by a board of directors, with the Government limiting itself to the role of stockholder'. The Mission made various recommendations about the industries which might do well if persevered with.[1]

Largely as a result of this Report, a more elaborate and better worked-out Six-year Plan was prepared and set out in the 1954 Budget statement by the Finance Minister. Under the premiership of Kotelawala a Central Planning Secretariat was formed. In 1950 a cement factory was built at the little port of Kankesanturai, on the Jaffna peninsula, near some extensive deposits of limestone. The cement produced was not at first popular with users in Ceylon. But a second factory has since been put up, and now locally made cement represents 40 or 50 per cent of the total consumption. The plywood and leather factories carried on, with some reorganisation; the rest closed down.

[1] *The Economic Development of Ceylon. Report of a Mission organised by the International Bank for Reconstruction and Development.* September 1952, Part II, Chapter 15.

In the 1954 Plan stress was laid on the part which the private sector could play in the development of industry. This, like other ideas, was inspired by the Mission's Report. But it did not go down well with the Bandaranaike Governments, which claimed to be socialist in policy. However, they adopted the idea of public corporations to run certain industries. Such corporations have been set up for cement, ceramics, textiles – one spinning and one spinning and weaving mill – sugar, chemicals, paper, hardboard, mineral sands, leather, oils and fats, and plywood. It is too early yet to make any attempt to estimate their actual or future success. The chemical, and oils and fats corporations made losses in 1962, the former of Rs 8 million: the others seem to be at least paying their way, so far. A certain number of industries have been started with foreign aid. The U.S.S.R. has afforded aid for the setting up of an iron and steel mill and for a rubber tyre and tube factory. A Czecho-Slovakian firm tendered successfully for the construction of a sugar factory. A Chinese corporation has entered into a contract for a textile mill. A Polish organisation has negotiated about the establishment of a hardware and small tools manufacturing plant. Britain has made available a big credit for telecommunication equipment. An interesting experiment is the setting up of an industrial estate near Colombo, run by a corporation. Another corporation has been established to foster small industries such as boat building, tile making and furniture.

It is claimed that Ceylon is now self-sufficient in thirty-three industries. All this has been made possible by very severe curbs put on imports, by prohibition, by quotas, and by heavy duties, not only for the purpose of protecting nascent industries, but also to conserve foreign exchange. Since these curbs have been tightened, in 1963, there has been quite a rush by Ceylonese to fill the gaps by starting new industries in the private sector. According to an official report over 300 industrial projects have been put forward by small companies and individuals.

These various industrial enterprises do not yet seem to have had much effect on the unemployment situation nor on the balance of payments; it is the import curbs which have affected the latter. It remains to be seen how far it will be possible to make these projects efficient. A number of young Ceylonese have been sent abroad for technical training, and there has been a constant flow of foreign experts from various parts of the world to advise or to initiate a number of industrial enterprises. Where an enterprise is started by a foreign firm, strict conditions are laid down for the employment and training of Ceylonese, and for ultimate Ceylonisation. The Government, however, has done its best to offer terms which will prove attractive to foreign capital, promising legislation to safeguard profits, dividends and the repatriation of capital. So far this does not seem to have been successful where private investors are concerned, and a recent statement that something must be done to reduce the amount of Rs 62 million which goes out of the island annually to Britain and the sterling area is hardly likely to encourage further investment.

Banking has so far been interfered with comparatively little. Up to the beginning of the second world war the commercial and exchange banks had it all their own way. The first inroad on their monopoly was the establishment of the Bank of Ceylon with government help and backing in 1939. Ten years later the Central Bank was founded, with a capital of Rs 15 million furnished by the Government. It was started off on the right lines by an American expert from the U.S. Federal Reserve Bank, and has functioned well. On numerous occasions its governing body, the Monetary Board, has been able to give timely advice to the Government. The Bank of Ceylon was merged with it in 1961. In 1955 the Ceylon Development Finance Corporation was started, for the purpose of financing private agricultural and industrial ventures, and up to the end of 1960 it had made advances to the amount of Rs 20 million for thirty-eight projects. The State Mortgage Bank, founded in 1929, and the Agricultural and Industrial Credit Corporation (1943) also continue to function. The Ceylonese always complained that the commercial banks confined their activities to the financing of the export industries, and were chary of local enterprises. Politicians have frequently attacked them for this, and there is always the possibility that legislation may be passed which will freeze them out. At present, however, the banking system of Ceylon seems soundly based, and the commercial banks have been useful in taking up Government loans.

A feature of Ceylon's economic life which has created some instability in recent years is the large number of strikes. On the whole the Governments since independence have paid plenty of attention to labour matters, and there has always been a Minister of Labour. Legislation on labour matters has been in accordance with modern trends, though trade unionism has tended to be a rather political growth, led by middle class Marxists, not by workers themselves. Among the harbour workers much trouble has been caused by rival unions with leaders from the differing Marxist groups. It is interesting to note that out of 900 registered trade unions in 1960, 516 were unions of public servants. The tendency has been to start far

P

too many small unions. The only really large one is among the plantation workers, the Ceylon Workers Congress, formerly known as the Ceylon Indian Congress. The employers, too, have their organisations, the Employers' Federation of Ceylon, and the Ceylon Estate Employers' Federation, the latter of which grew out of the Planters' Association. There were at the end of 1960 over 700,000 members of trade unions exclusive of plantation workers, who numbered 440,000. A whole conciliation and arbitration machinery of Industrial Courts, Joint Industrial Councils, Labour Tribunals and Wages Boards has been set up fot the settlement of industrial disputes, but strikes have been numerous,[1] and sometimes for trivial causes. Factory Acts, a Shop and Office Employment Acts, and an Employment of Women, Young Persons and Children's Act were passed in the fifties; some of these, however, have proved very hard to enforce.

[1] See Appendix D.

Chapter 16

Ceylon's Crucial Problems, 11

THE PROJECTS, agricultural and industrial, of the Bandaranaike Governments, indicated in the previous chapter, arise mostly out of the Ten-year Plan drawn up under government direction by the Central Planning Commission in 1959, estimated to cost Rs 13,661 million, and from a short-term Three-year Plan devised in 1961 with the idea of coping with the parlous economic and financial situation to which Ceylon had come. All these projects, however well conceived and carried out, inevitably require capital. The market for capital inside the island is very definitely limited, and therefore a proportion of it will have to come from foreign investment. But during the fifties the flow of capital was in the reverse direction – an outflow. The plantation companies, although to some extent they did continue to plough back some of their profits into their estates, were becoming increasingly nervous of doing this. The coming in of a more socialistic Government, with the threat of nationalising foreign-owned estates at the tail of its programme, further diminished their inclination towards any fresh investment. For some time the Government had been able to draw on its sterling assets (see p. 165) which in 1956 stood at Rs 1,200 million. By October 1962 they had gone down to Rs 492 million; this was, in point of fact, the nadir, for they have since gone up to Rs 600 million, owing mainly to some very strenuous measures taken by the Government.

It is clear from the last chapter that the Government has set itself some very large and costly tasks. It has succeeded in keeping down the cost of living, which in the last few years has gone up in Ceylon less than almost any country in the world. But this has been done by heavily subsidising food, especially rice, and by vigorous import controls. If the rice subsidy were suddenly removed, the cost of living index would soar like a balloon. The situation was summed up by the Finance Minister in his Budget statement of 1961, when he said that Ceylon lacked domestic capital, foreign exchange and technical skills. He also remarked that, whereas the gross national product had increased by 2·4 per cent, the population over the same period had increased by 2·8 per cent.

The major difficulty is to obtain foreign exchange, which is essential if capital equipment is to be bought for industrial and other projects. To obtain this, recourse has been had to all kinds of expedients. The already strict system of exchange control is constantly being tightened. Foreign travel by Ceylonese has been ruthlessly cut down, and even when one of them gets permission to undertake it the amount of money he is allowed to take out of the country is very small indeed, and even this is taxed; only for educational purposes abroad is there any relaxation, any allowance which can be described as adequate. Increasingly strict import control has been imposed; almost any article which can be described as a luxury is either forbidden to be imported, or the duty imposed on it is so high, sometimes 200–300 per cent, as to be practically prohibitive. Some of these import controls are for the purpose of protecting nascent industries, but for the most part their object is to improve the balance of payments and to earn foreign exchange.

The financial situation has been made much worse by the fact that for the last four years the terms of trade have operated against Ceylon's financial position, as indeed they have against so many countries which export primary products. But as well as this, there is no gainsaying the fact that the deficit budgeting to which the Government has resorted has been due to food subsidies, government investment in various enterprises, and increased social welfare. In 1959/60 there was a deficit of Rs 251 million, in 1960/61 of Rs 326·2 million, and in 1962/63 of Rs 491 million. The recently announced deficit in the 1963/64 Budget is estimated at a little over Rs 600 million. These deficits have been partly met by the fact that there has been much, rather inefficient, underspending by government departments, which means that some of the projects devised for increasing the gross national product are presumably not being properly carried out, or anyhow slowed down. The Opposition in Parliament has constantly criticised the Government for making use of foreign aid to help balance the Budget, on the grounds that such aid ought to be devoted to specific projects of a capital nature designed to increase prosperity. In 1961, when there was the deficit shown above, Rs 122 million was received from foreign sources, of which Rs 93 million was in the form of loans and credits, and Rs 29 as outright gifts.

The normal method of balancing a Budget is, of course, by increasing taxation. Under Bandaranaike's Government a number of new taxes were introduced, in addition to increases in the income tax – a wealth tax, a national development tax, an expenditure tax, a capital gains tax, increased taxes on companies, and a land tax of

15 per cent on landholders of above 100 acres. Changes have been introduced by the Finance Ministers of the present Government, such as a tax of Rs 400 a year on passport visas of non-nationals, a special tax on professional people – up to Rs 10,000 on Queen's Counsel, and a levy on non-national firms and businesses: the land tax and the national development tax have been abandoned, but the general level of taxation has not gone down, and people in the upper and middle income brackets are probably as heavily taxed as in almost any country in the world. The present Finance Minister, Ilangaratne, in his 1963 Budget has raised the exemption limit on income tax from Rs 2,500 per annum to Rs 3,000, but there are increased rates on incomes over Rs 20,000. Duties on kerosene, flour, and cotton and artificial silk piece goods are reduced. These various concessions appear to be of the kind which Oppositions are apt to denounce as vote-catching, Government supporters as 'soaking the rich'. He has introduced a business turnover tax, a tax on foreign exchange, and a national lottery.

The Budget deficit is expected to be reduced by Rs 44·6 million underexpenditure, Rs 220 million local investment in government securities, Rs 25 million from government agencies and funds which deposit with the Treasury, and Rs 175 million of foreign aid. New taxation is estimated to bring in Rs 88 million, leaving Rs 50 million as unfinanced deficit.

Some figures recently published by a United Nations agency on the expenditure of Asian countries are illuminating. These given for Ceylon, Rs 2,017 million in the financial year 1962/63, are analysed as follows:

(millions of rupees) Defence	69
Subsidies	226
Economic services	196
Social services	506
Local government grants	31
Investments	550
Loans, etc	10
Other expenditure	463

As a good harvest is expected in 1963, it is estimated that subsidies to paddy growers are likely to go up to Rs 336 million. The guaranteed price is 91 cents a measure: it is sold at 25 cents.

The Finance Minister said that he did not expect much foreign private investment and admitted that the stoppage of aid from the U.S.A. was something of a blow. In 1960 it amounted to Rs 52 million, to which must be added Rs 26 million by the CARE organisation for feeding school children. He did not specify from what quarter he expected foreign aid to make up for this.

The 1962 Budget statement was a depressing one. Dias Bandaranaike, then Finance Minister, said 'The point has now been reached when external reserves are down to a level below which they cannot fall without untoward consequences to the economy, and unless measures are taken to limit the monetary demand, the effect of import restrictions would be to create a scarcity of supplies and competitive bidding for those supplies unless . . . increased domestic production makes up for the reduction of imports.'

Ilangaratne's statement was much more optimistic. He had some reason for this, as the terms of trade had turned more in Ceylon's favour, and the heavy import controls turned the balance of payments similarly. Exports have increased by 4·3 per cent and imports have declined by 2·5 per cent. The exports of the main cash crops all increased in volume, but not in price. Considerable efforts are being made to increase tea exports to the Middle East, the people there being apparently willing to take low-grown tea which is of inferior quality to that supplied to the London market, still Ceylon's biggest customer. The Minister quoted statistics to show the increase of the gross national product, of the land under cultivation, and of the yield per acre, of the volume of exports, of industries, which had gone up from 5·2 to 6·6 of the total product. These increases, he stated, had more than kept up with the rate of increase of the population.

The last problem to be faced can be simply stated, but it may be the most difficult of all to solve – the phenomenal increase of the population, which is one of the highest in the world. The results of the 1963 census put it at 10,640,000, an increase of 2·4 million over that taken in 1953.[1] The first decennial census was taken in 1871, and the population then was 2,400,000. The present rate of increase of about a quarter of a million a year is quite frightening. It is, of course, one which faces several other Asian countries, and is caused by the improved health conditions which have brought about a big excess of births over deaths, and a longer expectation of life for the average Ceylonese. The high increase is the penalty which Ceylon has to pay for having a better medical service than almost any other Asian country. It is, of course, all to the good from every human point of view – except the economic. A quarter of a million extra mouths to feed, extra individuals to be clothed, housed and to receive the benefits of education and various welfare services is a large problem.

[1] For statistics see Appendix E.

The only real solution to the problem is the increase of productivity. The extra quarter of a million per year means that extra number of producers, as they grow up. But for some years to come, anyhow, Ceylon must remain a primarily agricultural country. It is certainly possible to open up more land and to increase production on land already under cultivation; to grow more rice, tea, rubber, coconuts and other crops. There is a big acreage of land in the dry zone uncultivated, and much jungle uncleared. But it is not limitless, as it may well seem to be in parts of Africa; and, in the opinion of some experts, much of this land is uncultivable, or at least quite uneconomic for cultivation. The areas on which the three export crops can be grown are even more limited, especially that which grows high quality tea, and there is also a limit to the amount of these three crops that can be increased by better cultivation. New markets for these products are not easy to find – witness the efforts put forth by the Tea Propaganda Board in various countries. Saturation point is easily reached, and competition is keen, especially for rubber, with synthetic particularly, and coconut products, for which there are the products of rival crops, such as groundnuts.

There are two other solutions which are sometimes suggested for overpopulation. One is emigration. The Sinhalese would like to see this applied to many, most, or even all of the Indian Tamils. As far as they themselves are concerned, they have no desire to leave their native island, unlike those same Tamils whose descendants are found today in various parts of the world – incidentally, creating somewhat similar problems to that in Ceylon. The other, and more obvious solution is birth control or, as it is fashionably styled today, family planning. There is a movement for pushing this in Ceylon, but it needs a vast amount of propagandist work to 'get it across' to the average villager; moreover, as a Sinhalese remarked the other day, it does not apply to Roman Catholics, so why should it to Buddhists. Neither of these two solutions, as far as one can see, could be anything but temporary palliatives.

To sum up the general economic position, can the increase of productivity be brought to measure up to the increase of population and the raising of the standard of living? The answer of this woman Prime Minister's Government is that it can, and that the method by which it is to be accomplished is by planning on the basis of socialism. Agricultural production must be increased; that is clear, and has been discussed earlier in these pages. To do it requires more intensive work on the land, and a certain amount of capital, especially for opening up fresh land for cultivation. Then, industries must be developed. This, too, requires capital, and technical knowledge. As far as industry is concerned, this postulates managerial as well as technological skill. The outstanding difficulty here, experience has shown, is to get technicians of what may be called the foreman type, whose technical knowledge and knowledge of the way to handle men is apt to need years of experience in 'doing things'.

Obviously one of the first requisites is to find capital; and it would appear that in order to get this there must be a supply of foreign exchange, to get which there must be a belief, in the minds of possible suppliers, in the political stability and economic potentialities of the country. The Ceylonese themselves cannot, as conditions are today, furnish enough domestic capital for the purposes required.

Ultimately then, the economic future of Ceylon is going to depend on the way in which the various enterprises which have got or are getting under way are going to be handled. The method which the Government evidently prefers is that of public corporations rather than private enterprise. To make these succeed, the middle class have to prove that they can produce the managerial skill necessary to make them work, and show a profit, and to do the same in private enterprise in commerce and industry. With public corporations there is always a danger of undue interference by purely administrative officers – bureaucrats – and by politicians. There has been some of this already, and not only foreign experts, recruited temporarily to show the way, but also some of the Ceylonese who have occupied high positions in some state corporations have become dissatisfied at such interference, and resigned. Then there is the question of integrity. No one who reads the Ceylon newspapers, or the reports of parliamentary proceedings, can fail to be struck by the numerous allegations of corruption that are freely bandied about. In a sense this is a good sign, meaning that corruption is not taken for granted, as it seems to have been – maybe for centuries. But it has penetrated deeply into national life. The author of this book keenly remembers being horrified when credibly informed of some of the things that went on behind the scenes in the Colombo General Hospital, and in local administration. Standards in public life will have to be raised.

In the last resort, however, everything depends on the people, on those who have to do the work; the mass of the people have to work intelligently, and work hard. The Sinhalese in the past have not always been noted for this. Sir Ivor Jennings, in his book on *The Economy of Ceylon*, written admittedly, soon after his arrival in the island, while describing the Ceylon Tamils as 'hard working, persistent and thrifty', speaks of the Sinhalese as 'apt to be lazy, easily discouraged and careless'. In an early Report of the Registrar of Co-operative Societies, the writer said 'the Sinhalese has a high standard of leisure'. But with the great improvement in the health of the island, the removal of the dread scourge of malaria especially which has had a weakening effect for countless generations, and with the revived national spirit that demonstrated itself in the 1956 election – though that had its bad as well as its good side; national-ism always has – it is possible that hard and intelligent work may be forthcoming. The success of the co-operative movement may well be a criterion of this. The Sinhalese man is a very adaptable person; he is capable of real craftsmanship, and possessed of considerable mechanical ability. The resources are there, and can be developed. The financial situation, if at present shaky, can be retrieved. There is a good system of communications, a legacy of the British occupa-tion, and a good prospect of a much improved system of education on modern lines – a national, though one may hope, a not too national system. No one who, like the author of this book, has spent the greater part of his working life in the lovely island of Ceylon can do anything but hope and believe that her people, Sinhalese, Tamils and the rest – his very good friends – can and will work together, work towards that destiny which should rightly be theirs, and build up a happy and prosperous nation.

Conclusion

I T IS perhaps rash for one who has not visited Ceylon for over two years to attempt an estimate of the political situation as it is at the time of writing. Mrs. Bandaranaike's position does not seem very stable, though she should be able to hold on till 1965 if she so desires, especially as, if the Finance Minister's optimism in his 1963 Budget statement is justified, the economic position is recovering. Much of the strength of her party derives from her own personality. The memory of her husband's martyr-like death may be dying out – from the electoral angle that is – but she still enjoys sympathy as his widow. She seems to understand the rural masses, and is personally popular with them, and she has a strong following among the women of Ceylon, many of whom are proud that one of their sex should have risen to a high position such as hers. As a Kanydan aristocrat she has much support in that traditionally conservative community. With the general run of Sinhalese her genuine devotion to Buddhism – though she was educated at a Christian school – is unquestioned, and counts for much. These are all intangible currents of public opinion, and only the next election can test their true significance. In her Government there still seems to be a right and a left wing. The Prime Minister, like her husband, is handicapped by a lack of ministerial talent. Her first Finance Minister, Dias Bandaranaike, now Minister of Agriculture but still her Parliamentary Secretary, is undoubtedly able. He represented her with credit at the Commonwealth Prime Ministers' Conference in 1962, and she still places much reliance on him. When he resigned, his place was taken, at two removes, by Ilangaratne, who has held one or another office ever since 1956. He has had a somewhat stormy political career. He was originally a government clerk, dismissed for his activities in provoking unrest among his fellow employees. He entered Parliament in 1949, but had to vacate his seat as the result of an election petition. He was for a time very much under the aegis of the Marxists, but joined Bandaranaike's party quite early on. He is well to the left, and has the reputation of being strongly anti-Western; while Minister of Commerce he certainly showed a keen desire to establish relations with communist countries. He may well stand or fall by the results of his 1963 Budget. These two Ministers are not supposed to be greatly drawn towards each other. Felix Dias Bandaranaike is not particularly popular with his ministerial colleagues. He is able, but considered arrogant and apt to be somewhat contemptuous of his colleagues' abilities. Like his uncle, he comes from the 'upper crust' of Sinhalese low-country land-owners, though his father and grandfather earned great respect as judges. He may suffer somewhat in popular estimation from being of the Christian religion, though he strives very hard not to let this in any way interfere with his politics. These two, with C. P. de Silva, Leader of the House of Representatives, solid and reliable, but in poor health seem to be the most able figures in Mrs. Bandaranaike's Cabinet.

Opposing her in Parliament is, first, the United National Party, led, with increasing confidence, by Dudley Senanayake. His party, having reformed its organisation, which probably needed a certain amount of cleaning up, is trying to consolidate, and to project a better image of itself on public opinion. The party puts forward a programme not very different from that of the Government, but rather less socialistic. It has been remarkably successful in the municipal elections in Colombo and Kandy, and has also scored in a number of elections for local authorities: in those two towns it made an almost clean sweep. It will be interesting to see what happens when, as has been recently decided, the former *kachcheris* run by Government Agents, and condemned as relics of colonialism, are replaced by elected District Councils.

As for the rest of the Opposition, there is the Tamil Federal Party, threatening another *satyagraha* campaign in October 1963. Recently G. G. Ponnambalam has come out very strongly against this. What the results will be, the readers of this book may know before it is in print. The most interesting new development is the closing of the Marxist ranks. For some time they were very tolerant towards the new Government; but this did not last. The three groups, N. M. Perera's LSSP, Philip Gunawardana's MEP, and the Communist Party, have come together under the name of the United Left Front. Time alone will show how they find themselves able to reconcile their ideological differences, further complicated by the Sino-Russian divergence, which has appeared even within the Communist Party itself. The difference on 'Sinhala only' seems to have been reconciled by a recognition of the *status quo*: Sinhalese to be the official language, with Tamil as a regional language.

This last move may have remarkable consequences. Philip Gunawardana, of the MEP, has prophesied that there will be a coalition of the SLFP and the UNP. So – the next election?

Postscript

SINCE writing the above, the author has been able to pay a very brief visit to Ceylon, and also to meet some prominent Ceylonese politicians of the three main parties, as well as others in different walks of life.

Among the Western-educated he found a somewhat alarming degree of pessimism about the island's future, especially on the economic side. Labour troubles seem to be endemic in Colombo. Reference has been made in several places in this book to the excellent system of roads; but the condition of the roads themselves has sadly deteriorated.

The villagers appear to be a little better off than formerly, though this would seem, to some extent anyhow, to be due to the heavy subsidies which enable some of them to grow paddy profitably, and others to buy imported rice at a cheap and quite uneconomic price. This is made possible only by heavy taxation; and such taxation is apt, after a time, to come under the law of diminishing returns.

The financial situation has seriously deteriorated, as Ceylon's external assets have gone down to about Rs 400 million, Rs 100 million less than had been anticipated. As certain foreign loans are due for repayment during 1964, the situations is causing the Government grave concern. Travel abroad has been temporarily stopped. The Government has also decided to ration textiles.

The Government managed to survive a considerable parliamentary crisis over the matter of a commission appionted to deal with the question of taking over the press, though arising out of it has been the resignation of the Speaker of the House of Representatives. The Prime Minister has again said that she has no intention of going to the country till the end of the Parliament's five year spell – which is 1965.

The United National Party and the United Left Front (from which a section of the Communist Party has split) have each gained a seat in by-elections, whereas the votes for the Sri Lanka

Freedom Party have dropped – though this is always a likely happening in by-elections, for the party in power.

So the big question mark remains – what will the rural voter do when the Prime Minister does see fit to go to the country?

Books

IT WAS tempting to try to compile a fairly full bibliography on Ceylon history and politics, but too large a task, even if it had been confined to secondary authorities. In the footnotes through the text will be found references to a number of books which I have found useful in writing this book, and which would be of interest to anyone desirous of reading more about Ceylon.

A full bibliography of the island's history up to the end of the fifteenth century will be found in Volume One of the *History of Ceylon,* by various writers, on the model of the *Cambridge Medieval History,* and published by the University of Ceylon Press Board. An abridgement of this, by Professor Paranavitana and C. W. Nicholas, makes easier reading. The second volume of the *History* is under preparation, and will doubtless cover in its bibliography the original and secondary authorities for the later period. For the more recent years there is a useful bibliography in Mr. Howard Wriggins' book *Ceylon: Dilemmas of a New Nation,* referred to in the text. It gives some original authorities as well as a comprehensive selection entitled *Books and Pamphlets.*

The late Fr. S. G. Perera, a learned Jesuit, from his deep knowledge of his country's history wrote a *History of Ceylon for Schools,* covering the years from 1515 to 1911. He collected his facts admirably, and the book is most useful for the periods of the Portuguese and Dutch occupations, for which there is otherwise no single connected narrative. Mr. Sydney Bailey published in 1952, in Hutchinson's University Library series, a useful short history, *Ceylon,* for the non-Ceylonese general reader. Professor E. F. C. Ludowyk has recently (1963) published an entertaining *Story of Ceylon* (Faber & Faber). Mention should be made, too, of the late Humphrey Codrington's *Short History of Ceylon,* a real pioneering piece of work based on a long and enthusiastic lifetime of historical research by a British civil servant in his leisure time.

The books of Dr. G. C. Mendis, Sir Charles Jeffries and Mr. B. H. Farmer have been referred to in footnotes, and are well worth perusal; also Dr. Colvin de Silva's *Ceylon under the British Occupation, 1795–1833,* originally a doctoral thesis, but completed by this active politician when an unkind Government during the Second World

War placed him under detention. Another book of which special mention may be made is Sir Charles Collins's *Public Administration in Ceylon*, a Chatham House study published by the Oxford University Press. Sir Charles had a long and successful career in the Ceylon Civil Service, and always took a genuine interest in the island's history and affairs.

Miss Elsie Cook's *Geography of Ceylon*, originally published in 1931 and brought more up to date (1951) by Mr. Kularatnam is valuable. Mr. B. K. Sarkar's *Demography of Ceylon* provides an interesting statistical study.

On the constitutional side, in addition to the works of Sir Ivor Jennings referred to in the text, Mr. S. Namasivayam's *Legislatures of Ceylon*, which goes up to 1948, and his *Parliamentary Government in Ceylon*, covering the succeeding ten years, are learned and helpful.

In the text are mentioned books by Leonard Woolf, *The Village in the Jungle* and J. Vijayatunga's *Grass for my Feet*. In addition to these entertaining works I feel I must recommend the late John Still's delightful book *The Jungle Tide*.

Detailed monographs on Ceylon history are not listed here; the author is glad to see that some of these are now coming out as the result of research done in the University Department of History, which he started and with which he was for a long time connected.

Appendix A

Exports of Tea and Rubber

(thousands of lbs)

YEAR	TEA		RUBBER		Percentage of total exports	
	Quantity	Value (Rs)	Quantity	Value (Rs)	TEA	RUBBER
1952	314,485	723,048	209,798	373,025	51·3	25·8
1953	335,555	825,090	217,326	337,583	55·5	22·1
1954	361,262	1,122,798	209,354	285,394	65·5	16·1
1955	302,235	1,194,227	209,355	350,348	63·8	18·0
1956	348,129	1,043,847	194,694	391,773	63·2	17·7
1957	367,732	1,021,346	208,614	300,299	64·3	18·9
1958	410,723	1,130,969	207,201	258,109	68·5	15·6
1959	383,494	1,045,013	205,756	297,820	61·8	17·6
1960	409,784	1,095,679	234,604	378,373	61·7	21·3
1961	425,721	—	193,753	—	—	—
1962	451,632	—	223,652	—	—	—

Appendix B

Co-operative Societies

Year	No. of Societies	No. of Members	Turnover (thousands of rupees)	
1921	154	18,000	132	
1931	600	24,000	1,243	
1941	1,852	79,000	4,458	
1952	8,239	1,267,000	186,087	(Primary Societies)
1960	13,962	1,536,000	526,483	(Primary Societies)

The types of co-operatives in 1960 were:

1	Credit	3,886
2	Thrift and Savings	423
3	Consumers' (Primary)	964
4	Agricultural Production and Sales	256
5	Cottage Industries	948
6	Production and Sales (excluding 4, 5 and 7)	454
7	Multi-purpose	4,741 { Integrated credit, distribution, production and marketing activities.
8	School Co-operatives and Youth Clubs	1,835
9	Other Primary	185
10	Secondary	298

Total: 13,990

Total turnover: Rs 2,212 million

Ownership of Tea Estates
(31 December 1961)

	Acres	Per cent
Sterling companies (registered in United Kingdom)	209,388	35·6
Owned by non-Ceylonese individuals	34,039	5·8
Owned by rupee companies (registered in Ceylon)	122,575	20·9
Estates and smallholdings owned by Ceylonese individuals	221,399	37·7

Ownership of Rubber Estates
(31 December 1961)

Sterling companies	88,441	13·2
Non-Ceylonese individuals	16,156	2·4
Rupee companies	85,562	13·2
Estates and smallholdings (Ceylonese individuals)	477,671	71·2

Appendix D

Labour Unrest

Year	Number of Strikes	Workers involved
1949	94	480,286
1950	110	28,271
1951	102	312,817
1952	75	11,523
1953	87	378,082
1954	114	101,831
1955	107	22,370
1956	214	88,760
1959	304	367,301

Growth of the Population of Ceylon

(as taken from the census figures)

Year	Population	increase per cent
1871	2,400,380	—
1881	2,759,738	15·0
1891	3,009,789	9·0
1901	3,565,954	18·6
1911	4,106,350	15·2
1921	4,498,605	9·6
1931	5,306,871	18·0
1946	6,657,339	25·4
1953	8,097,895	21·6
1963	10,640,000 (*approx*)	30·0

1953 Census:

Low Country Sinhalese	3,469,512
Kandyan Sinhalese	2,147,193
Total Sinhalese	5,616,705
Ceylon Tamils	884,703
Indian Tamils	974,098
Ceylon Moors	463,963
Indian Moors	47,462
Burghers and Eurasians	45,950
Malays	25,464
Veddahs	803
Europeans	6,508

INDEX

Index

A

Adam's Peak, 31
Agricultural colonies, 146, 149
Agriculture, 34, 70 and *n*, 82,
  141, 145–6, 165, 166, 169,
  210, 217–9, 219–20, 231
  see also Coconuts, Coffee, Rubber, Tea
Air raids, 137
Amarasuriya, H., 169–70
American Mission, 22, 99
Ananda College, 101
Anuradhapura, 28, 30, 32, 33,
  35–7
Arunachalam, Sir Ponnamba-
  lam, 87, 117, 119, 120, 201
Ayurveda, 95, 147, 180, 211

B

Banda, M. D., 181
Bandaranaike, Sir Solomon, 140
Bandaranaike, S. W. R. D.
  early career, 140, 141, 142,
    170–1
  founds *Sinhala Maha Subha*,
    140, 155
  Minister, 140, 159, 171
  Leader of the House, 170, 171
  national dress, 171
  leaves UNP, 170–2, 173
  wins 1956 election, 177, 179–
    80
  and Tamils, 186–8, 196, 201–2
  Prime Minister, 181–9, 197

  foreign policy, 206, 207
  Executive Committees, 144
  assassination, 189–90, 192
Bandaranaike, *Mrs. S.*
  leads SLFP, 190–2
  Prime Minister, first woman,
    193, 198
  domestic policy, 194, 231
  foreign policy, 205, 207–9
  position in country, 193, 234
Banking, 78, 81, 148–9, 213, 225
Barnes, Sir Edward (Governor),
  52, 55–6, 63, 70, 71
Bell, H. C. P., 113
Bevin, Ernest, U.K. Foreign
  Secretary, 172
Bhikkhus, 29–31, 54–5, 180–1,
  185, 189–90, 196, 211–2
Board of Ministers, 128, 134–5,
  136, 137, 168
Brownrigg, Sir Robert (Gover-
  nor), 52, 53–4, 99
Buddha, Gautama, 28–9, 177
Buddhism *and* Buddhists
  Committee of Inquiry, 31, 66,
    181
  education (*pirivenas*), 22, 196
  festivals, 30–1
  Jayanti year, 176–7, 181
  religion, 22, 27–32, 36, 37, 39,
    47, 53, 101, 112, 118, 140,
    176–7, 181, 197, 211, 234
Burghers
  Dutch, 18, 19, 58, 195
  Portuguese, 18, 19
  Others, 19
  Representation, 115, 117, 120,
    121, 122, 131, 158 *n*
Burrows, Sir Frederick, 144
Butler, Sir Geoffrey, 125, 126

249

Printed in Great Britain by C. Tinling & Company Limited, Liverpool, London and Prescot.

DATE DUE

MAY 2 1 1968			
GAYLORD			PRINTED IN U.S.A.